The Critique of Nonviolence

The Critique of Nonviolence

Martin Luther King, Jr., and Philosophy

Mark Christian Thompson

Stanford University Press
Stanford, California

STANFORD UNIVERSITY PRESS
Stanford, California

©2022 by Mark Christian Thompson. All rights reserved.

No part of this book may be reproduced or transmitted in any form or by any means, electronic or mechanical, including photocopying and recording, or in any information storage or retrieval system without the prior written permission of Stanford University Press.

Printed in the United States of America on acid-free, archival-quality paper

Library of Congress Cataloging-in-Publication Data

Names: Thompson, Mark Christian, author.
Title: The critique of nonviolence : Martin Luther King, Jr., and philosophy / Mark Christian Thompson.
Description: Stanford, California : Stanford University Press, 2022. | Includes bibliographical references and index.
Identifiers: LCCN 2021045650 (print) | LCCN 2021045651 (ebook) | ISBN 9781503631137 (cloth) | ISBN 9781503632073 (paperback) | ISBN 9781503632080 (ebook)
Subjects: LCSH: King, Martin Luther, Jr., 1929-1968—Philosophy. | Race—Philosophy. | Nonviolence--Philosophy. | Ontology. | African American philosophy. | Philosophy, German. | African Americans—Civil rights.
Classification: LCC E185.97.K5 T455 2022 (print) | LCC E185.97.K5 (ebook) | DDC 323.092—dc23
LC record available at https://lccn.loc.gov/2021045650
LC ebook record available at https://lccn.loc.gov/2021045651

Cover art: Robert Motherwell, *In Plato's Cave No. 1*, 1972. Acrylic on canvas, 182.9 x 243.8 cm (72 x 96 in.)

Typeset by Newgen in Minion Pro 10/15

For my wife, Kerri

Love is an ontological concept. Its emotional element is a consequence of its ontological nature. It is false to define love by its emotional side. This leads necessarily to sentimental misinterpretations of the meaning of love and calls into question its symbolic application to the divine life. But God is love. And, since God is being-itself, one must say that being-itself is love.

—**Paul Tillich** (*Systematic Theology, Volume One* 1951, 279)

Table of Contents

Acknowledgments xi

INTRODUCTION
    Ontology and Nonviolence   1

1   Being and Nonviolence   27

2   Nonbeing and Nonviolence   45

3   Black *power* as Nonviolence   70

4   Gnosticism and Nonviolence   95

5   Divine Nonviolence   110

CONCLUSION
    Eros as Nonviolence   137

    Notes   149

    Bibliography   165

    Index   197

Acknowledgments

I would like to thank everyone at Stanford University Press who read and worked on this book. I am particularly grateful to Erica Wetter and Kate Wahl for their interest and belief in the project, and to two anonymous readers for their encouraging and illuminating reviews. I thank early readers Nan Z. Da and Anahid Nersessian for their invaluable input, along with my colleague Jeanne-Marie Jackson for her continual support. As always, I give my deepest thanks to my wife and children for making this book possible in the most fundamental way.

Introduction
Ontology and Nonviolence

I. King's Black *power*

WHAT IS BLACK POWER? On June 16, 1966, in the wake of the James Meredith shooting, Stokely Carmichael publicly announced his preliminary formulation of Black Power, which he continued to refine for years after.[1] It was an occasion Martin Luther King, Jr. recalled with great restraint in *Where Do We Go from Here: Chaos or Community?* (originally published in 1967), given that Carmichael admitted to having used him to gain the widest audience possible for the announcement. Representing the Southern Christian Leadership Conference (SCLC), King, along with Carmichael, then chairman of the Student Nonviolent Coordinating Committee (SNCC), and Floyd McKissick, the national director of the Congress of Racial Equity (CORE), organized a joint march meant to continue activist James Meredith's solitary "March Against Fear." In the wake of the Voting Rights Act (1965), Meredith had set out to walk from Memphis, Tennessee, to Jackson, Mississippi, to rally Blacks to vote. He was shot June 6, 1966—the second day of his march. Having survived the attempt on his life, Meredith remained hospitalized as the SCLC, SNCC, CORE, and any other Civil Rights organization that would join, immediately continued his journey, now dubbed Meredith's Mississippi Freedom March.

"Once during the afternoon," King recounts,

> we stopped to sing "We Shall Overcome." The voices rang out with all the traditional fervor, the glad thunder and gentle strength that had always characterized the singing of this noble song. But when we came to the stanza which speaks of "black and white together," the voices of a few of the marchers were muted. I asked them later why they refused to sing that verse. The retort was: "This is a new day, we don't sing those words any more. In fact, the whole song should be discarded. Not 'We Shall Overcome,' but 'We Shall Overrun.'" As I listened to all these

comments, the words fell on my ears like strange music from a foreign land. My hearing was not attuned to the sound of such bitterness. I guess I should not have been surprised. I should have known that in an atmosphere where false promises are daily realities, where deferred dreams are nightly facts, where acts of unpunished violence toward Negroes are a way of life, nonviolence would eventually be seriously questioned. I should have been reminded that disappointment produces despair and despair produces bitterness, and that the one thing certain about bitterness is its blindness. Bitterness has not the capacity to make the distinction between some and all. When some members of the dominant group, particularly those in power, are racist in attitude and practice, bitterness accuses the whole group. (King 2010a, 182)

Stunned by the sound of this "strange music from a foreign land," King seeks to decipher this new musical language in conversation with Carmichael. It is then King realizes that Carmichael has used him to announce the "Black Power" slogan to mainstream America, and the world. Carmichael admits to his ruse and rejects nonviolence, calling the new movement "Black Power" after refusing in private King's request he use some less aggressive alternative.

The fact that Martin Luther King, Jr. suggested names for Black Power to Stokely Carmichael may seem odd.[2] Yet, King already possessed his own definition of "Black Power" before Carmichael went public with his. In his trenchant response to the movement increasingly identified with Carmichael's use of the "Black Power" slogan in 1966, King writes: "There is a concrete, real black power that I believe in. I don't believe in black separatism, I don't believe in black power that would have racist overtones, but certainly if black power means the amassing of political and economic power in order to gain our just and legitimate goals, then we all believe in that. And I think that all white people of good will believe in that" (King 1998, 320). How to avoid the "racist overtones" of "black separatism," yet orient political and economic goals based on racial community, begs the question of racial ontology. How is the distinction between racial essence and racial existence decided and exceeded?[3] How can there be racial communities in the absence of essential difference, where race is not a matter of ideological and historical contingency? Once Black political and economic power is amassed and equality achieved, will race disappear from American society?

In other words, Black Power intellectuals including King did not present a systematic understanding of racial ontology. That is, they did not explicitly ask, what is the being and end of race? What is the being and end of Blackness? What is racial being and what are the ends of race? Of course, it is perfectly understandable they did not. With more practical matters in mind and a wider public to reach, Black Power leaders did not bother to expound theories of gnostic being and eschatological end. Nevertheless, they could engage in high theory in public speeches, meetings, and writings; among Black radicals, reading philosophy and philosophizing were thought crucial to understanding racism.

Additionally, when they posited Black community in the face of white supremacy, Black radicals made philosophic decisions to clarify their practical aims. Although concerned with the material means and ends of racial oppression, their mode of apprehending racism's concrete causes and conditions identifies race as a naturalized (when not natural) phenomenon. Rarely distinguishing between race as a construct and race as a metaphysical truth, many Black radical thinkers of the period left ambiguous how they understood Blackness ontologically, as either a cause, product, or event. Indeed, their conceptual separation of Black and white went beyond race as the ideological imposition of white supremacy, implying instead a metaphysical force. In this understanding, race's teleological unfolding has been either unjustly altered or is about to undergo revolutionary change according to a greater plan of justice. In other words, even though Black Power thinkers do not overtly describe a racial ontology, they nevertheless still possess one, both as an effect of the philosophical tradition in which they intervened and as a condition of their practical analyses of racial oppression.

While that tradition includes Fanon, Du Bois, Douglass, Wells, and many others, it also means Plato, Augustine, Marx, and Marcuse. Many studies have examined Black Power's relationship to philosophers belonging to the Black radical tradition, but this study concentrates on Black Power's investment in European philosophy.[4] Black Power thinkers took all philosophy seriously, and they absorbed the philosophic principles of those thinkers they admired and appropriated, both Black and white. *The Critique of Nonviolence* does not deny the living presence of the Black radical tradition in Black Power philosophy; to do so would be absurd. Instead, it addresses the question of racial ontology as adduced in European philosophy and disputed in the Black radical tradition. Focusing on Martin Luther King, Jr.'s anti-racist, anti-humanist metaphysical thought, this book asks: How did the most prominent Black radical conceive an anti-racist racial ontology, and how might the answer to this pressing question continue to be relevant today?[5]

To respond to these questions within Black Power's hermeneutic circle, King requires an ontology of race, free of Black separatism. This book thus explores Martin Luther King, Jr.'s way of Black *power*, which distinguishes itself philosophically from the Black Power directly confronting him as a race-based alternative to nonviolence. King countered with his own understanding of Black *power* as a rejection of essential, hierarchical racial community, privileging instead the beloved community of radical human equality. Black *power* was the ability to forgive and to integrate while still retaining historical specificity, cultural traditions, and significant racial attitudes. In conceptualizing Black *power*, King did not develop a theory of Blackness as a series of positions and practices; to do so would have been contrary to his anti-essentialist and anti-relativistic understanding of race to human separation.

For Carmichael, "Black Power as a slogan" demanded that an "organization which claims to speak for the needs of a community . . . speak in the tone of that community, not as somebody else's buffer zone" (Carmichael 2007, 17). Criticizing King's nonviolence as "somebody else's buffer zone," Carmichael sees Black Power as community advocacy and self-defense for "those who do not attach the fears of white America to their questions about it" (Carmichael 2007, 17). Carmichael identified members of this fearless group as "black Americans [who] have two problems: they are poor and they are black" (Carmichael 2007, 17). Here, class and race converge in the articulation of Black Power, with neither category reducible to the other.[6] Although addressing two "problems" simultaneously, Black Power nevertheless theorizes race and class separately, as two categorically discrete yet conceptual related fields. In so doing, Black Power ultimately seeks to transcend white supremacy's definition of "black Americans."

Throughout his career as an activist and public intellectual, Carmichael insisted that Black Power possessed a longer history, in a global network of racially oppressed communities, than the one he could provide.[7] Even as early as 1966 he insisted "the concept of Black Power is not a recent or isolated phenomenon: it has grown out of the ferment of agitation and activity by different people and organizations in many black communities over the years" (Carmichael 2007, 19). Despite this, neither Carmichael's direct expression of Black Power nor any aspect of the deeper, more complex history to which he alluded became the basis for Black Power's popular image among those unsympathetic to its cause. The highly distorted, derogatory notion of Black Power as the promulgation of separatist violence in the name of insurrectionary anti-white hatred derives from the suppressive ideological exploitation of Black Power ideas and imagery.[8]

This presentation of Black Power obscures the movement's social, political, and philosophical complexity, and collapses all Black radical movements into a single caricature.[9] Combating this form of marginalization, the specialized literature devoted both to Black Power, the historical movement, and to Black *power*, the movement into history, continues to grow.[10] Thus, while Black Power can appear two-dimensional in the popular imagination, both it and Black *power* can also be found in their diverse, multilayered mode of being, encompassing an array of philosophies and approaches to the longer Black Freedom Movement.[11]

The popular, negative misconception of Black Power lay partly in the misapprehension that Black nationalism and Black radicalism are synonymous.[12] Yet, as Bogues has shown, Black nationalism

> is a different species of intellectual practice from that of a political intellectual, although the latter includes some elements of the public intellectual. Because even though "speaking truth to power" as a form of social criticism is to some degree a political act, any observation of black radical intellectual production would illustrate that the central figures of this tradition were explicitly political, seeking to organize, having the courage to stand by or break with organizations and programs while developing an intellectual praxis that made politics not a god but a practice for human good. Theirs was not just a practice of social criticism but oftentimes of organized efforts to intervene in social and political life. (Bogues 2015, 7)

In other words, Black radicals sought to change the political system to integrate it more fully rather than separate further from it. For Bogues, Black radicals provide a critique of modernity and not a wholesale rejection of it. From this perspective, Joseph's contention that Black Power begins at Bandung, Indonesia, in 1955 rather than later in the United States makes historical and philosophical sense (Joseph 2006a, 7). As Joseph writes:

> Presided over by Indonesian president Sukarno and convened by the prime ministers of Indonesia, India, Burma, Ceylon, and Pakistan, the conference featured representatives of twenty-nine nonwhite nations whose populations together exceeded one billion. Bandung's declarations against racism, colonialism, and imperialism represented a watershed event: a "third bloc" opposing both capitalism and totalitarianism. (Joseph 2006a, 7)

In this way, Joseph "reperiodizes the Civil Rights–Black Power era by pushing the chronology of black radicalism back to the 1950s and forward into the

1970s" (Joseph 2006 8). In so doing, he rebrands Black Power as a constituent part of Black radicalism and working in tandem with the Civil Rights Movement, all toward the same goal of Black freedom.[13] Differentiating between Black nationalism and Black radicalism, then, performs an essential historiographic function.

Robinson differentiates even further by insisting on separating Black nationalism from "a black version of ethnic pluralism" he sees as prevalent in the 1960s and 1970s (Robinson 2001, 2). While this may be so, ethnic pluralism itself took on many forms and would need further clarification. That said, of the many Black ethnic pluralist groups, the Black Panther Party (BPP) seemed the most capable of reflecting the doctrines and agendas of each in the popular imagination. Indeed, according to Spencer, "Panther imagery was a reflection of the connective tissue linking protests nationwide" (Spencer 2016, 22). While Panthers, Morgan comments, "self-represented to promote Party doctrine and agendas," their images also represented the connections between various Black Power philosophies and practices (Morgan 2018, i). This sometimes led to merely surface distinctions between Black radical groups and movements. The Panthers' specific trajectory stretches back to Newton's and Seale's life experiences and early involvement with underground East Bay groups in the 1950s. As Kathleen Cleaver and Katsiaficas insist, the "question of the underground was a principal issue for the Black Panther Party from its inception. Prior to founding the Black Panther Party for Self-Defense with Huey Newton, Bobby Seale was a member of the Revolutionary Action Movement, but Seale did not share RAM's insistence on the revolutionary vanguard being clandestine. RAM preferred primarily to interact with the public through mass front organizations; RAM structure, membership, meetings, and other activities were secret" (Cleaver and Katsiaficas 2001 6). Ultimately, as Spencer relates, the culmination of these experiences and influences created the BPP belief

> that revolution was both internal and external and strove to create an organization that would be a microcosm of the world they were trying to create. Party members grappled with sexism, classism, individualism, and materialism and attempted to create alternative structures, institutions, and lifestyles. Their goal was not only to challenge and change the conditions in America but to politicize their membership and their mass following. In short, Black Panther Party members not only tried to transform the world; they tried to transform themselves. (Spencer 2016, 4)

A major part of these beliefs was the conviction that violent self-defense was necessary. "With the Panthers, of course," Lazerow and Williams write, "the issue to some extent has always been about violence. But their critics make violence the only issue, and they remain frozen in one moment in time" (Lazerow and Williams 2006, 7). In the wake of urban rioting, by 1966 many Black Power activists rejected nonviolence as ineffectual and even accommodating. The question of tactical violence included that of leadership. As Austin and Brotz note:

> Martin Luther King Jr., Bayard Rustin, Ralph Abernathy, Roy Wilkins, and James Farmer balked at a change in tactics; traditional protest measures had secured substantial public support and laws that ostensibly brought about a new day in race relations. Since most movement people understood that established leaders would not, indeed could not, change tactics at a time when things seemed to be improving, the younger, less experienced activists had to answer the question of who was going to lead this next phase of the movement. Would it be the older, more middle-class oriented blacks? Would it be the college-educated, the group W. E. B. Du Bois had dubbed the "Talented Tenth"? Would it be the mass of workers who made up the bulk of black America? Or would it be the dispossessed, the unemployed and underemployed people who lived by their wits; those who had no stake in the system, the group that Karl Marx and later Huey Newton dubbed the "lumpen proletariat"? (Austin 2006, xx)

Chappell sees that the "core belief of King's 'militant' opponents was that only defensive violence would deter the offensive violence that had long defined life in cotton field and ghetto" (Chappell 2021, 516–517).[14] This suggests that "militants" saw King as wittingly or otherwise in collusion with racially oppressive forces. They did not understand King to be espousing Black Power; rather, they took him to be preaching Black submission. This, of course, was a strategic misunderstanding meant to change the terms of Black radical leadership seen to have grown ineffective. As Chappell also insists, "King was often willfully misunderstood in his lifetime and remains widely misunderstood today. King's critics seized on his word nonviolence" (Chappell 2021, 516). For some Black Power leaders, "nonviolence" meant abandoning the right to self-defense in everyday life and not solely at historical inflection points when cameras were rolling. The threat of Black reprisal was meant to curtail lawless acts of violence between individuals, committed away from the public sphere. King's nonviolence was criticized as organized civil disobedience that acknowledged the legitimacy of the racist state power it transgressed against.

Yet as a manifestation of Black *power*, King's nonviolence may have been far more radical than a way of preserving the constitutional order by aligning it more effectively with its normative principles. As Hills and Curry suggest, Black *power* is "a universal call for justice, which he engages as the transition from 'thingification' to personhood. #BlackLivesMatter is the theopolitical demand for Black personhood, which we believe to be housed in King's philosophy of Black Power" (Hills and Curry 2015, 454). In this understanding of Black *power*, the idea's most fitting image would not be that of Huey P. Newton armed and enthroned, but rather that of Dr. Martin Luther King, Jr. describing his dream to the world in Washington, D.C.[15]

That said, there is not an either/or choice to be made between the images' representative quality; both display versions of the same struggle equally well. They form part of what Terry calls the "comprehensive cartography of Black Power contestation," which

> would cover roughly eleven themes: (1) political violence, (2) the politics of "self-determination," (3) identity and culture, (4) the social theorization of the ghetto, (5) gender, sexuality, and the family, (6) the political agency of the poor, (7) theories of racism, (8) social justice in an age of emerging postindustrial capitalism, (9) mid–Cold War geopolitics, (10) the political critique of African American religion, and (11) philosophical reflections on hope and pessimism. Constraints of space here do not allow for a full elaboration on each of these domains, but I hope to use the more familiar theme of violence—especially as topics of integration and racial identity are covered elsewhere in this volume—as a generative point of entry toward a sketch of this larger terrain and King's movements therein. (Terry 2018,a 295)

A philosophy of race is not included among these eleven themes. Citing "self-determination," "identity and culture," and "the social theorization of the ghetto," Terry's "comprehensive cartography" instead charts an *ethics of race* that tacitly identifies racial ontology with group formation and social responsibility. This is what Terry calls elsewhere "the ethics of oppressed groups," while pointing out that the

> one great difficulty in explicating the ethics of oppressed groups stems from the need to balance our deeply felt personal interests, such as dignity and self-respect,

with the claims for consideration, fairness, care, and even mercy that others in and outside the group have on us. King hoped that nonviolent, mass direct action could incorporate these myriad considerations without a "slide to subjectivism," as Charles Taylor might put it. The angst that he suffered throughout his career stemmed from his visceral understanding of how human interconnection was especially heightened among the oppressed: how reckless rebellion could invite indiscriminate group repression, how selfish accommodation could entrench group stigmas of inferiority, and how political violence can tragically delimit the indeterminate horizons of how and with whom the world should be shared. (Terry 2018b 62)

While this is certainly understandable, it also risks deferring questions of racial legitimacy and the metaphysics of authenticity at racism's origin and thereby effectively ensuring that racism persists in some Platonic-like form. For it remains to be seen if social problems can be solved without first or simultaneously addressing philosophical differences in ontology and formulating an alternative means of envisioning being together as a political goal. This would be not a "slide into subjectivism" but rather a negotiation of the objective, competing values defining human being among various groups, each attempting to be recognized as such. Ontology must be considered, not to take it seriously as an explanation of human being, but rather to take it as a way of understanding the fundamental attitudes preventing the full resolution of racially motivated inequality and injustice. Indeed, King avoids a slide into the subjectivism of racial categorization by considering and overcoming racial ontology as part of his Black *power* philosophy. In this way, King calls for the end to race and any other category of human being that creates division and, by extension, injustice.

In so doing, King is both true and false to his philosophical training. While he embraced the basic categories of the Western metaphysical tradition, he refused its essentialism to articulate an ontotheological theory of human difference made commensurable in what I call Being-in-love. Positing equality beyond racial distinction, King rejected racial essentialism before ever having practiced nonviolence publicly. This means King possessed an anti-essentialist ontology of race in advance of his work as a Civil Rights activist. He developed it studying philosophy, and in particular German philosophy, during his studies at Morehouse College, Crozer Theological Seminary, Boston University, and individually. King's thought, then, has its ontological roots in this tradition as well as in the Black experience. This understanding of King's philosophy is not meant to supersede or exclude any other but rather is intended to supplement and enhance King's already significant standing in African American philosophy.

II. King and African American Philosophy

Stephen Ferguson and John McClendon's recent history of African American philosophers sees King as so well known as an African American philosopher that the authors find it unnecessary to dwell on him in a vital project designed to recuperate lesser-known figures. This decision seems even more appropriate given that King's life and work command their own branch of study. Within King studies, a restitution project has been under way insisting on a more radical reading of his political philosophy and on a thorough understanding of the ideological function King's image plays in contemporary culture.[16] Both aims of this project entail rescuing King's legacy from its right-leaning appropriation as commemorative and memorializing, yet without any politically transformative capability. As Rose insists, "King's legacy is purposely deployed to promote the neoliberal idea that America has overcome its struggles with racism, poverty, and militarism, thereby discouraging contemporary Americans from engaging in the work necessary to combat these forms of structural injustice" (Rose 2019, 4). In other words, the radical force of King's philosophy has been neutralized by its acceptance in mainstream political discourse as edifying and complete. This result would be considered essentially right-wing because it protects institutional and interpersonal racism as having been overcome.

Part of this project of recuperation has been made possible by the much wider availability of King's unpublished work combined with a fuller documentary history of his movement. Livingston notes, "Reading King's best-known works, like *Where Do We Go from Here?*, in a broader historical context outlined by his unpublished speeches and movement documents reveals not only a radical King, as much recent scholarship has sought to recuperate, but a militant theory of nonviolence that resists the domesticated portrayals of civil disobedience" (Livingston 2020, 702).[17] Shelby and Terry see the reevaluation of the radical King as produced by consideration of a wider range of topics in his work, as scholars no longer "neglect King's well-considered and wide-ranging treatments of many important philosophical and political issues, including labor and welfare rights, economic inequality, poverty, love, just war theory, virtue ethics, political theology, violence, imperialism, nationalism, reparations, and social justice—not to mention his more familiar writings on citizenship, racial equality, voting rights, civil disobedience, and nonviolence" (Shelby and Terry 2018, 2). According to this recent work, part of the problem has been the misrepresentation of King's nonviolence, in which his acknowledged, extortive threat of violence is obscured for a more congenial, appropriative presentation of the Civil Rights leader (Hinton 2018, 50).

Another radical, dangerous aspect of King's philosophy is its understanding and conscious manipulation of white racism as a set of "irrational fears" paradoxically provoked by American democracy itself and preventing the recognition of Black humanity at the level of cognition (Terry 2018b, 14–15). King used these fears to provoke scenes of white violence while limiting that violence under threat of violent Black revolt behind nonviolent civil disobedience. Because, as Scheuerman points out, King's philosophy of nonviolence "appealed to traditional (mostly Christian) natural law ideas when explaining why some (unjust) laws could potentially be violated by prospective civil disobedients": any violence it brought about would be justifiable before God (Scheuerman 2015, 429). This calls into question both the nature of Christian (non)violence and that of the civil disobedient.

Relying on traditional Christian natural law to legitimate its violence, King's nonviolence implies an ontology in addition to a faith. As King writes in *Stride Toward Freedom* (originally published in 1958), "There is something about the protest that is suprarational; it cannot be explained without a divine dimension. Some may call it a principle of concretion, with Alfred N. Whitehead; or a process of integration, with Henry N. Wieman; or Being-itself, with Paul Tillich; or a personal God. Whatever the name, some extra-human force labors to create a harmony out of the discords of the universe" (King 2010b, 82). Referring to the 1955–1956 Montgomery bus boycott, King carefully avoids writing "supernatural," choosing instead "suprarational," which refers to the ability to comprehend the protest, and nonviolence generally, rather than to the protest's inherent quality. As a quality of mind, then, the protest transcends human reason without surpassing humanity itself. In other words, King understands the protest philosophically first, and only then possibly theologically, indicating his epistemological approach by referencing the philosopher Whitehead, along with the philosopher-theologians Wieman and Tillich, with both of the latter forming the joint subject of King's dissertation. While the dissertation's subject division is nearly equal, King betrays a clear preference for Tillich's philosophical theology, showing particular interest in Tillich's Heideggerian concept of Being-itself. Indeed, King studied Heidegger's philosophy closely, writing in a longer version of "Pilgrimage to Nonviolence" (originally published in 1960):

> During the past decade I also gained a new appreciation for the philosophy of existentialism. My first contact with this philosophy came through my reading of Kierkegaard and Nietzsche. Later I turned to a study of Jaspers, Heidegger and Sartre. All of these thinkers stimulated my thinking; while finding things to question in each, I nevertheless learned a great deal from study of them. When I finally turned to a serious study of the works of Paul Tillich I became convinced that existentialism, in spite of the fact that it had become all too fashionable, had grasped certain basic truths about man and his condition that could not be permanently overlooked. (King 2013, 73)

King did not overlook them; instead he incorporated them into his Black *power* philosophy.

Indeed, King's Black *power* philosophy is grounded in these "basic truths," and specifically in how Heidegger's fundamental ontology articulates them. That said, King's use of Heidegger identifies and rejects the German philosopher's putative racism while maintaining Heidegger's understanding of Being and critique of metaphysics. In this sense, King's thought falls well within Cornel West's general understanding of "philosophy and the Afro-American experience" (1977). Surprisingly, West begins this metaphilosophical essay with a lengthy explanation of Heidegger's correlative importance for African American philosophy's basic critical assumptions (or *basic truths*). As an anti-Cartesian, indeed anti-Platonic philosophy meant to question all the Western philosophical tradition's assumptions about human being, Heidegger's fundamental ontology provides the metaphilosophical basis for African American philosophy's challenge to Western metaphysics. West writes:

> Afro-American philosophy appropriates from Heidegger the notion of philosophy as interpretation of what it means to be for people who, as a result of active engagement in the world, reconstruct their past, make choices in the present and envision possibilities for the future. Yet Heidegger's conception of philosophy is inadequate. His understanding of the "historicality" (*Geschichtlichkeit*) of Dasein, or the way in which historical circumstances influence individuals' choices in the

present, is unsatisfactory. His constitutive categories of "historicality," namely, fate, destiny and heritage, fail to incorporate the current perceptions of the historical forces which constrain human activity. (West 1977, 9)

For West, Heidegger's critique of ontology is essential to African American philosophy, which appropriates it as a condition of its existence. That said, Heidegger's philosophy fails as a historical account of the material forces shaping social existence, for which West looks to Wittgenstein and Dewey. Yet as the critical negation of the Western tradition in metaphysics, Heidegger's philosophy articulates the ontological or "human" condition of African American experience. A fundamental ontology that could speak meaningfully to the history of racism and other forms of dehumanization premised by Western metaphysics would satisfy well West's metaphilosophical conditions for defining African American philosophy.

Bernard Boxill takes a different view of the relationship between African American philosophy and the white Euro-American tradition. Leaving aside Western metaphysics and metaphilosophical speculation, he suggests the "history of African American political thought can be divided into two great traditions—the assimilationist and the separatist. The assimilationist tradition maintains that a society in which racial differences have no moral, political, or economic significance—that is, a color-blind society—is both possible and desirable in America. The separatist tradition denies this, some separatists maintaining that a color-blind society in America is not possible, others maintaining that it is not desirable" (Boxill 1992, 119).[18] Notably, Boxill holds this view regarding African American political thought and not African American philosophy. His understanding of African American philosophy can be described as a critical conversation with the Western philosophical tradition "about the nature of justice, liberty, equality, individuality, community, tolerance, solidarity, and other important political values, a conversation that stretches back for centuries," in which "Martin Luther King, Jr. is as much an interlocutor about when civil disobedience is permissible as are Ronald Dworkin and John Rawls" (Shelby 2010, 344). In addition to his reading of King as a philosopher of civil disobedience decisively influencing the work of Dworkin and Rawls while revising Thoreau considering the African American experience, Boxill's use of Locke to consider African American reparations provides another example of his integrative philosophical practice.[19] Boxill is not engaging in ontological speculation; rather, his concern is analytical and legal, starting from the premise that traditional arguments in Western philosophy can illuminate African American activism, while African American philosophy can clarify, rather than destroy, positions within the tradition.[20]

In what would be agreement with Boxill, West labels Heidegger's philosophy inadequate to the specificity of African America's historical experience. Yet West's tacit appropriation of Heidegger for a form of African American meontology is problematic both for Boxill's conception of African American philosophy and for reading Heidegger in philosophical and historical context, for West conflates African American experience with fundamental ontology, to ambiguous result. Heidegger's destruction of metaphysics is not experientially descriptive, as West himself points out; it addresses the ontological conditions facilitating the thinking of Being. In other words, Heidegger's concern is only partially anti-Cartesian critique, and therefore not solely negative. His is not meontology; it is ontology. In this respect, any appropriation of Heidegger's philosophy is an ontological investment in Dasein's existential analytic. To avoid the potentially crushing weight of its burden, West has stopped short of racial ontology. Yet as Naomi Zack points out, "If we give race a fraction of the kind of systematic thought reserved for traditional philosophical topics and begin to sort out some of the current disagreements in the literature with the standing tools of the trade, it is obvious that race is not a burdensome subject. It is not difficult to get the empirical and semantic facts about race right. Even if the full and final theory is elusive, plausible abstract clarity can be brought to the issues. If individuals who are not philosophers find the ontology of race conceptually confusing and emotionally distressing, this does not mean that philosophers, who for the most part do earn a professional reputation of detachment, need be confused and upset" (Zack 1999, 249–250). Implicit or overt, racial ontology forms a part of any definition of African American philosophy. Is there, however, an African American ontology?

The fact that Kwame Anthony Appiah's 1992 question, "African-American Philosophy?," for example, remains silent on the matter speaks to these issues of metaphilosophy and ontology. To answer "African-American philosophy?" it might be best to interrogate the query's construction. For Appiah's essay title does not ask, "What is African American philosophy?" Yet an essay entitled "African-American Philosophy?" must offer an example of African American philosophy, assuming the essay meets the conditions articulated. Appiah's essay does not do this. Pointing out that Africana philosophy and African American philosophy are not the same thing, the essay argues instead for subsuming both under the heading "ethnophilosophy": "the attempt to explore and systematize the conceptual world of Africa's traditional cultures" (Appiah 1992, 17). This approach assumes African American philosophy exists and has been clearly defined, only to deconstruct this definition and place its existence under erasure in ethnophilosophy's wider text.[21] Appiah's suggestion would appear to be very similar to what Lucius Outlaw described in 1987 as the "deconstructive appropriation of philosophy as a privileged notion and its decentering extension to products of the intellectual labors of Africans in the New World" (Outlaw 1987, 78). For Appiah and Outlaw, debates on philosophy are "inherently ideological and political" rather than essential (Outlaw and Roth 1997, 35). Yet Outlaw differs from Appiah insofar as ideological-political context signals a difference within Africana philosophy between the various diaspora discourses, indicating the existence of a related yet unique African American philosophy.

George Yancy develops Outlaw's approach when he writes, "African-American philosophy emerges from a socio-existential context where persons of African descent have been faced with the absurd in the form of white racism" (Yancy 2011, 551). Yancy theorizes "the meaning of African-American philosophy within the context of Black sub-personhood" as construed within the American ideological-political context (Yancy 2015, 1145).[22] In addition to Blackness as a diasporic condition of contingent African American Blackness, African American philosophy investigates the ideological-political complex that is American whiteness. This "racial contract," as Charles Mills would describe it, also means, as Lewis Gordon suggests, that "whiteness premises itself on ignoring blackness, and blackness premises itself as a relation to whiteness (and other symbolic purveyors of thought), leads to a subverted realization: Whiteness is only universal to the extent to which it ignores reality. It is thus a particular asserting itself as universal. That blackness admits its relationality means that it is, albeit not the universal, more of a universalizing commitment. This observation is found throughout African Diasporic thought" (Gordon 2014, 96). From this, Gordon concludes that "blackness, broader in scope, unmasks the false security of whiteness" (Gordon 2013b, 730). As Howard McGary insists, it reveals the moral paradox of racial universalism, for "people cannot be said to have made a moral judgment if they intend their judgments to apply only to members of their family, religious sect, or race" (McGary 2009, 4). Rather than a moral imperative, race is defined contractually among the dominant group. This "domination contract," as Mills puts it, "makes exclusion conceptually central, which corresponds to the actual historical record. Instead of taking 'person' as gender- and race-neutral, it makes explicit that maleness and whiteness were prerequisites for full personhood" (Mills 2000, 453).

In this respect, Mills's racial contract relies on philosophical anthropology for its basic definition of human being. Along with Mills, Gordon also draws out the philosophical implications of defining blackness in this anthropological sense. He writes, "Philosophical anthropology examines what it means to be human. Unlike empirical anthropology, which presupposes the legitimacy of the human sciences, including their methodologies, philosophical anthropology challenges the methods themselves and the presuppositions of the human offered by each society, and by doing so, offers the transition from method to methodology and methodological critique. That area of research makes sense for Africana and black philosophy from the fact of the challenged humanity of Africana and black people in the modern world" (Gordon 2013a, 48). By framing the question "African American philosophy?" in this way, it becomes clear why Gordon seeks to honor that "the political commitments of Africana studies and Black studies sometimes elided the importance of their location in academic institutions. Those proponents' search for a practice or praxis, although well intentioned, at times undermined the value of thought" (Gordon 2020, 42–43). He understands these commitments as fundamentally different from other disciplinary tendencies, which suffer from "the problem of 'compartmentalism' and 'disciplinary decadence,' two tendencies that continue to be features of not only much race theory but also most disciplinary practices in the academy. The former offered disciplines under a separate but equal rule, which, if history has taught us anything about such formulations, is never actually so. The latter sought methodological conquest. These constrained what one could talk about when it came to human matters and how one is supposed to do it" (Gordon 2018, 30). In philosophy, this is the result of a colonial attitude that accepts "the historical rise of a particular cultural group as the self-avowed sole progenitor of philosophical practice" (Gordon 2019, 17). The danger of this self-understanding is the reinscription of racial essentialism, and therefore racism, through contractual exclusion within Africana philosophy itself. As Henry Louis Gates, Jr. writes, "We cannot, finally, succumb to the temptation to resurrect our own version of the Thought Police, who would determine who, and what, is 'black.' 'Mirror, Mirror on the Wall, Who's the Blackest One of All?' is a question best left behind in the sixties. If we allow ourselves to succumb to the urge to build an academic discipline around this perverse question, we will, like the fairy-tale witch, die from our own poison. For if the coming century in this country is black and brown, it is a blackness without blood that we must pass on" (Gates 1992, 9).

To avoid this mistake, that of essentialism, Gordon defines Blackness within the parameters of an existentialist humanism. He writes, "Critics of existentialism often reject its human formulation. Heidegger, for instance, in his 'Letter on Humanism,' lambasted Sartre for supposedly in effect subordinating Being to a philosophical anthropology with dangers of anthropocentrism. Yet a philosophical understanding of culture raises the problem of the conditions through which philosophical reflections could emerge as meaningful" (Gordon 2017, 105). Gordon sees an opposition between existentialist African American philosophy and essentialist phenomenology, which for him is anti-humanist and therefore unconcerned with the complex experience of racial oppression. The division he articulates refers to his discussion of Black studies' development and the critical disciplinary division between literary critical and philosophical method, where the former is essentialist and the latter existentialist.[23] Africana and African American philosophy are epistemic enterprises that concentrate on existential ideological and political phenomena and their historical contingency. African American theory engages in ontological speculation, sometimes without attention to the philosophical history embedded in its method.

Bearing the essentialist/existentialist disciplinary division in mind, Anita Allen writes:

> African-American philosophy has played at least six broad roles: (1) to critique law and government authority; (2) to critically analyze power, and institutions and practices of oppression, subordination, slavery, class, caste, colonialism, racism, sexism, and homophobia; (3) to articulate the bases of African-American identities and the grounds of responsibility, community, solidarity, and collective action; (4) to express African-American existential, spiritual, psychological, and moral joys and discontents; (5) to celebrate and interpret African-American art and culture; (6) to assess the discipline, canon, and history of Western philosophies, by reference to gaps, logical and moral inconsistencies, methodological limitations, epistemologies, and exclusions. (Allen 2013, 19)

Critique, analysis, articulation, expression, interpretation, and celebration: these are the activities that define African American existentialist philosophy. Nowhere in this list, however, does Allen suggest the aesthetic activity of "rendering," in the sense of "service" and "cause to be." African American philosophy does not render African America or African Americans. While it may perform a duty, there is no aspect of creative "making" in this service; it never "causes to be" through an act of creation. In philosophy, ontology provides this service. It is the task of ontology to articulate being through critique, analysis, expressivity, interpretation, and even celebration. Most of all, however, ontology describes being creatively, insofar as being cannot merely be said to be, or described, but must also be enacted. African American philosophy also enacts being. The salient question, then, is, does it enact essential African American Being, and being that is contingently African American? This ontological question of African American being has been left to African American Theory, and not to African American philosophy.

Yet ontology is at the heart of African American philosophy. Without it, there is no way to know the answer to "African American philosophy?" without making a series of unphilosophical decisions. These decisions would assign essential meaning to "African American" instead of interrogate it; they would determine the definition of race in any configuration (essentialist, constructivist, situationist, etc.) instead of questioning its conditions of possibility; they would assume a common professional experience instead of suspecting a layered field of engagement; they would assume a common personal formation and motivation for the study of philosophy instead of positing diversity of background. From this wide perspective, African American philosophy can be defined as philosophical critique that doubts Western philosophy's fundamental assumptions about what it means to be human. This is ontology not as racial essentialism but rather as critique. This was King's philosophical project.

Whereas in the 1980s Outlaw began the deconstructive project of articulating African American philosophy as a counterdiscursive force or differend within Western thought, Gordon and Appiah changed course in the early 1990s and attempted to define African American philosophy as a part of Africana philosophy, or even more broadly as an example of ethnophilosophy. One effect of this shift was to make African American philosophy's ontological concerns those of the diaspora. Realizing the inadequacy of this definition, Allen and Yancy present a philosophy specific to African American concerns while avoiding any articulation of Black ontology that would subsume these issues completely under the heading of Africana philosophy or ethnophilosophy. Their philosophy owes much to Gordon's existentialism in outline while being more attuned to the characteristics that define the singularity of African American life.

That said, neither Yancy nor Allen suggests anything like an African American ontology, which would rely on the validation of race as African America's *ens realissimus*. Also avoiding articulating racial ontology, Charles Mills's racial contract acts as a powerful conceptual tool for understanding African American singularity politically and socially without recourse to metaphysics, or "Blackness" as "being," in any sense. Doing so, however, assumes a uniform African American experience, without which the racial contract becomes the transcendental analytic by which all African Americans are subject to the same form of racist elaboration. From this perspective, Yancy's, Allen's, and Mills's sociopolitical philosophies would be parts of a critique of "pure" racist reason that recognizes uniformity of African American "being" in relation to the racial contract itself, whereby all African Americans were recognized and discriminated against in the same way.[24]

III. King and Ontology

Before showing how King alters Heidegger's thought to contextualize this uniformity ontologically, it may be useful to lay out broadly those aspects of Heideggerian philosophy King adopts, beyond West's more schematic approach. Heidegger's fundamental ontology articulates the "conditions constitutive of the interpretability of entities as the entities they are" (Carman 2003, 85). Dasein, or being-there, is "the kind of entity that in each case we human beings are" (Wrathall and Murphy 2013, 1). As entities, or beings, we are situated in the world at a certain time, which we discover though our intentionality, or care, which Heidegger understands as Dasein's fundamental structure (Denker 2013, 71). "Being-in-the-world" names Dasein's intentionality, with "the world" as the structure of intentionality's content, and "being-in" the way Dasein means that content (Richardson 2012, 87). Furthermore, because "Dasein is a temporal unfolding, because it is finite and must die, it constitutes a unified 'structure.' Heidegger calls this 'structural whole' 'being-toward-death'" (Trawny 2018, 37).

Dasein is attentive to these structures as they are reflected in language. "For Heidegger, the key feature for understanding language is to focus on our responsiveness to it, the way that it shapes and guides our understanding of ourselves and the world around us 'before we are speaking'" (Wrathall 2005, 89).[25] As "the house of being," as Heidegger puts it in the "Letter on Humanism" and elsewhere, language "is a medium in which Being takes hold of us, appropriates us, and allows us and all beings to come into our own" (Polt 1999, 177). We come into our own in the world, which itself is conditioned by "earth," a later and notoriously esoteric Heideggerian concept. As Trawny puts it, "'World' is the 'openness' in which the earth's coming forth can unfold itself. 'Earth' is the 'sheltering' on the basis of which 'world' can be founded" (Trawny 2018, 96). "From this perspective," Trawny continues, "the 'reciprocity' between 'earth' and 'world' is a 'struggle.' Heidegger considers this 'struggle' to be characteristic of the 'truth of being'" (Trawny 2018, 96–97). Finally, "'Earth' here does not, of course, refer to the globe but rather to the specific 'place' of an 'origin,' i.e., the 'homeland'" (Trawny 2018, 97). Dasein's experience of "earth" as the ground in which it is rooted as in the world is shared communally as the "homeland" of a people or Volk. The "openness" of world allows the earth to come forth to a people so that they may recognize themselves as such in "the house of being."[26]

How does this relate to King's philosophy? King, too, seeks to render the conditions under which beings encounter each other in their truth, believing that racial segregation has obscured and obstructed the fundamental truth of human being, the ontological drive toward unity. In attempting to describe the current social situation, King seeks the terms under which it may be interpretable. The autobiographical accounts of his intellectual journey provide the narrative basis for the attempted elaboration of a legitimate epistemological standard with which to encounter Being existentially as Other. To this end, King fully accepts that the existential priority of human being is Dasein or being situated in and constituted spatially and temporally by a fundamental relation to finitude. King's promised land is not to be attained in the afterlife; it is reached in human existence by striving toward the freedom defined by the philosophical critique of segregation, through which God's presence in history is revealed ontologically. For King as for Heidegger, Dasein is structured by care, which in King's philosophy means care for the self and other, conditioned by God's love. Care is the intentional expression of God's unconditional love as realized in the confrontation with human finitude or being-toward-death. Said differently, the fear of death and anxiety of living bring Dasein to seek God's love for comfort and meaning in existence. God's love can only be experienced existentially in the authentic relation to others provided by certain knowledge of the self as ontologically conditioned by it. In so doing, the subject thrown into the world and confronted with finitude finds the plenitude of meaning in existence through the experience of God's love in the beloved community of others who have also encountered and acknowledged this truth.

Because the truth of Being can only be intuited and experienced obliquely in the unity of community, "essential" designations of human difference serve to pervert being. For King, race (like any other segregated category of human being) is sinful, because it is a tool by which the experience of God's love, ontologically premised on community, is prevented. This beloved community is one of care for the self and other, as premised by Being and mediated by language as an inherently nonviolent mode of communion between self and other, and between the community and God. While language can be made violent, King's notion of language as the vehicle of ontological truth is one of love's expression. All languages at base are meant to express care conditioned by God's love. This is because all peoples share the same origin of earth as God's creation. Race is a displacement of Being's truth as the unity of human being discovered in the anxiety of existential experience and realized in care as the beloved community.

King accepts there is a fundamental ontological relation that precedes and conditions existence. This ontology accepts Dasein as Heidegger defines it, and Dasein's situatedness in time and space. These existential qualifications ultimately disclose the dimensions of Being, or for King, Being-in-love, as it is disclosed in worldly existence. In this respect, King's existentialism is Heideggerian *Existenzphilosophie*, in that Heidegger's existential analytic, or systematic exhibition of "the conditions necessary for the discovery of meaning," is translated as pious acts of love performed in response to Dasein's realization that God's love precedes and determines existence (Martin 2013, 112). King does not suggest that the existential analytic synthesizing acts of neighborly love in God's name reveals the path to salvation after death; rather, he thinks, it shows the way to the direct and immediate amelioration of life in existence qualified by death.

For King, attaining the promised land is possible on earth; his is not an ontology of the afterlife, but is oriented toward daily existence lived within the light of Being. This worldly attainment creates the beloved community, within what he calls the World House. The beloved community consists of those who live life oriented toward Being and therefore against Nonbeing, which for King is death understood as human separation. Importantly, King here removes Heidegger's linguistic qualification, to eliminate essentialism from his philosophy. God's love strives to bring all humanity together equally in Being, grasped in existential acts of love reflecting this ultimate, universalist reality. Humanity's segregation propagates Nonbeing, the dialectical negation of God's love, hence King's need to excise linguistic hierarchy from the House of Being. For King, then, salvation and damnation occur on earth, the former as the beloved community and the latter as Nonbeing, or segregation. Earth, or "the promised land," discloses the type of community Dasein recognizes as historically, existentially valid, and therefore Dasein's fate in the eyes of God. The clearing allows Dasein to encounter its choice, its judgement. This powerful existential choice—for love or for Nonbeing—is revealed in potentially violent confrontation, with nonviolence striving toward the Being of the beloved community and violence embracing alienation from God's love as Nonbeing and death.

Along with presenting his ontology, *The Critique of Nonviolence* demonstrates its relation to King's political-theological reflections on police violence and the state of exception. It shares several concerns with a key early text in these debates in Germany, Walter Benjamin's "Critique of Violence" (1921). A comparative reading of King and Benjamin, along with later philosophers such as Jacob Taubes and Giorgio Agamben, reveals the depth of King's ontological attack on police violence as the illegitimate appropriation of the state of exception. For King, police violence against African Americans is the basis of sovereign American being. In part through its ontological appropriation of German philosophy and theology, King's philosophy condemns the perpetual American state of racial exception that permits unlimited police violence against Black lives.

Reading King with Benjamin, then, shows how King's ontology of what I call *divine nonviolence* condemns police violence as the consummate exercise of illegitimate power. Benjamin and King's critique of police violence can mean an overcoming of racism in divine violence. While the ontological basis for King's nonviolence belongs to Heidegger, the formal, political elements of the argument are like Benjamin's. They come from direct consideration, mainly through Rudolf Bultmann's work and other sources in contemporary Continental theology, of the same debates in Germany that shaped Benjamin's essay, such as political theology, Gnosis, eschatology and cultural crisis, and renewed philosophical speculation on Saint Paul's political ontology. In this vein, Heidegger presents an anti-humanist ontology that King corrects with systematic theology and a theory of divine violence as radical nonviolence. Through this theological commitment in his ontology of nonviolence, King accepts Heidegger's philosophical commitments while rejecting what I refer to as their "racist realism."

IV. The Aim of This Book

Ultimately, this book speaks to how King thought of nonviolence ontologically, and how racism in philosophical concepts led him to develop a different ontological understanding of racist police violence. That said, *The Critique of Nonviolence: Martin Luther King, Jr., and Philosophy* does not intend a biographical account of King's journey in philosophy (he provided that himself); rather, it considers King's philosophy in relation to other philosophers who drew on the same intellectual source for thinking about racial ontology, and racism in fundamental ontology.[27] I realize that much of what follows will seem new and counterintuitive to those well versed in the philosophers discussed and equally disorienting to those with a more general impression of the book's figures. I also understand that the way in which academic philosophy is presented here may seem unrepresentative or even unfair to those involved in it. However, the purpose of this book is not to reinvent the wheel regarding King, Benjamin, or Heidegger studies, or to misrepresent academic philosophy. This book brings under one roof, so to speak, philosophers and ideas that are seldom configured together in this way. While plenty of work has been done on Heidegger and anti-Semitism and race, when Heidegger's philosophy is brought into dialogue with King's, or any philosopher's outside "established channels," both philosophers' work changes in ways we cannot predict. We cannot expect to have the same Heidegger we have when we read his work with King's that we have when we read his work with, say, Arendt's. Yet when we read Heidegger within the framework of King's philosophy, and vice versa, the product will be different from that which is produced when we read Heidegger with Arendt or Marcuse, or King with Malcolm X or Rawls. This does not mean a reading that puts a very different and potentially strange face on familiar debates is wrong or destructive; it indicates instead the expansiveness of the topic in its ability to support a diversity of approaches and views. The inclusion of diverse, rigorous, new work on established philosophers and themes only serves to underscore the importance of previous scholarship and strengthen their already significant appeal.

Although the aim of this book is new, its novelty should not be understood as an attempt to contribute to reception history, or to the body of work devoted to King and political philosophy. This book's argument, then, has to do with King's ontology and not directly with his political philosophy. While welcome and exciting, the recent work on King's political philosophy does not consider this aspect of his thought. This book concentrates on ontology in King's thought to establish the structure and exigency of King's Black *power* as Being-in-love, and divine nonviolence as ontology.

Referencing works by Huey P. Newton, Cornel West, Lucius Outlaw, Bernard Boxill, George Yancy, and others, the book begins by presenting a theory of ontology in African American philosophy and the central place of King's thought within it. It then suggests that King's ontology was strongly influenced by Martin Heidegger's. After unpacking the aspects of Heidegger's philosophy most important to King's thought, the book then describes how King dealt with racism in fundamental ontology. Specifically, it grounds King's thought in 1920s German academic debates between Heidegger, Karl Barth, Paul Tillich, Rudolf Bultmann, Hans Jonas, Carl Schmitt, Eric Voegelin, and others on divine Being, Gnosticism, humanism, violence, and sovereignty.

The philosophical and theological history of this period in Germany provides King with responses to Heidegger's essentialism without having to reject his philosophy in toto. Indeed, King's focus on Paul Tillich's theological *Existenzphilosophie* is instrumental in facilitating his appropriation of Heidegger's fundamental ontology. To show this, the book concentrates on King's dissertation about Tillich, and on other key texts from his speculative writings and speeches, describing his ontotheological concepts of love and sin. The book then posits King's understanding of divine love (Being) and carnal sin (Nonbeing) as Heideggerian fundamental ontology articulated socially in racial integration and segregation.

To be clear, this book is an examination of race and racism in fundamental ontology that discusses King and Heidegger, and King and Benjamin. It is a reflection on the philosophical concept of race that, to this end, reads King's Heideggerian thought strictly within this concept. To show this, the book follows a straightforward methodology of inference and speculation. That is to say, the book's method does not rely on direct proof of reception because it takes as axiomatic that intellectuals in America had heard of King and possessed familiarity with his arguments.[28] The book uses inferential and speculative readings of related concepts between King's thought and Benjamin's. Although the book does not rely on readings of reception and direct influence, it does make use of historical connections between the philosophers treated. It reads King reading Heidegger through Tillich, and notes King's own acknowledged familiarity with Heidegger's philosophy, and with German Idealism generally. "King and philosophy," then, means "King and fundamental ontology," which for Heidegger was philosophy. Likewise, it signifies a specific, metaphilosophical attempt to think through ontology to reject racism as inherently violent. In other words, the title and subtitle should be read in the full sense of reciprocity inherent in the dialectic they present.

Chapter One examines King's interest and training in modern philosophy, paying particular attention to his interest in existentialism and Heidegger's ontology. Specifically, the chapter is interested in how their thought converges around anti-humanism, discussing King's own avowed anti-humanism as the point at which he connects Heidegger's philosophy with anti-racist social ontology. The chapter then briefly sketches out the how racism in Heidegger has been viewed, and how King dealt with it philosophically. Next, the chapter looks at King's social gospel and materialist philosophies in his thought. The chapter ends with King's description of nonviolence as a unique form of anti-racist fundamental ontology informed by social realism and historical materialism.

Chapter Two takes a closer look at King's appropriation of Heidegger's philosophy through his engagement with Paul Tillich's systematic theology. The chapter then engages in an extended reading of King's dissertation on Tillich as the general conceptual framework for nonviolence as a "basic truth" of human being. It situates King's doctoral work within the German philosophical tradition by linking it through Tillich's systematic theology to Heidegger's fundamental ontology. The chapter closes by showing how King's training in German thought informs his anti-essentialist view of civil rights.

Chapter Three considers King's form of Black *power*. It discusses how King rejects, philosophically, Malcolm X's and Stokely Carmichael's views, and those of the Black Panther Party, as racial essentialism. The chapter then examines Huey P. Newton's racial Platonism, which Newton adapts from his extensive readings of the *Republic* as a form of revolutionary love, or eros. To differentiate his own Platonic understanding of agape from a form of racial essentialism, King rejects any racially motivated preference for eros as the drive to separate and conquer. Rejecting eros as *libido dominandi*, King, following Tillich, insists agape transforms eros into "essential libido," the ground of beloved community.[29] The chapter closes with an in-depth discussion of King's dialectical reliance on Platonic eros to define agape in ontological relation to nonviolence.

Following on King's ultimately ontotheological presentation of nonviolence, Chapter Four considers political theology in King's "Letter from a Birmingham Jail" (1963). It suggests King exploits the Gnosticism and eschatology latent in fundamental ontology to theorize justice as divine nonviolence. The chapter shows that King's "Letter" can be read productively through interwar debates in German philosophy and theology about Gnosticism and eschatology. In so doing, the chapter shows that King's Gnosticism presents a theory of democratic political theology as the justification for civil disobedience.

Against this philosophical backdrop, Chapter Five connects King's thought on violence and sovereignty with Walter Benjamin's in his "Critique of Violence" (1921). Specifically, Benjamin's concept of divine violence offers a way to think of American anti-Black police violence as illegitimate within the political theological paradigm King proposes. Through its comparative reading of King and Benjamin, the chapter concludes, with King, that police violence in America is the illegitimate use of law-making sovereignty.

The conclusion traces how the critical theoretical reception of King's nonviolence misunderstood or ignored his use of eros, from Herbert Marcuse's initial reaction to Martha Nussbaum's more recent misreading. The book closes with bell hooks's recuperation of eros in King's philosophy as a return to the revolutionary praxis of Black love.

In summary, King rejects Black separatism, which he sees as Platonic in nature, and enlists Heidegger to distinguish agape as anti-essentialist. This leads to his appropriation of Tillich's thought as an anti-humanistic, anti-racist elaboration of fundamental ontology. Adapting Tillich, King overcomes "erotic" separatism with agape as the anti-essentialist expression of Being-in-love, King's combination of Heidegger and Tillich. This concept yields an understanding of nonviolence as political theology informed by the Gnostic eschatology that shaped fundamental ontology in Germany in the 1920s and 1930s. For King, divine nonviolence is the social and political articulation of Being-in-love as the veiled ground of history's teleological development toward beloved community. Like Benjamin, King sees the state as inherently violent; divine nonviolence posits beloved community as the state's successor and the inaugurator of history redeemed. That is, divine nonviolence is the Gnostic indication of history's end of state sovereignty, especially that which nonviolence is exercised and preserved in police violence. When this end occurs, beloved community begins as the new, authentic form of existential being.

1 Being and Nonviolence

I. King's Anti-Humanism

MARTIN LUTHER KING, JR. would occasionally pepper his sermons with brief philosophy lessons. In one such instance, he says:

> There is a school of modern philosophy called existentialism which starts out with the premise that man creates himself. Says it[s] most outstanding exponent: "It is a doctrine according to which existence preceded, and eternally creates the essence. Man first exists, and in choosing himself he creates himself: in acting he makes himself." Stated in more concrete terms this theory merely says that man is the measure of all things; man, rather than God, creates himself; and that whatever man is he himself achieved. But no Christian can believe this. From the deeps of our moral consciousness springs the conviction that what we are, we owe. (King 1994f, 574)

Citing Sartre as the "most outstanding exponent" of this "school of modern philosophy," King rejects existentialism as a humanism. Placing "man" before God, existentialism of this variety has nothing to offer the Christian community.

This level of antagonism in King toward existentialism may seem odd, given that at Crozer he studied with George Washington Davis, who in 1957 published *Existentialism and Theology: An Investigation of the Contribution of Rudolf Bultmann to Theological Thought* (1957). In 1958, Davis "sent a copy of his [Bultmann] book . . . to King with the inscription: 'With my warm compliments and with cherished memories of our days together as professor and student, friend and friend, on Crozer campus and in my home'" (Carson et al. 2008, 76). The book had been published by the Philosophical Library, with a subtitle that indirectly identifies Rudolf Bultmann as a philosopher with something to offer theology. Yet like King's, Bultmann's thought can confound this distinction. Bultmann was a Marburg theologian, and his work strongly reflected that of Martin Heidegger, his close colleague at the university from 1923 to 1928 and closer friend, with whom he maintained a correspondence for fifty years. Heidegger's importance to twentieth-century theology is not limited to his friend Bultmann's thought. As John Macquarrie writes, "More than any other contemporary philosopher, Heidegger has exercised a powerful influence on continental theology" (Macquarrie 1967, 3). Indeed, Walter Marshall Horton's 1938 study, *Contemporary Continental Theology: An Interpretation for Anglo-Saxons*—a book with which King was thoroughly acquainted—can hardly explicate its subject without reference to *Being and Time* and other works by Heidegger and treating them in some detail. King used Horton's book as a standard reference in Davis's two-term course Christian Theology for Today. In this year-long seminar, King encountered, along with Bultmann, the continental "crisis theologians," whose views King describes in negative terms (King 1994b, 124). For the crisis theologians, "man" has become absolutely alienated from God and can only return through crisis. Otherwise, "man" dwells alone in the world, far beneath a distant God. Naming Karl Barth as the contemporary exponent of crisis theology, King sees him as Kierkegaard "arisen from the grave" (King 1994b, 133). The crisis theology of Kierkegaard, a Christian existentialist, is still too invested in "humanism" for King.

That said, King draws inspiration from a version of existentialism associated with Bultmann's thought. On another occasion when existentialism figured in a sermon, King says:

> There is the tension that comes as a results of man's general finite situation. Man has to face the fact that he's finite, that he is inevitably limited, that he's caught up within the categories of time and space. And he faces this thing that he may not be. That's why one great school of modern philosophy, known as existentialism, cries out that the great threat of modern life is the threat of nonbeing, and every man has to live under the threat of nonbeing, that he must face this fact sooner [or] later in his life, that hovering over him is the threat of nonbeing. He finds his self asking with Shakespeare, "To be or not to be, that's the question," but he faces the fact that he may not be. And he knows that there will come a moment that he will have to go into his room and pull down the shades and turn out the lights and take off his shoes and walk down to the chilly waters of death. And he confronts this threat of nonbeing that drives through the whole structure of modern life. And because of that he lives in tension and dismay and despair because he knows

that hanging over him is the cloud of nonbeing, the threat of nothingness. He wonders, "Where does it go from here?" This is the tension of modern life, and these things account for the tension. These things all come together and leave all of us standing amid the tension of modern life. (King 1994f, 264)

King strongly approves of this "school of modern philosophy," this existentialism, which is different from that of Kierkegaard and Sartre, and to which Bultmann (but not Barth) belongs. Concentrating on the question of being in relation to finitude, King strikes a remarkably Heideggerian tone, suggesting that being's orientation toward death distinguishes life as the struggle against Nonbeing. "One great school of modern philosophy, known as existentialism," shows how being is "caught up within categories of time and space" and, due to modernity's emphasis on the human priority of being, struggles with Nonbeing as alienation from Being as *ens realissimum*. Striking Kierkegaardian and Sartrean notes of "despair" and "nothingness," King cites *Hamlet* and the question of being-unto-death as the problem of humanism. Ultimately, however, King rejects Kierkegaard and Sartre for an existential analytic of being, and "time and space" qualified by Nonbeing, making his anti-humanism more Heideggerian than not.

Perhaps conscious of this, King understandably credits Jacques Maritain for his anti-humanism instead of Heidegger, despite having more in common philosophically with the latter.[1] He is struck by Maritain's Manichaean views, in which "the age of humanism is marching toward its own 'liquidation.'" Humanism takes "human aspiration for Ideal Values. This view is often referred to as Humanism. The essence of this view is that God is to be found in man's highest social experiences, not in any reality beyond man" (King 1994a, 441). The previous age of humanism was that of Idealism, in which God is a "mere Idea" as "man begins to trust in his ability to dominate nature single-handed, by his own science and technology" (King 1994b, 123). This was preceded by the first age of humanism, where God "becomes the guarantor of man's success (Bacon, Descartes) in dominating nature" (King 1994b, 123). Yet King is most impressed by Maritain's anti-humanism, in the sense that the phases of humanistic thought Maritain describes are characterized by varying degrees of anthropomorphic thought in which "man" comes to value his own powers above God's.

Although the student paper in question may seem to reproduce Maritain's work through Horton's summary, King still took Maritain's basic point about humanism to heart, expressing it in his own reflections on Jeremiah. King writes:

> Jeremiah was opposed to any form of humanism in the modern sense. It might be well that those of us who are opposed to humanism in the modern world would speak out against it as did Jeremiah and set out to give a rational defense of theism. It seems to me that one of the great services of neo-orthodoxy, notwithstanding its extremes, is its revolt against all forms of humanistic perfectionism. They call us back to a deeper faith in God. Is not this the need of the hour? Has not modern man placed too much faith in himself and too little faith in God? (King 1994b, 166)

King understands humanism as "anthropocentrism," or "man's" valuation of human being above God. He accepts Maritain's history of anthropocentric humanism as humanity's increasing confidence in its own abilities, and with Maritain sees human arrogance reflected in modern philosophy, which presumably would need to be overcome in order for Christianity to return to its theocentric orientation of thought. Elsewhere King refers to "Modern Humanism—the cult of modern science," and calls it "man having too much faith in himself" (King 1994f, 369). In his most pointed formulation, King writes, "Humanism is another answer frequently given to the question, 'What is man?' Believing neither in God nor in the existence of any supernatural power, the humanist affirms that man is the highest form of being which has evolved in the natural universe" (King 1994f, 330n). From this point of view, although oriented differently in terms of disciplinary object, King's critique of humanism has much in common with Heidegger's "Letter on Humanism" (1946).

Any account of or intervention in African American philosophy framed by Heidegger's fundamental ontology must address racism in Heidegger's thought, historically and philosophically.[2] Without first doing this, the work risks reproducing the racism in Heidegger's thought, naively or through misguided intention. Terms like "Being" and "Blackness" are not in themselves or by force of rhetoric counterdiscursive. Where Heidegger's philosophy forms the basis of the ontological gesture, a full acknowledgment of the historical contexts and debates that shaped his thought provides a fuller understanding of the African American philosophical enterprise itself. Indeed, King could not have appropriated Heidegger's fundamental ontology without recognizing and conceding the possibility of its racism, given Heidegger's well-known complicity with the Nazis. While King did not voice his opinion on this directly, he nevertheless intervened in the Heidegger question perforce, in his statements on humanism.

II. Heidegger's Racism

Heidegger's "Letter on Humanism" has often been read as a source document for understanding his racism. As Janicaud notes, the "Letter" does not clarify this relationship in light of Nazi crimes; it enhances them as "a complete blurring of the ontological specificities of the political dimension" (Janicaud 1989, 139; Rabinbach 1994, 33). Nazism in the "Letter" is not a "humanism," as Lacoue-Labarthes suggested, but rather, as Derrida insisted, the conflation of spirit with race (Rabinbach 1994, 34–35). Indeed, "Derrida's reading of Heidegger highlights the presence within our response to Nazism of a philosophical problem as well as a need for moral condemnation. He draws out uncomfortable overlaps between the biological racism of the Nazis, the spiritual racism of Heidegger, and the metaphysical thinking informing much of our universalism" (Bevir 2000, 122).[3]

That said, in Heidegger "spiritual racism" is not the same as anti-Semitism, which views "world Jewry" as a product and problem of modernity, rather than as a category of fundamental ontology.[4] Yet, as Fritsche writes, insofar as

> the question of the role of world Jewry has to be framed as the ontological question of the truth of modernity, it is not primarily a racial question. However, the answer to it can very well refer to a race, and according to Heidegger it does so: the type of humanity claimed by the truth of modernity and the racial essence of the Jews are the same. Only because destiny has sent a truth that the Jews, in virtue of their race, have always already practiced before modernity, and which essentially-racially only the Jews could practice, was it possible for them to disseminate their racially determined empty rationality and calculative ability and, in this way, increase their own power. And only for this reason could they take on from Being the world-historical task of becoming the protagonists of machination and of uprooting all beings. (Fritsche 2018, 323).

As in King, race in Heidegger is not biological; it is ontological in the sense of a natural affinity to Being. Unlike in King, however, Heidegger sees this affinity as belonging to a specific, historical people, as revealed both in their philosophical relation to language and in their language itself (Aboutorabi 2015, 415).

For this reason, it is hard to imagine, as Bernasconi does, that Heidegger's "turn" responds to any rejection of racism a philosopher like King might recognize, and to the need to account for this rejection in fundamental ontology (Bernasconi 2000, 62). While Heidegger certainly rejected scientific racism, his alternative is in some ways much worse. Although Bernasconi seems to realize this, his highly selective historicism prevents him from grappling with distinctions between "person" and "work" and between "work" and "Weltanschauung" (Ansell-Pearson 1994, 507). In other words, Bernasconi mistakes the history of philosophy for history, a grave error that allows him to imagine Heidegger as anti-racist.

More realistically, as Sharpe shows, "Heidegger's martial language in the *Rektoratsrede* echoes his near-contemporary description of 'the essence of Truth' as *Kampf* and, soon after, his characterization of the relation of 'earth' and 'world' in artworks as '*Kampf*,' as well as his 1935 association of 'the political' with founding *Gewalt*" (Sharpe 2018b, 197).[5] *Gewalt* names the "ontological dimension of Heidegger's interpretation of *Geschichte*." As Love and Meng explain, it is "the political aspect that attends his notion of *Geschichte* as an act of creation—as an act, more precisely, of violence—that Heidegger is obviously engaged in himself: his notion of *Geschichte* and his history of Being amount to creative rejoinders to the world's increasingly technocratic condition. It would be difficult to view Heidegger's intervention in any other way in light of his interpretation of history" (Love and Meng 2018, 101–102). As Feldman, in a more "realist" vein, writes, Heidegger's use of Hölderlin and "earth" advances his

> attempts to "prepare the ground" for a post-liberal awakening to end the present interregnum that is impeding the return of an authentic culture ceases to be innocuous. Indeed, even his later "non-Nazi" philosophy assumes a much more intense political undertone and carries a much more noxious legacy than heretofore appreciated, a realisation perfectly understood by contemporary fascists themselves. Thus, for example, Heidegger's meditations on Hölderlin become political exhortations for a future that finally overcomes the baleful legacy of Socratic humanism. For this German poet takes centre stage in Heidegger's later work as (in his view) the first gnostic to mourn the loss of the spiritual in a constantly unfolding Greek tragedy on the withdrawal of Being. Although this play nearly reached a triumphant climax under National Socialism, what seemed a final curtain signaled only an interval. (Feldman 2005, 193)

In this regard, Waite also provides important context:

> Heidegger's lecture on Hölderlin's elegy "Homecoming / To the Relatives," was first delivered in the main auditorium of Freiburg University on June 6, 1943, the

centennial of Hölderlin's death, during the definitive German retreat from the USSR. Heidegger's concepts of *Heimat* and *Heimkunft* now welcome the Wehrmacht and Waffen SS home as those "relatives" who are hereby readied to fight another day if no longer (only) in military battle, then (also) in spiritual. (Waite 2008, 118)

The idea that Heidegger "turned" his philosophy because of concerns over racism neglects this history. Rather, as Lafont sums up Habermas's conclusion after decades of thought on the issue, "Heidegger's path to his famous 'turn' (*Kehre*) is better explained by external factors related to Heidegger's political involvement with Nazism than by the internal development of his philosophical project as originally conceived in *Being and Time*" (Lafont 2018, 49). Even if these factors are ignored, the development of Heidegger's philosophy offers no line of imminent anti-racist thought, for, unlike King after him, Heidegger could not specifically equate being's existential analytic with racist essentialism in the first place. He reserved this classification conceptually, if not definitionally, for humanism, and the tradition of metaphysics generally. In the "Letter," the issue with humanism is that it is not essentialist enough, drawing ontological attention from race as the fundamental horizon of being.[6]

For Heidegger, before and after 1933, philosophy is fundamental ontology, or the ontological structure in which human beings constitute themselves in relation to a world. Attacking the theological turn at German universities in the 1920s (whose theologians, such as Barth, Bultmann, and Tillich, would later exert a great influence on King's thought), Heidegger condemned theology as a science. According to Heidegger, theology posits Christ as the ground for the structure of existence in the world. Yet, in the case of fundamental ontology, or simply philosophy, the analysis of existence proceeds from the ontological structure of being; the Christian belief in rebirth in Paradise rejects this structure in favor of an element conditioned by it (Kleffmann 2009, 254). In this "scientific" sense, theology is like Marxism, Christian existentialism, or Sartre's existentialism, in that it denies Being as the ontological ground of human being. Indeed, the distinction between human being and animal being relies on the rejection of human being as a "rational animal," to be known in its truth "biologically" (Long 2017, 185). Situating Heidegger's understanding of science in relation to philosophy as fundamental ontology, Trawny writes, "If philosophy always had to refer to something real, then it would be a particular science like biology. The 'object' of philosophy, however, seems to be a philosophical problem" (Trawny 2017, 437). The "philosophical problem" is that of philosophy itself as the investigation into human being's ontological structure as the basis for all experience. As Rae notes, "only fundamental ontology can disclose the truth of human being" (Rae 2010, 28). The shift in focus in Heidegger's later thought from the existential analytic of human being to the unmediated interrogation of being is to ensure that this conviction will be clearly understood (Rae 2010, 28).

Heidegger uses the occasion of Sartre's misreading of his "humanism" to begin to clarify his position in this new way. In the "Letter on Humanism," Heidegger insists that "the essence of humanism lies in the essence of human being" and not, as Sartre would have it, in the inversion of metaphysical statements (Kakkori and Huttenen 2012, 352). For Heidegger, fundamental ontology rests on the ruins of the Western metaphysical tradition, not within it as its reversal (Kelley 1997, 203). The presentation of this understanding was promised in *Being and Time* and elaborated in Heidegger's late work, which sought to continue the project of overcoming metaphysics. In 1946, the same year Heidegger writes the "Letter," he "criticizes that the Nazi regime despised the spirit, but in the same year says that 1933, the year Hitler came to power, was the attempt of 'overcoming metaphysics' and the 'opportunity for a possible total consciousness (*Gesamtbesinnung*) of the Occident'" (Fuchs 2015, 96). Developing this thought, Fritsche writes:

> Initially, Heidegger thought that the empirical National Socialism proffered a movement for the consummate overcoming of liberalism. After 1937–1938, however, he came to regard really-existing National Socialism as the fulfilment of liberalism and metaphysics that did not transcend them in any way. This meant that he acknowledged that his fight, since the time of *Being and Time* at the latest, against liberalism and its intensifications had been in vain. This changed perspective of the empirical National Socialism prompted both Heidegger's *Kehre* [turn] and his discovery of the "true," timeless, National Socialism. (Fritsche 2018, 322)

As Karl Jaspers—whose philosophy King studied closely—indicated in *The Question of German Guilt* (1946), Heidegger's inability to confront National Socialism through anything beyond the categories of fundamental ontology was the source of his initial embrace of it, as well as the reason he rejected it in anticipation of a truer version of itself (Grunenberg 2007, 1010).[7] Strenski sums up the matter well: "Heidegger's reversal, then, was not so much away from a spiritual ideology which he genuinely believed Hitler embodied, but merely away from the Führer's failure to live up to Heidegger's Nazi ideals" (Strenski 1982, 60).[8] Placing this thought in relation to Heidegger's anti-Semitism, Fritsche writes:

> In my view, the answer to the question of Heidegger's anti-Semitism is much simpler. His thinking was not since 1931 prone to contamination. Rather, in *Being and Time* he voted fundamental-ontologically and in the history of Being historically for National Socialism. In addition, after 1938 he remained committed to National Socialism. In all this, he will have been aware that there was, to say the least, no contradiction between his anti-Semitic opinions since 1916, at the latest, and his philosophizing. (Fritsche 2016, 595)

Viewed from this perspective, as Sheen notes, "the problem then becomes how to read the philosophy that Heidegger produced over the sixty years stretching from 1912 to 1976. Is there anything at all in the 102 volumes of his *Gesamtausgabe* that is not contaminated by either anti-Semitism or Nazism?" (Sheehan 2015, 368). Taking "philosophy" in Heidegger's sense as fundamental ontology, all his philosophical writings would have to be weighed against his anti-Semitism. Because of the "pervasiveness" of anti-Semitism in the Black Notebooks (Pégny 2018, 302), it seems either hopelessly naïve or vaguely malevolent to accept the idea that, while "Heidegger's conduct during the 12 terrible years of the Hitler dictatorship may have been less than heroic—he did not risk jail or death by openly opposing the regime—it is a revisionist exaggeration to read totalitarianism or anti-Semitism into his work" (Demske 1994, 30).[9] That said, anti-Semitism is not the sum of Heidegger's philosophy, which has been used, without misunderstanding or disreputableness, to less pernicious ends.

If anything, the Heidegger controversy yields a sense that, whatever the critical orientation, Heidegger's ontology and his politics could not be separated without some explanation.[10] For King, systematic theology achieves this separation, serving as the *philosophical* explanation of an anti-racist fundamental ontology. Likewise, any appropriation of Heideggerian philosophy would have to account for the politics that motivated its development (Rockmore 2016, 234). King provides this account in his "Pilgrimage to Nonviolence," which is as much an exposition of an anti-racist philosophy that nevertheless draws on racist aspects of the European philosophical tradition as it is a résumé of reading. This list would have to include, in the spirit when not in the letter, a reading of Heidegger's later work, which Rockmore and others take to be an extension of his

Nazi-era thought, insofar as it seeks to obscure and extend that earlier thought (Rockmore 2016, 234). This later philosophy is marked by the humanism debates in Germany in the 1930s and 1940s and the attempt to address "human being" in terms of language rather than an overt politics (Grassi and Krois 1980, 84). Grassi, another of Heidegger's many former students, would develop his own existential humanism, and publish his teacher's "Letter on Humanism" (1946/1947) with its 1942 prelude and companion piece, "Plato's Doctrine of Truth" (Rubini 2011, 450).

Indeed, for Heidegger, as Smith relates, this "long itinerary begun with Plato has culminated in the 'unfettered' Platonism of Nietzsche for whom truth itself is nothing but a value" (Smith 1995, 448–449). The "Letter" completes Heidegger's extended interpretive analysis of Plato's philosophy as the doctrine of "truth," with the transformation of Heidegger's understanding of Platonic truth shifting from unconcealment to correctness, to conformity of statement (assertion) to things (Kovacs 2003, 42). As "history," Heidegger's "long itinerary" from Plato to fundamental ontology charts a very specific course, one that risks ending where it began. Realizing the potentially metaphysical basis for his historicism, Heidegger attempts to avoid producing "a self-refuting historicism by a simple and perhaps profound device. Heidegger maintains that all fundamental historical changes in man's understanding are products of the disclosure of Being itself" (Lampert 1974, 587). This conceit would include changes to the understanding of human diversity, the history of which would paradoxically require a less historical account to identify the transhistorical element motivating its development. In this way, Heidegger's interrogation of being's motivating agent or idea determines the historical ground of Dasein's self-understanding in diversity. This, however, does not solve the question of human diversity's historicity in relation to Being without risking a return to metaphysics. Following this path would bring Heidegger's philosophy back to philosophical theology, no matter how circuitous the route. Indeed, this return to theology will be King's philosophical path through Heidegger's ahistorical Hellenism, or what the Civil Rights leader would understand as fundamental ontology's one-way street to racial essentialism.

In the 1930s, Heidegger's ahistorical Hellenism brought the scrutiny of Nazi race ideologues such as Alfred Rosenberg, who were concerned that this Third Humanism, or humanism based on Greek *paideia*, was not direct enough in its racial essentialism and as a result obscured their racist ideology of the *Volk* (Rabinbach 1994, 16). Heidegger derived his "primal meaning," or the cause of the fourfold causes in fundamental ontology, from his reading of the Greeks, and in particular Plato (Noschka 2014, 338). For Nazi race ideologues, "primal meaning" had to stem from the race as the ontological category, and not from ontological categories themselves. Indeed, the humanism debates of the 1930s and 1940s often placed Plato at their center, as a means of providing an ontological understanding of the *Volk* that could be considered steeped in the humanist tradition while rejecting universalism based on race (Fleming 2012, 87).[11] One could go so far as to say that Plato, not Nietzsche, was the Nazis' preferred philosopher (Sharpe 2018a, 347). In other words, twentieth-century racial readings of Plato's cave allegory such as Huey P. Newton's have their origin in the German Hellenism debates of the 1930s. To accommodate Nazi calls for Platonic readings providing a more overt racial understanding of being, Heidegger shifts the focus of his thought in the early 1940s from Dasein's existential analytic to the truth of being (Rae 2010, 24). This strategy, emerging from Nazi humanism debates over Plato, led to Heidegger's seminar on Plato, the Doctrine of Truth, and the distortion of the difference between fundamental ontology and politics on the grounds of humanism rather than human being.[12]

III. King's Attitudes

Although King studied contemporary German philosophy and theology, he may not have been aware of the details of these debates. Nevertheless, their content obtains in Heidegger's philosophy itself, which alters in the late work after *Being and Time* (1926) to accommodate rapidly changing social paradigms and political demands. Any appropriation of Heidegger's philosophy would have had to account for its politics, even if the facts of its intellectual antecedents were unknown. King did this by combining Heidegger's ontology with philosophical and sociological sources devoted to "social and ethical theories."

Among those influences, Walter Rauschenbusch's *Christianity and the Social Crisis* (1907) was crucial to King's development as a philosopher.[13] King tells of how struck he was by Rauschenbusch's insistence on a Christianity attentive to social and economic inequality, despite his book's "superficial optimism concerning man's nature" and nationalist tendencies (King 2010b, 110). Rauschenbusch's "social gospel" impressed King to such an extent that he began serious study of "the social and ethical theories of the great philosophers, from Plato and Aristotle down to Rousseau, Hobbes, Bentham, Mill, and Locke" (King 2010b, 111).[14] The idea that Christianity has a specific social mission expresses itself philosophically, rather than theologically, in King's thought. Indeed, philosophy for King is the secular, socioeconomic arm of religious faith; it fills in the gaps in theology, which in King's view deals mostly with spiritual matters as distinct from contemporary issues of social and economic inequality.[15]

This interest in moral philosophy as a supplement to theology leads King to Marx, whose *Capital* (1867) and *The Communist Manifesto* (1848; written with Engels) he closely studies. The result is an overwhelming dislike for Marx's communism, a political idea that for King possesses three insurmountable errors. The first is its atheism and related embrace of materialism as the engine of history. The second, following from the first, is the belief in the state as the highest legal and moral authority, an idea that for King allows legal and moral relativism to prevail in society. This in turn permits "the moral justification of destructive means," which signifies a violent, immoral state practicing the theory that "the end is preexistent in the mean" (King 2010b, 112). King's third objection is the logical outcome of the previous two. He rejects communism's totalitarianism, which he finds unavoidable because of the communist state's atheism and moral relativism. While King appreciates Marxism's origin in social justice, as well as its critique of exploitive capitalist culture, he ultimately cannot tolerate its reduction of the individual to the "collective enterprise" (King 2010b, 115). That said, King openly and readily accepts Marx's dialectical method, which he adopts in the process of reading Marxist philosophy.

During this time, King's "faith in love was temporarily shaken by the philosophy of Nietzsche," whom King reads while considering communism's totalitarianism, atheism, and moral relativism.[16] King sees "Nietzsche's glorification of power" in *The Genealogy of Morals* (1887) and *The Will to Power* (1901) as protofascism fueled by a withering critique of Christianity and by the evolutionary belief in the superman. To avoid the hint of compromise with the philosopher whose thought represents the strongest refutation of his own, King writes that "perhaps" Nietzsche shook his faith in love. Yet while King's encounter with Nietzsche's texts certainly had a profound effect on him, he avows that their influence was temporary, and that he overcame Nietzsche with a renewed faith in love, inspired by Gandhi's life and writings.

King was "electrified" by a sermon he heard on Gandhi's "life and teachings," inspiring him to learn more about satyagraha and the power of love to achieve social reform. Crucially, King reads Gandhi as the first person in the twentieth century to collectivize and politicize Christ's instruction to "turn the other cheek" in response to the enemy's blow, which Christ himself recommended only for the individual. The account King offers of Jesus's pacifism and Gandhi's adaptation of it assiduously avoids the suggestion of revolution in either's social thought. Indeed, King's entire account of his intellectual development sidesteps the radicalism of the religious thinkers he mentions, leaving the suggestion of it to philosophers. For King, true religious thought is not radical; it does not promote revolution. Rather, it seeks reform and correction. The reason for this is simple: the legitimate state takes its authority from divinity, and so to revolt against the legitimate state would be to rebel against God. Furthermore, as God's love rejects violence, the illegitimate state cannot be removed by revolutionary means, and King's faith in love assumes such means to be a priori violent. The existing state must be converted to "true" religion through faith in love alone if it is to be legitimated. As divine love incarnate, Christ could not have been a revolutionary thinker; as his non-Christian spiritual heir in social thought, Gandhi must be a reformer rather than a revolutionary.[17]

At King's invitation, then, commentators consistently discuss his philosophy of nonviolence as a Christianized version of Gandhi's. The reason for this is obvious enough, given King's own testimony regarding Gandhi's inspirational presence in his life and thought. In thinking about King, nonviolence, and intellectual influence, the desire to take King at his word can suppress the suspicion that he may have had strategic reasons for aligning himself so strongly with Gandhi's thought, to the exclusion of the philosophy in which he trained. This can lead to an overestimation of Gandhi's influence in King's articulation of nonviolence as ontology as well as insurgency. While King's nonviolence is not seen as entirely derivative of Gandhi's, the inevitable comparison produces a surface reading of King's original contribution to ontology. Doing this means that King's philosophy is not permitted to speak for itself.

By her own admission, Martha Nussbaum provides such an example:

In my recent book *Anger and Forgiveness: Resentment, Generosity, Justice* I argued that King follows closely the thought of Mohandas Gandhi about anger and resentment and advises a complete removal of those emotional attitudes, on the ground that a wish for payback is a conceptual part of them. Instead, both thinkers recommend an attitude that may criticize and express outrage about bad deeds, but that always eschews retribution, and that, furthermore, always extends to the wrongdoer a generous type of love and a hope for a future of cooperation and constructive work. Since, however, my concern in that book was to provide an argument of my own about the foundations of revolutionary justice, I studied King and Gandhi together (linking them, eventually, with the thought of Nelson Mandela), and thus did not provide a separate textual analysis of King's specific attitudes, though I did include many textual references. It is time to perform that further task. (Nussbaum 2018, 105)

Though her essay is the occasion for completing this task, she again subordinates King to Gandhi, ending with:

To conclude: King is in some respects less philosophically explicit than Gandhi. In other ways, however, he fleshes out and further develops Gandhian ideas, but also contributes creative insights of his own. And in the two areas in which he departs from Gandhi—his qualifications about violence in self-defense and his refusal of a total Stoicism about emotions—he appears to me to have the more philosophically defensible position. (Nussbaum 2018, 126)

In Nussbaum's discussion, Gandhi is never far behind King, and no truly "separate analysis of King's specific attitudes" is provided. Perhaps the reason for this is that for Nussbaum King has specific *attitudes* rather than philosophical positions. Inspired partly by Gandhi, to be sure, King saw nonviolence as human dignity reflected in the practice of freedom and the right to self-invention. He believed in civil disobedience governed by strict rules of self-purification, emotional control, and a realist's belief in self-determination and shared governance. While not color-blind, King rejected essentialism in view of the coming color-blind society, the beloved community. His conception of freedom was accordingly nondenominational and republican, defending the right to vote as the highest expression of human dignity. Segregation, racism, capitalist exploitation, militarism, and sexism all undermine human being as dignity embodied and ensouled. The individual's synthetic realization in community is the only bulwark against the ever-encroaching forces of nihilism. While his philosophy is action-oriented, King is more than a "philosophical man of action"; he is a philosopher who took action.

Taken as a specific philosophical position, King's *attitudes* have been seen as personalism. The identification of King's thought as personalism rests on courses he took at Boston University and the intellectual narrative he provides in "Pilgrimage." Yet King's dissertation ultimately had nothing to do with personalism, treating instead the idealist-existential theology of Paul Tillich. Given that the dissertation is the summation of any doctoral candidate's intellectual journey and the promise of her future intervention in the discipline, it appears existentialism and idealism made far more of an impact on King's development as a thinker than did personalism alone. Furthermore, while personalism provides a convenient culmination to the narrative of his spiritual development as an intellectual, it does not provide an adequate explanation of his thought in isolation from or above his various other philosophical commitments. King had to know that "personalism," as the name for his eclectic thought, would play better publicly than "German Idealism" or "*Existenzphilosophie.*"

Still, today it is perhaps better to think of King as a personalist or existentialist rather than an idealist in the philosophical sense, even when the former positions require a simplification of King's philosophy as well as of personalism and existentialism. To be sure, where all three are treated fully, inconsistencies between them still arise. Likewise, to understand King as primarily a religious thinker whose critical-theoretical tendencies, no matter how philosophically informed, are subsumed in "image of God" speculation would also be a mistake. Once more, King chose to write on Tillich for several reasons, one of which was Tillich's hybrid status as philosopher, theologian, activist, and existentialist. Like Tillich, "King belongs to several traditions and . . . the character of his work doesn't derive from a strictly academic undertaking" (Birt 2012, 4). Following Tillich, King presents a dialectical synthesis of personalism and existentialism, mediated by the German Idealist tradition.

Ontology is by far the aspect least explored by scholars of King's philosophy. That said, King's ontology is sometimes addressed as "philosophical anthropology." This designation, however, is at once too general and too specific to accommodate King's philosophy. King's theological commitments make the designation of philosophical anthropology difficult to sustain; yet his existentialism lends itself to the identification. Relying on empirical investigations in culture to explicate the human condition, philosophical anthropology facilitates speculative conclusions on human nature as embodied in the human person. The human person, however, is not to be confused with human being, and ontology, while part of philosophical anthropology, cannot be reduced to it. While King's personalist and existentialist concerns are anthropological, his theological idealism embraces metaphysical speculation on being beyond being-in-the-world. Because King's philosophy offers no easy distinction between the human person and human being, ontology must take priority over philosophical anthropology.

This is evident in King's account of personalism while at Boston University. In the final paper for L. Harold DeWolf's seminar on personalism, King writes, "Personalism's insistence that only personality—finite and infinite—is ultimately real strengthened me in two convictions: it gave me metaphysical and philosophical grounding for the idea of a personal God, and it gave me a metaphysical basis for the dignity and worth of all human personality" (King 2010b, 121). Until discovering personalism, King had no metaphysical basis for the socially conscious aspects of his faith. Indeed, for King philosophy is tasked with social concern, whereas theology is concerned with spiritual matters pertaining to the individual alone. Personalism allows him to unite these two disciplines and address social inequality while maintaining the individual's personal relationship to God. Importantly, the basis for this disciplinary union is metaphysics, which King sees as a field of intellectual inquiry that mediates the relation between philosophy and theology.

That said, it would be wrong to think exclusively of King as a personalist. For DeWolf's course on personalism, King wrote an end-of-term position piece outlining and criticizing the philosophy. In this brief yet rich work, King rejects personalism as dualistic or humanistic, as it "stresses epistemological dualism while absolute idealism stresses epistemological monism. For the 'typical' Personalist the thing series and the thought series are numerical[ly] two rather than one" (King 1994b, 111). King prefers absolute idealism because "it satisfies the mind's demand for unity. Moreover, it gives an easy explanation of interaction" (King 1994b, 111–112). King, however, sees personalism's appeal as an explanation for evil "without attributing it to the Absolute," and notes that "creation can be a real factor with the personalist, but not so with the Absolute idealist" (King 1994b, 111–112). For this reason, instead of personalism alone King proposes a combination of the two positions, or what he refers to as "practical absolutism," as the solution. This would be a socially responsible idealism that accounted for evil by acknowledging "we can never make a claim to absolute certainty. This is certainly the emphasis of a method of coherence and that I accept. But while we cannot be theoretically certain about any issue, we are compelled to act. And certainly, we have a right to act and accept any belief until one better is found if it does not contradict experience" (King 1994b, 112). In other words, "practical absolutism" is open to alteration yet acts as if the truth it holds is absolute. King accepts the truth of gnostic duality on the condition of unconditional unity as faith in action. For King, epistemological uncertainty is overcome by ontological truth known in a way different from humanistic prescription. Personalism alone remains too invested in human being, and therefore too humanistic for King's philosophical and theological sensibilities. For these reasons, it cannot be said with Burrow that "the philosophy of Personalism provided the intellectual framework for [King] to ground that doctrine in a formal way" (Burrow 2014, 229). In the personalism piece, King clearly finds German Idealism more useful.

Because of this, it is perhaps unsurprising that King closes the narrative of his intellectual pilgrimage to nonviolence with his encounter with Hegel. Having read and studied Hegel's *Phenomenology of Spirit* (1807), *Philosophy of Right* (1821), and *Lectures of the Philosophy of History* (1837), King concludes that, despite what he sees as its irrationalism, Hegel's philosophy has much to offer. He recounts that Hegel's "contention that 'truth is the whole' led me to a philosophical method of rational coherence. His analysis of the dialectical process, in spite of its shortcomings, helped me to see that growth comes through struggle" (King 2010b, 121). Having with personalism already bridged the divide between socially conscious philosophy and a rigorously personal understanding of theology, King adopts an important methodological aspect of his work from Hegelian Idealism. In Hegel's philosophy, King's personalism finds processual structure in the idea that "truth is the whole." This means that the unity of individual and collective in God's love can be expressed as a process. For King, following Hegel, this process is dialectical. Hegel's dialectic describes the movement of social struggle within the spiritual continuum of God's love. This movement is phenomenologically psychological, political in the sense of right, and eschatologically historical in its ends.

King calls the immediate product of his doctoral work the development of "a positive social philosophy," yet after leaving Boston University and beginning work as a pastor in Montgomery, he is faced with a social dilemma that calls for pragmatic civic leadership. At this point, King's positive social philosophy exhibits what he describes as "the power of nonviolence," borrowing the title from Richard Gregg's work.[18] During the Montgomery crisis, the "power of nonviolence" is given popular utterance as King's "philosophy of nonviolence." King's pilgrimage to "sacred" nonviolence ends in the social application of theologized philosophy, denuded of its *libido dominandi*.

Of course, King did not use philosophical terms or jargon to express his thought. Because of his desire to reach a popular audience, King rarely uses philosophical terminology, and when he does, he is sure to explain it in accessible language meant to educate and edify. This "translation," however, brings with it a disciplinary shift, changing the intellectual context of King's rhetoric from philosophy to spiritualism. King considers this translation, or correlation, of his intellectual development to be a "pilgrimage" to nonviolence. The end of his intellectual journey through philosophy is the spiritual center of redemption through divine love and boundless faith. This attainment is expressed conceptually and rhetorically in King's journey away from philosophy's technical language to that of a shared vocabulary of spirituality. King's "pilgrimage," then, is from the communication of philosophical learning to the expression of spiritual attainment. This, after all, is the overt story he tells in the "Pilgrimage to Nonviolence," and it is the rhetorical strategy of his literary work. The conclusion to be drawn is that the Heideggerian thought that culminated in King's doctoral work on Paul Tillich never falls away.

2   Nonbeing and Nonviolence

I. King's *Denkformen*

MORE THAN TO MARITAIN, King's avowed anti-humanism also owes much to existentialist philosopher and theologian Paul Tillich.[1] King's dissertation focused partly on Tillich, a German émigré who adapted Heidegger's philosophy to Christian existentialism.[2] King's work on Tillich allowed him to synthesize the German Idealism and *Existenzphilosophie* in which he grew interested as student in a way that informed his commitment to theology. Tillich's work was also important to King for its view of psychological existentialism as an investment in a contemplative, therapeutic approach to daily life (Tiebout 1959, 607). Tillich, though, was most well-known in the United States as a philosopher, where he was associated generally with German Idealism and *Existenzphilosophie* (Gilkey 1990, 566). In this view, "Tillich emerges . . . as a kind of Hegel redivivus—with the benefit of the correction of Existentialism and related disciplines" (Mueller 1966, 501). For greater accuracy, Tillich's contemporary critic would have done well here to label him a kind of Heidegger Christianus, as Tillich conceived a theologically oriented *Existenzphilosophie* based on Heidegger's fundamental ontology to express Dasein's existential analytic in terms of finitude and what he called "Being Itself" (Sturm 2016, 199). As Thomas summarizes,

> According to Tillich, there are four levels of ontological concepts, including that of the basic ontological structure of self and world and that of the elements of the structure of being. There are three sets of polar ontological elements which apply to all levels or dimensions of being: individualization and participation, dynamics and form, and freedom and destiny. Because God is the ground of being, the ontological elements can be appropriate symbols of the divine. The subjective side of the polarities can symbolize the existential relation between God and humanity; thus, humans can see God as personal, dynamic, and free. (Thomas 1996, 87)

Tillich employs Heideggerian ontological categories to theological ends by positing a systematic correlation between the two disciplines' concepts (Thomas 1953, 10). Put succinctly, "the distinction between philosophy and theology, in Tillich's view, is essentially one of definition: philosophy describes the 'structure of being' with objectivity and detachment while theology seeks the 'meaning of being for us' with existential concern" (Van Hook 1977, 73).[3] Through this distinction Tillich offers a picture of Dasein's "awareness of the divine ground of being from which man is existentially estranged, but with which he is essentially united, and the 'memory' of which union is never lost, even in the most estranged forms of existence" (Williamson 1972, 206). Ultimately, Tillich strives "to unite or have us see the proper union of the ontological category of Being (ultimate reality) and the axiological category of ultimate value, God. So God, as the Ground and Power of Being, is most real and most valuable" (Kegley 1960, 179).

From this perspective, Tillich differs from Heidegger only in that he desires the transformation of metaphysics into theology, and not its destruction (Schüßler 1995, 193). The strong structural relationship between Tillich's Christian existentialism and Heidegger's fundamental ontology helps to differentiate their thought according to Being, which Tillich believes not to have been suppressed or ignored in Western metaphysics but rather incorrectly expressed systematically (O'Meara 1968, 249). In this respect, Tillich's existentialist thought is Heideggerian in *Denkform* yet not in content (O'Meara 1968, 251–252). Tillich understands Heidegger's philosophy primarily as metaphysics and not existentialism (O'Meara 1968, 252). Perhaps the reason for this was that Tillich, and other religious thinkers influenced by Heidegger, sensed that Heideggerian fundamental ontology lacked any moral basis for the recognition and condemnation of evil (McDonald 2010, 891).

Tillich's reading of Heidegger must have been convincing to King, as he, too, is Heideggerian in *Denkform* while infusing this thought with a moral rigor it originally lacked. King is particularly impressed by Tillich's Heideggerian anti-humanism, writing approvingly in his dissertation, "Theocentric concern leads Tillich . . . to the further assertion that God is not man. Both are averse to anything that smacks of humanism" (King 1994b, 518). Indeed, he seems attracted to their thought due to its "cry against the humanism of our generation" (King 1994b, 519). He then expands on this anti-humanism using Tillich's Heideggerian terms: "As we have seen, Tillich's ontological analysis leads him to affirm that God must not be confused with man in any sense. God as being-itself infinitely transcends all beings. He is not a being, not even a 'highest being' or a 'most perfect' being. He is the power of being in everything that has being" (King 1994b, 518).

Drawing powerful conclusions such as these from Tillich's philosophical theology, King's thought never strayed far from it. For example, after being arrested October 19, 1960, for "trespass" at a whites-only dining hall in Atlanta, King writes Coretta Scott King from the state prison at Reidsville, Georgia, to ask her to bring a few books when she and the children visit: "Please bring the following books to me: *Stride Toward Freedom*, Paul Tillich's *Systematic Theology Vol 1&2*, George Buttrick *The Parables of Jesus*[,] E. S. Jones *Mahatma Gandhi, Horns and Halo*, a Bible, a Dictionary and my reference dictionary called *Increasing your Word Power*. This book is an old book in a red cover, and it may be in the den or upstairs in one of my [strikeout illegible] bags" (King 1994e, 532). The short list of essential reading is telling. King requests his own *Stride Toward Freedom*, Tillich's *Systematic Theology* (1951), along with a book on Jesus's parables, an interpretation of Gandhi's life and work, the Bible, and an old, weather-beaten copy of a "Word Power" dictionary.

Seen as a whole, the book selection suggests that King is attempting to go over the past to find a way forward in his present situation. That is, he appears to want to rephrase past statements and recast prior events for popular consumption without losing the essence of their complex philosophical content. While King commonly cited scripture and referred to Gandhi and Jesus in the same context of nonviolent resistance innumerable times—and the Word Power dictionary would help him find the most impactful phrases—*Systematic Theology* is included among the handful of books King requests from prison because it contains the philosophical content to be represented to a popular audience by references to Gandhi, Jesus, and King's own past statements. He did not cite Tillich directly often enough or in depth, outside the dissertation, to warrant this inclusion otherwise. In King, Tillich translates Heidegger, Gandhi transforms Tillich, and Gandhi makes Jesus meaningful to King's audience as the sovereign legitimation of nonviolent civil disobedience. For this reason, King cites Jesus and the Bible often and directly while frequently referring to Gandhi, seldom mentioning Tillich, and remaining virtually silent on Heidegger.

That said, when King does cite Tillich, the effect is always definitive. This is especially the case when King discusses Kairos, or "creative moments" of decisive action taken at the perfect time:

> We know that the most creative moments in history are those moments when individuals are left free to think. The thing that makes man is his freedom. This is why I could never agree with communism as a philosophical system because it deprives man of freedom. And if a man is not free, he is not fully man. If a man does not have the capacity to deliberate, to decide, and to respond, as Paul Tillich would say, he is not a man, for a man is man because he is free. And, therefore, communism is on the wrong road because it denies freedom.[4] (King 1994f, 448)

King looks to Tillich to describe "creative moments in history," or times at which human freedom can be known and exercised as the courage to be.[5] For King, the political context of this decisive moment, or Kairos, cannot be that of Soviet communism because, as a "philosophical system," Soviet communism "deprives man of freedom."[6] Without freedom-in-Kairos, a being cannot be fully human.[7] Freedom defines the fullness of human being as deliberative, decisive, courageous action in response to the world. Communism would deny these human rights. Tillich's "philosophical system," his systematic theology, embraces freedom as the ability to respond to existence at the appropriate time. Along with limiting deliberative thought and discussion, communism compromises the ability to act at the right time, in response to material challenges. Communism disrupts the continuum of freedom and action, which for both Tillich and King also determines the temporality of human being. "Being and time" provide the optimal moment to act, in the expression of human freedom.[8] In this respect, freedom and temporality are mutually constituting aspects of being-in-the-world, where obstructing one frustrates the other.

Tillich's *Systematic Theology*, then, helps King think about social action as Kairos, insofar as it offers a theory of temporality in relation to freedom and being. With the exception of Tillich's text, the books King lists for Coretta to bring to him in jail all provide material relating to past actions, writings, and sermons. *Systematic Theology* offers a way to theorize the return of these past works in a new form, as the creative act defining human freedom and the human condition. In other words, *Systematic Theology* is the organizing principle for King's theological correlation of various textual traditions as a social act.[9]

King's focus on correlation as social action guided by philosophy and faith in God leads him to suggest a spiritual relativism between the different conceptions of divinity. As he suggests in a 1967 sermon,

You may not be able to define God in philosophical terms. Men through the ages have tried to talk about him. (Yes) Plato said that he was the Architectonic Good. Aristotle called him the Unmoved Mover. Hegel called him the Absolute Whole. Then there was a man named Paul Tillich who called him Being-Itself. We don't need to know all of these high-sounding terms. (Yes) Maybe we have to know him and discover him another way. (Oh yeah) One day you ought to rise up and say, "I know him because he's a lily of the valley." (Yes) He's a bright and morning star. (Yes) He's a rose of Sharon. He's a battle-axe in the time of Babylon. (Yes) And then somewhere you ought to just reach out and say, "He's my everything. He's my mother and my father. He's my sister and my brother. He's a friend to the friendless." This is the God of the universe. And if you believe in him and worship him, something will happen in your life. You will smile when others around you are crying. This is the power of God. (King 2000, 138)[10]

In listing him among Plato, Aristotle, and Hegel, King associates Tillich exclusively with philosophers who use "high-sounding terms." He then suggests that his audience may need to know God "another way." Here, King speaks of action rather than continuing to talk about terms. In so doing, he nearly imperceptibly transitions from philosophical discourse on being to knowledge of God through social action. For King, these two "ways of knowing" are coextensive; God is known not through theological study but rather from action taken after the study of philosophy—which is the path to action King describes in his "Pilgrimage to Nonviolence." Social action determined by and productive of spiritual imperatives develops from the study of philosophy. For King, systematic theology is the bridge between philosophy and social action; it names the moment at which a decision born of deliberation turns to direct, nonviolent intervention.

Of all those mentioned in King's brief intellectual autobiography, Tillich exercised the greatest influence over King's thought. Yet the "Pilgrimage," which mentions him only once in the narrative, appears to have been written to distance his thought from Tillich's for the public record. In converting his training in philosophy to a popular spiritualism and "life philosophy," King entirely effaces the basis of that training and its link to theology. Tillich's reappearance in the "Letter from a Birmingham Jail" as a theologian indicates the extent to which the work allows the entirety of King's thought to shine forth in an example of rhetorical genius and mastery that was able to express the interrelatedness of his thought perfectly. That said, King does not merely appropriate Tillich's thought and then place it in a new social context; he criticizes key aspects of Tillich's conception of God, arriving at his unique, socially conscious understanding of God's love and human freedom. Investigating Tillich's own philosophical sources—such as Kant, Hegel, Nietzsche, and above all Heidegger—King shows that Tillich's theology is in fact theological philosophy lacking the pronouncement of faith provided by close textual involvement with scripture.

Elsewhere, King refers to Tillich as "the great philosopher and theologian of our age," placing his thought firmly in the present as the moment's definitive statement:

> And this is the man who stands up in the greatness of life. He discovers the power and the creativity of the human will, and he faces any circumstance with the power and the force of his will. And he has a sort of dogged determination. This is what Paul Tillich, the great philosopher and theologian of our age, means when he writes a book entitled *The Courage to Be*. He says in that book that all around man is the threat of nonbeing. The man who has adjusted to modern life, the man who lives with creativity in the modern world, is the individual who stands amid the thrust of non being and has the courage to be, in spite of all. (King 1994f, 362)

Referencing *The Courage to Be* (originally published in 1952), King introduces the idea of "nonbeing" as the medium of "modern life" that nihilates creativity, promoting unfreedom. For King, creativity is freedom's expression; therefore, "the courage to be" is the courage to create. Tillich's "existentialism" identifies the nihilating ground of existence, and the intellectual and emotional fortitude necessary to counter this influence on the spirit in relation to the structurally Heideggerian "Being Itself." For Tillich, "Being Itself" is obscured by Nonbeing, or the nihilism of finitude and historicity. The courage to be speaks of the bravery to believe in Being that stands outside of history and mortality, revealing itself only in freedom's creativity. As King writes elsewhere:

> Courage can take the fear produced by a definite object into itself and thereby conquer the fear involved. "Courage," says Paul Tillich, "is self-affirmation 'in spite of' … that which tends to hinder the self from affirming itself." It is self-affirmation in spite of death and non-being. He who acts courageously takes the fear of death into his self-affirmation and acts upon it. This courageous self-affirmation which is a sure remedy for fear is not to be confused with "selfishness." Self-affirmation includes the right self-love and the right love of others. Erich Fromm has pointed

out in convincing terms that the right self-love and the right love of others are interdependent, and that selfishness and the abuse of others are equally interdependent. (King 1994f, 539)

This courage, then, is self-affirmation in the face of Nonbeing, which Tillich and King perceive as self-love; this is to be understood not as selfishness but rather as the ability to know love as the affirmation of all human freedom and creativity. In choosing for personal freedom, the love necessary to do so is revealed as transitive and is then felt for others. As in Heidegger, self-affirmation occurs "in spite of death and nonbeing." Quoting this line from Tillich, King understands self-affirmation as the existentialist's courage to transcend "being unto death" through love of the self, as loved by Being Itself.

Because of this aspect of his thought, Tillich's name shows up in King's "Pilgrimage" under "existentialism" (King 2010b, 111, quoted earlier). Here, King offers a clear genealogy of Heideggerian existentialism but not of the Sartrean version, given the exclusive concentration on German philosophy. Seeing Sartre instead as a variant of Heideggerian *Existenzphilosophie*, he leaves the philosophy's place ambiguous on his pilgrimage's timeline. Other pilgrimage entries are linked with events, such as doctoral study, and have a clear beginning and end. *Existenzphilosophie*, however, is presented as indeterminate and ongoing. The reason for this is that King has not ceased to be influenced by existentialism. Indeed, his list of existentialist philosophers is given chronologically in the order of their birth, ending with King's contemporary Tillich, with whom he corresponded and met. Tillich's work convinces him that *Existenzphilosophie* need not mean atheism or philosophical spiritualism, and that it could entail a philosophical method by which to bridge faith, personalism, and social intervention. Tillich provides guidance about how to translate moral philosophy and philosophical theology into a spiritual vocabulary for individual action.[11]

King sees Tillich's thought as a form of "personalism" combining theology and *Existenzphilosophie*, where both are informed by Heidegger. "Being Itself" is the personal God:

> Now I am aware of the fact that there are devout believers in nonviolence who find it difficult to believe in a personal God. But even these persons believe in the existence of some creative force that works for togetherness, whether we call it a principle of concretion as in Whitehead, a process of integration as Henry Nelson Wieman, Being Itself as Paul Tillich, an impersonal Brahma as Hinduism, or a

personal being of boundless power and infinite love. We must believe that there is a creative force in this universe that works to bring the disconnected aspects of reality into a harmonious whole. There is a creative power that works to bring low gigantic mountains of evil and pull down prodigious hilltops of injustice. This is the faith that keeps the nonviolent resister going through all of the tension and suffering that he must inevitably confront. (King 1994f, 325)

Modifying Heidegger for theology, Tillich's "Being Itself" names a personal God that, according to King, is nevertheless objective in its cultural and historical manifestations. The personal God King posits relates to the individual as self-love and self-affirmation, allowing her to transcend the existential condition of Nonbeing and extend human being to all others. However, this personal God has no specific attribute beyond Being as the dialectical negation of the nihilating finitude. King's personal God is spiritual, yet not in any strict, religious sense. It is made "visible" not conditionally, but rather as unconditional love received without ritual restriction or moral stricture, in the embrace of nonviolence. Nonviolence is as much a social practice as it is a spiritual regimen, making King's understanding of it both practical and esoteric. Ultimately for King, nonviolence is the polymorphic practice of "Being Itself," "an impersonal Brahma," "a principle of concretion," and "infinite love." However, the system in which King understands Being is Tillich's Heideggerian existentialism. King's focus on correlation as social action guided by philosophy and faith in God leads him to suggest a spiritual relativism between the different conceptions of divinity.

King thus adopts Heidegger's ontology through Tillich's method of correlation to understand his own physical and spiritual pilgrimage to nonviolence. The "ontological polarity" King addresses in Tillich's dialectical method holds dualistic elements in suspension such that they support each other without destroying the other's particularity. These elements can only be unified into a single, synthetic being when the opposition of being and Nonbeing is resolved by God. As King reads him, Tillich understands salvation as the reconciliation between being and Nonbeing in God, which in turn resolves all other dialectical tension as the ontological ground of history. In this respect, God as logos is active in history through correlation with humanity, insofar as the dialectical tension between divine and human being forms a part of the ontological polarity inherent in Being. As opposed to Barth, who strongly criticized Tillich's dialectical ontology on these grounds, King's Tillich sees God as systematically active in human history much in the same way Hegel understands the self-expression of the Absolute Idea in history.

Indeed, King openly states that Tillich's concept of correlation, as the set of questions and methodological procedure for his entire systematic theology, are taken from philosophy, writing that the "method of correlation shows the interdependence between the ultimate questions to which philosophy is driven and the answers given in the Christian message" (King 1994b, 351). This assertion sets up a strong opposition between philosophy and theology, only for Tillich to negate it without conflating, or synthesizing, the two opposing terms. "Such a method," King writes, "seeks to be dialectical in the true sense of the word. In order to gain a clearer understanding of this method of correlation it is necessary to discuss its negative meaning" (King 1994b, 352). This discussion occurs without dialectical sublation or distinction within negation. Methodologically, this means that the same Heideggerian ontological polarity shaping the critical voice in Tillich's work is also at work in King's. Indeed, Tillich's and King's critical methods appear to merge, making it difficult to distinguish the two in King's dissertation. Unlike his discussion of Wieman, in which he keeps a wide critical distance, King allows himself a dialectical intimacy with Tillich's thought that at times creates a unity of content and expression. This is most obvious in King's account of disciplinary differences between philosophy and theology in Tillich's thought, where it becomes difficult to distinguish the two authors' views.

This difficulty becomes exacerbated when King discusses Tillich's views on the difference between the theologian and the philosopher. For King, "neither the theologian nor the philosopher can avoid the theological question," as both inquire after the structure of being (King 1994b, 366). In this sense, in their basic task philosophy and theology are united. However, King draws a distinction in the intentional structure of either inquiry. Philosophy investigates the meaning of being's structure in itself, whereas theology evaluates being's meaning for us. This differentiation depends on the tenuous distinction between being-for-itself and being-for-us, and on where the two modes of being coincide, as they do in Heidegger's existentialism, which King's dissertation references in this regard. Here again King, following Tillich, establishes an ontological polarity, only to undo its binary structure by revealing that the two elements are two aspects of the same phenomenon. Being-for-itself and being-for-us are two manifestations of the same human orientation toward being, displaying a commonality of critical belief, or doxa.

King suggests this when he writes that the difference between the philosopher and the theologian is ultimately their attitude toward being. The philosopher "seeks to maintain objectivity toward being," whereas the theologian collapses this distinction. This approach to being derives from the recognition of a categorical difference in sources of epistemic certainty. The philosopher looks to reason alone, or logos, for objectivity, while the theologian embraces Christ as logos, as understood by the church. Once again, however, King allows Tillich to complicate the difference between two seemingly opposed attitudes toward being, those of reason and of faith. He insists, quoting Tillich, that all philosophers rely on passion and creativity for rational thought, and therefore each one "is a hidden theologian" (King 1994b, 368).

The strongest example of ontological polarity King offers is between "man" and the world, from which being's "basic ontological structure is derived."[12] This means for King's thought, however, that "man" and world do not actually stand in fundamental opposition, and that reconciliation between them is possible, in the form of redemption. In this sense, King has once again taken an existential view of being's "basic ontological structure," combining being-for-itself and being-for-us to arrive at a philosophical position distinguishable from theology only in terms of critical vocabulary and dialectical method. The point of this is to posit the necessity of accepting God's activity in the world, and history as logos, in effect supporting Tillich against his detractors. This is important for King's thought because his defense of Tillich leads to King's embrace of the social gospel instead of the acceptance of resignation in the anticipation of salvation after death. For King, salvation comes in the now-time of eschatological history.

King thus accepts with Tillich the "basic ontological structure" of reality as that of experience premised on the distinction between subject and object (King 1994b, 385–387). Originating with Heidegger, King writes, this understanding is noncategorical, relying instead on apposite polarity for the generation of experiential meaning.[13] The comprehension of this structure is both philosophical and theological; it depends on the cognition of being-for-itself in its intentional meaning as being-for-us. In other words, King views through Tillich dialectical thought as the methodological equivalent to ontological polarity. In this view, the "basic ontological structure of reality" is revealed to be a unified field of object and subject. The subject and object are irreconcilably different in experience, yet their ontological orientation to the world is the same.

This orientation is determined by freedom. For King and Tillich, freedom and destiny form the most important dialectical pairing in ontological polarity, revealing the basic ontological structure of human being in its essential expression. Because freedom is here a mode of being rather than an element of it, the will cannot be said to encompass its articulation as decision. The will is not free to choose because freedom does not belong to the will, existing instead for itself as part of a dyad in the basic structural scheme of ontological polarity. Likewise, the claim of indeterminism in decision cannot be maintained, as this, too, would run afoul of freedom by replacing human agency with destiny. In either case, the distinction between freedom and destiny dissolves, and the ontological specificity of human experience descends into one form of necessity or another. To avoid this, King posits, with Tillich, that freedom is not an element of either the will or destiny; it is in fact the ontological determination of human being.

According to Tillich, freedom is "experienced as deliberation, decision, and responsibility" (Tillich 1966, 184). Each subject takes the totality of her experience as the starting point of decision, rendering this choice objectively in the world. Deliberation occurs above the matter at hand, with decisions made in the full light of reason, after careful consideration of all motives and material factors. Because of this, the subject takes full responsibility for each of her decisions, and all decision reflects the totality of her being-in-the-world. In this respect, freedom is the culminating expression of the inevitability inherent in each subject's decisions, based on the totality of the experience, character, and capacity for reason. This destiny does not limit freedom in any way; rather, it expresses the fullness of its being as the basic narrative structure of a life.

In ontological polarity, freedom and destiny are integral aspects of all other polarities, and all experience. Freedom is not, however, guided by destiny. For King and Tillich, the two exist in dialectical relation. That said, freedom is united with finitude. Here King reads Tillich as following Heidegger in the belief that Nonbeing "presupposes an ontological basis" (King 1994b, 396). This means that Nonbeing exerts force on being, and in history. Referring to Parmenides, King states that finitude negates infinite being and in so doing affirms "the totality of finite existence" (King 1994b, 396). Next moving to Platonic thought, King suggests that Nonbeing is the space in which the self unfolds as possibility, or freedom. He concludes by rejecting, along with Tillich, the assumption that Augustinians say Nonbeing is a purely "privative" understanding of sin's medium. It is, rather, dialectical, providing the basis for decision.

As in Heidegger, for King and Tillich finitude provokes anxiety. This feeling is distinguished from fear because fear is directed toward an object and can be allayed by action. Anxiety has no object and is brought about by the human condition, defined by finitude. Indeed, anxiety is a constant presence, making the subject aware of finite existence and the predicament of being. Through anxiety, the subject becomes aware of freedom in its unity with finitude. Anxiety responds to the freedom of decision made possible by the finitude of Nonbeing, in which the choice between sin (Nonbeing) and redemption (infinite being) is articulated as destiny. In this respect, freedom means for King and Tillich the ability to make for oneself the existential choice between being-for-itself (God) and being-for-the-self (finite subjectivity). Said differently, King highlights in Tillich the existential choice between agape and eros, in its spiritual-temporal context.

The anxiety provoked by finitude results in the realization that human being is troubled by its "lack of aseity," or "the self-sufficiency possessed by God alone" (King 1994b, 402). In this modification of Heideggerian *Existenzphilosophie*, "causality" is the dialectical negation of Nonbeing, maintaining human existence by confirming the contingency of being-in-the-world as the absence of self-creation. After making this strong ontological claim for Tillich, King leaves the theologian out of a brief engagement with Heidegger's thought, displaying a thorough knowledge of Heidegger's philosophy, independent of Tillich's treatment of his former colleague's work. Indeed, King ultimately reads Tillich's conception of God in structurally Heideggerian terms, suggesting that His omnipotence derives from His ontological status as Being. This Being stands in opposition to Nonbeing, or finitude, and the potential it creates for sin. The anxiety defining the human condition articulated to consciousness in the reaction provoked by human being's lack of aseity brings about human being's awareness of God's existence. Because human being's relationship to God is the substance of the basic structure of its ontology, no contingent factor can separate human being from Being. The ontological polarity structuring reality derives meaning from the struggle between Nonbeing and being, which resolves in Being, and is the meaning of God's omnipotence. Contingent sets of relations, such as those determined by nature and politics, cannot supersede God's love. King's introduction of God's love to the characterization of His omnipotence comes from his association of Tillich's Heideggerian theology with Saint Augustine's.

King compares Tillich's understanding of divine omnipotence with Augustine's, finding that the ancient philosopher's Platonism led him to believe that the experience of divine omnipotence was intellectual. For Augustine, according to King, God as logos was "implied in all knowledge," and could thus be known in philosophical speculation on worldly experience (King 1994b, 410). King believes that Tillich rejects this and posits instead human awareness of divine omnipotence "grasped by an ultimate concern" (King 1994b, 410). This "ultimate concern" is for finitude, or Nonbeing, which then—in a dialectical relation of ontological polarity—posits Being as divine omnipotence. King does not necessarily find connections in Tillich alone; he makes them between Tillich, Paul, Augustine, and Heidegger.

King also makes connections with Hegel's philosophy, and for him these connections play a methodological role in Tillich's thought that is complementary to Heidegger's *Existenzphilosophie*. That said, in describing the basic structure of being-in-the-world, the Hegelian dialectical movement of ontological polarity anticipates resolution in synthesis. Were this actually to happen, however, it would sublate ontological polarity in the dialectical thought of absolute being, rather than in divine omnipotence as Being. Hegel's dialectical method cannot lay claim to ontological priority, and the thought that it could is heretical to Tillich.

King brings out the philosophical aspect of this theological distinction in his discussion of Tillich and symbols. Tillich, King suggests, strongly differentiates between sign and symbol in language and iconography, insisting that signs diminish the referent, whereas symbols enhance the reality of their object. "Protestant Hegelianism" conflates sign with symbol, inadvertently undermining the perception of God's existential presence (King 1994b, 413). In other words, signs resolve a final identity between signifier and signified, whereas symbols resist sublation, leaving the polarized relationship of signifier and signified intact.[14] The negative, or Nonbeing, in language remains present as a means of revealing finitude in relation to Being as the existential horizon of being-in-the-world.

King then distinguishes Tillich's conception of God as unconditional Being from conditioning Being in a series of philosophical positions, including Heidegger, German Idealism, Platonism, mysticism, rational deduction, and Barthian theology. This means that, whereas these other, mostly philosophical approaches to God's Being are premised on the apprehension of a divine object, Tillich conceives of God as the unconditional presupposition necessary for engaging in conversation about God's existence. In other words, in order even to consider God's existence, the concession must be made that Being is present unconditionally in the basic ontological structure of being-in-the-world. God, then, "is not an object which we as subjects perceive or think about"; rather, He is the unconditional condition by which subjects think about objects (King 1994b, 416). God is the medial condition of thought about the subject in relation to objects.

For King reading Tillich, God's nature is creative. Acts of creation stand as testament to God's existence in freedom, which could then be defined as the unconditional expression of human being's nature. This is not to suggest that God could somehow be unfree or hindered in His acts of creation. As omnipotent Being, God provides the example of freedom in perfection, beyond the fetters of finitude. King and Tillich's example is that of unconditional Being and is valid for contingent being as eternal love projecting into history the ideal of unlimited freedom as the subject's salvation and redemption from Nonbeing. For the subject, freedom is the ability to express its nature, without obstruction. Social oppression, for instance, would act against God's will, or the truth of being-in-the-world.

While King distinguishes Tillich's conception of God from Hegel's Absolute and Barth's "Wholly Other," among other conceptions of God and Being, he devotes heightened attention to Plato's "Creator-God" and Platonic Ideas. This is due to the similarity of association of God with creativity in both Tillich's and Plato's thought. King forcefully differentiates the two conceptions of God by emphasizing that, for Tillich, God's creative act is not dependent on Ideas for its realization as the world. Rather, the Ideas are elements of the "divine mind"; they are the categorical expression of divine thought, a view shared with Neoplatonism and Augustine. King emphasizes this aspect of Tillich's thought to underscore the "originating creativity" of God's Being, and the fact that "the creature is rooted in the creative ground of the divine life" (King 1994b, 427). If the origin of God's creativity, as the expression of reality, were the Ideas, then it would be the case that "the creature" would be "rooted in the creative ground" of the Ideas. In this instance, the understanding of unconditional freedom present in Nonbeing—the historicity of being-in-finitude—would be a sign rather than a symbol of eternal Being. In other words, King's presentation of Tillich's philosophy embraces the unconditional negation of the symbol, as opposed to the enframing positivity of the sign. Because his reading of Tillich relies on the strong, Heideggerian implication that language is the house of Being, King can establish the active logos in speech as the true determination of human freedom, according to God's will.

The relation of God to human being is that of freedom conditioned by resistance. Human being as being-there, or Dasein, resists the finitude of Nonbeing, which is conditioned by being-in-the-world. The creative ground of being—the recognition of creation as an act of divine freedom—reveals human dependency on its "creative ground." This in turn creates a "double resistance" to Nonbeing and creativity, the tension between which preserves the world. In other words, King's Tillich establishes the existential basis for being-in-the-world as dialectical tension between Nonbeing and freedom, the synthesis of which belongs to God alone and would mean the end of history.

The order of history becomes, for King and Tillich, a question of providence. Looking briefly at divine creation, including either historical foreordering or foreseeing (*pro-videre*), King provides two possible ways of understanding historical unfolding eschatologically (King 1994b, 430). The first is that of a passive God observing history's preordained development. The second sees God actively intervening in history to achieve human salvation. The former understanding forecloses on free will, as it inscribes the event in history before it occurs. The latter allows for free will, to a certain degree. That said, King reads Tillich as rejecting both of these possibilities, favoring instead an eschatological understanding of providence privileging an openness to human agency in history. This openness is maintained by the unbreakable bond between God and humanity, as opposed to against, outside, or as a part of it. With this view, King highlights Tillich's emphasis on the soul's link to eternity as a structural one defined by the dialectical tension between freedom and finitude. King then recasts Tillich's thought "in Pauline terms" as the eschatological work of God's infinite love.

Tillich's eschatological thought raises the problem of evil for King with some urgency. For, according to King's reading of Tillich, God creates only creatures that are like Him, and that are therefore creative and free. Yet, human creativity is set in the finitude of Nonbeing, which is alien to God's nature. Divine creativity must guide individual experience and human history in a medium alien to it. As part of divine creativity, human creativity, the structural equivalent to Heidegger's Dasein, necessarily rejects both freedom as the ground of dependent being embedded in finitude, and of Nonbeing's unfreedom. The rejection is the basis for any existential analytic, as King might envision it. Because of Dasein's double resistance, its existential analytic question of evil in the world becomes bound with that of theodicy, where the affirmation of Being Itself, God's love, is the attempt to live in contradiction without the power to sublate the ontological polarity of creativity's oppositional elements. Theodicy enables subsistence in the basic ontological structure of being through the realization of God's love. It is only in recognizing and accepting God's love that the origin of evil as Nonbeing becomes tolerable to reason.

In order better to explain Tillich's complex understanding of God's creativity in eschatological history, King raises Tillich's objection of the "Aristotelian-Thomistic formula that God is *actus-purus*" (King 1994b, 433). For King reading Tillich, the dialectical bond between the dynamic and formal aspect of an idea, such as that between "potentiality" and "actuality," favors the object's form over its possible meaning. This means that "meaning" has formal attributes that are not accounted for, excluding possibility from participation in the structure of reality. The loss of possibility reduces the thought of divine agency in history to an unproductive, and therefore uncreative, binary choice between divine presence and absence. The fact of this choice demands ontological sublation, which does not fall within the purview of human being. The loss of potentiality's dynamism has serious consequences for the eschatological understanding of existence in which freedom and salvation are structurally embedded. King's Tillich avoids making this choice by maintaining that God acts both in actuality and potentially, in human history. Human being authentically resolves the tension of this ontological polarity not in deciding between binaural elements but rather in the acceptance of God's love as faith, or that which sustains logical contradiction as "the possible."

God's love is the possibility of infinite freedom in finitude. For unlike God's actual, unconditional freedom, human being's freedom is unconditional in theory alone. For this reason, the foreclosure on possibility cuts human being off from the experience of freedom in any positive, historical sense. Because freedom is only achieved eschatologically, as the historical project of humanity, it must be posited historically as possible in the present and, in its futurity, as destiny. For, in the divine creation, possibility and actuality are ultimately one, uniting freedom and destiny, finitude and eternity, in God's Being. As King writes, "There is an absolute unity and identity of freedom and destiny in God" (King 1994b, 435).

This unity depends on God's eternal presence; yet for Tillich, God does not exist outside of temporality. Citing Plato's sense of time as "the moving image of eternity" and Hegel's rejection of endless time as "bad infinity," King shows that Tillich believes instead in God's "omnitemporality," in which eternity is understood as "the power of embracing all periods of time" (King 1994b, 436). As a correlate to omnipotence, omnitemporality is the temporal expression of God's unconditional freedom. Omnitemporality allows Tillich to value time as an attribute of Being, rather than of Being's modality, insofar as time is an expression of Being's ability to encompass each of its moments, which are not infinite in number. As in Heidegger, Being contains the finite totality of being's temporality, avoiding Hegel's "bad infinities" and Plato's museum of the moving image.[15]

Because God fulfills all moments, God in history is both "possible freedom" and "freedom's fulfillment." Human destiny is reunion with God in unconditional freedom. This reunion would mean the end of individual existence in fusion with God. Because it is a reunion, King's reading of Tillich sees human being originally in union with God. The goal of eschatological being is the return to union with God, or the end of individual identity. As a process of individuation and de-individuation, eschatological being can be understood as conditioned by a "natural" tendency toward reunion with God. This return, then, would be motivated not by desire, but rather by the aspect of the divine in human being that seeks to return to Itself. King and Tillich call this aspect of the divine "love." Love, without desire, articulates the temporal movement of human being toward reunion with God. There are, however, forms of love that are moved by desire, and therefore do not motivate this movement toward God. King writes of libido, which is motivated by need; philia, or the attraction of equals; and eros, or the love of power. King uses the term "agape" to name God's love, which falls into none of these categories, and to name God as love. Agape is unconditional love, experienced ontologically in human freedom as possibility and destiny.

Justice is an attribute of love. Any violation of love as agape demands justice. This reaction, however, is to be thought of not as retributive but rather as, in Tillich's words, "the negation of the negation of love" (King 1994b, 442). This means that justice negates the rejection of reunification with God, and by extension with fellow human beings, as all humanity derives from the original unity with God. Performing justice entails negating desire, which motivates acts that value individual, ontologically isolated existence above loss of individuality in unity with God. *Justice sees desegregation as a natural progression toward reunion in divine love.* Ultimately, injustice limits the possibility of human freedom, requiring justice to reestablish the authenticity of human being in God's love. Justice, then, is not retributive, and can be seen as punitive only to those who reject the negation of love's negation. This choice leads to continued ontological isolation and alienation from God and fellow human being.

II. King's Being

The dissertation's philosophical sophistication obtains in its comparative and critical capacity for connecting Tillich's theology to the history of Western metaphysics. For example, King suggests that Tillich's concept of God verges on "absolute quantitative monism," which he understands as God's presence in all beings, and as divine participation in history. King then elucidates "absolute quantitative monism" further by insisting that Tillich's God concept is nearly identical in this regard to "Hegel's philosophy of Spirit and Plotinus' philosophy of the One" (King 1994b, 447). In these critical moments when he steps outside Tillich's thought to link it to an intellectual tradition, King always refers the theologian's "monism" back to a source in German or ancient Greek philosophy. That said, King sums up "monism" with Tillich's statement that "man's love of God is the love with which God loves himself," without mentioning the strong Augustinian aspect of this belief and declining to reinforce a basic element of Tillich's thought with its source in theology, despite having already discussed Augustine's more overtly philosophical concepts in the dissertation (King 1994b, 447).

The charge of monism brings King to point out an apparent contradiction in Tillich's concept of human freedom. For King, monism implies God's presence in human being to a determinative degree, undermining humanity's ability to act independently and according to free will. Tillich's concept of freedom, however, suggests a quantitatively pluralistic view of human being's relationship to divine Being, whereby divine presence is not immanent in everyone, acting instead as a medium in which human freedom is possible. The tension in Tillich's thought between these two quantitative analyses can be partially resolved by suggesting a difference between essence and existence in the relationship of human being to God's Being. In its essence, human being exists in unity with divine Being; however, the historicity of human being places it outside of God. Ultimately, King is not satisfied with this solution, insisting instead that Tillich's philosophy is irreconcilably contradictory on this point.

Indeed, for King this inconsistency in Tillich's thought is the point at which his dialogue with the theologian becomes critical and creative. King announces this shift in his dissertation's tone as a structural necessity of the work, and as a necessary part of the "creative integration" of his individual thought. King compares this "creative integration" to the conversion narrative of individuals in isolation, such as Paul and Augustine, as well as to the solitary trials undergone by Jesus and Buddha (King 1994b, 454). King's separation from Tillich, and to a lesser extent Wieman, is provoked by their acceptance of God's love as a dialectical bond between human beings, yet without consideration of the moral responsibility inherent in fellowship. In other words, King criticizes Tillich and Wieman for the fact that their conception of the ontological necessity of God's love for human freedom does not posit fellowship and goodness as ontologically given. King, then, is calling for a greater emphasis on the social responsibility inherent in God's love, which does not recognize essential racial difference. His concept of fellowship goes beyond God's love as "process," in Wieman's sense, or "Being-itself" in Tillich's: it posits divine love as "fellowship and communion" with God, based on knowledge and volition.

In this relationship, God's personality is revealed to be "goodness." For King, this means there "can be no goodness in the true ethical sense without freedom and intelligence." God's love is experienced in human freedom, and it is known intellectually through the divine fellowship of the beloved community. In this respect, "only a personal being can be good," because fellowship is found only in the interpersonal relationships between beings, as conditioned by God's goodness, and in the subject's personal relationship with God (King 1994b, 513). This "personal good" is the substance of divine fellowship, and the basis of divine love as social justice. Outside of the divine relation between human beings as absolute equality, love, freedom, and justice have no meaning.

King sharpens his criticism of Tillich by emphasizing the importance of the monism/pluralism contradiction in his work, attributing it to the theologian's lack of scriptural reference when discussing God's creation of human being. For King, Tillich's avoidance of scripture on this matter leads to the devaluation of freedom and responsibility as "co-creative" with God. This is to say, while God's original act of creation is unconditional and absolute, human freedom in finitude recalls this creativity as human being's social responsibility within God's love. Freedom, then, is determined by the responsibility to strive to achieve God's love in social existence. In short, King criticizes Tillich's lack of social engagement and suggests that this shortcoming in his philosophy is due to an inattentiveness to theology's foundation in scripture. Tillich is too much the philosopher of Heideggerian fundamental ontology to embrace the full, anti-essentialist implications of his thought.

Because King ultimately attempts to see Dasein as socially responsible, the problem of evil in Tillich's concept of God returns with force in the dissertation's last section, devoted to criticism. According to King, Tillich understands the cause of evil as threefold: physical, due to finitude; moral, because of "creaturely freedom"; and "the apparent fact of meaningless and futility" caused by, in Tillich's words, "the negativities of creaturely existence" (King 1994b, 530). The evil of meaninglessness, then, would be caused by an inherent, ontological property in existence, and thus be rooted in God Himself. Tillich explains this,

King believes, by positing the existence of an irrational aspect in God's nature, what Tillich calls the "abyss" of negation in God as logos. God's nature is itself dialectical, creating evil in the world in the form of meaning's negation. This irrationality in God's nature is not Nonbeing; it is the nihilism of inaction that conditions freedom within God and in the world. King finds this unacceptable, for an obvious reason. His theory of God's love as the attempt to achieve human freedom in history is mediated by the divine creative power, which, if abysmal, also justifies freedom's negation. As a social theology, an abysmal God is impossible; the problem of negation is historical and contingent rather than eternal and unconditional.

Insisting that "there is much in Tillich that is reminiscent of Spinoza and Hegel," and presumably Heidegger, King condemns what he sees as the theologian's pantheism on the grounds that, as an intersubjective eschatological development, Tillich's God weakens the distinction between individuals, and between the individual and God. In effect, human beings become aspects of God, recognizing in each other and themselves only Him. In sharp contradiction, King believes that the substance of "true religion" is in the distance between the individual and God, and between individuals. In this distance, subjects recognize each other, clothed in their humanity, and in so doing come into "true" relation with God. This relation "expresses itself in worship and love" (King 1994b, 532). True religion is absolute, unconditional surrender to God's love, which alone mediates social relations by making humanity's recognition of human goodness and divine justice possible.

Guided by this belief, King's final presentation of Tillich as a self-contradicting monist leads to his positing of human freedom in individuality, without recourse to the subject's divine determination in absolute Spirit or Being. King does not deny God's omnipotence; he insists instead that human being is radically separate from His divine nature. King's rejection of the idea that human and divine nature are to any extent combined leads him to charge Tillich with a dependence on philosophy that causes a crucial lack of engagement with scripture, and ultimately with social reality. Tillich's commitment to Heideggerian philosophy results in his self-contradictory presentation of human freedom, which in turn produces a false conception of God, and a fundamental misunderstanding of Being as a political force. Being instead inflicts divine violence through nonviolence by exposing the lie of racial essentialism.

King provides his mature vision of divine love as social force in the "World House" part of his 1964 Nobel Lecture, with an anecdote about an unwritten story. A one-line sketch for a future novel is found among a novelist's posthumous papers: "A widely separated family inherits a house in which they have to live together" (King 2010a, 177).[16] From this, King immediately conceives of the "World House." Thought of as a single family, humanity is brought together under one roof by science and technology. King imagines each group within the whole of humanity as an individual family member at odds with another member over diametrically opposed beliefs. Easterner is against Westerner, Black versus white, Jew contra Gentile, etc. In order to preserve the House, each binary pair must overcome the opposition that binds its two poles. Because they are in constant conversation, the relation between binaural elements is dialectical. Indeed, King sees the human family as composed of dialectical partners, each with the task of overcoming binary antagonism and uniting in peace and freedom. Once one antagonism is sublated, the new, unified being finds a new dialectical partner to dispute, until each antagonism is resolved, and a unified House prevails.

This means that each struggle is relevant to all the others, and that the totality of conflict is the House's history. Furthermore, because each dialectical pair is committed to conflict, its participants are not free to pursue other interests. Because of this constraint, King believes that conflict between members is unnatural, insofar as it reflects a rejection of the freedom to do something else. The resolution of individual conflicts, and the ultimate unification of the fragmented House, not only brings peace to the family, it also sets each member free. The goal of the House's history is peace and freedom through the recognition of the individual body as part of one body, or Dasein. Dasein here names not a totality but rather a common condition and orientation toward God. Humanity's "incorporation" as Dasein leads to the recognition of its unified sensibility in one Being. The House is the home of the human body and spirit, and for King its architect was God, or Being Itself. The House reflects God's creativity, represented historically in Dasein's existential analytic, as an architect and is built of His love. For King, divine love is reflected in the House's design, and in the substance of its timber—in the House's existential or ontic structure. The House's ontic structure—the course of its history—reflects humanity's own creativity, or existential analytic, which links human being to God, Who is Being Itself.

Shortly after having written his dissertation, King calls the result of a humanity unified in God's love the beloved community. Just as "World House" names Heidegger's "home," those who live in the House are "homeless" until they recognize each other in Being, at which point they become the beloved community, or a "people." In "Justice Without Violence" (originally published in 1957),

King suggests that the beloved community is formed in the wake of nonviolent protest, which can be distinguished from violent protest not by its execution but rather by its effects. Violent protest is defined by an aftermath of bitterness and further human estrangement. It condemns the fractured community to further damnation, where sinfulness is social dislocation and segregation. This means that for King redemption is found in friendship and "brotherly" love, or agape. Conversely, enmity stands in dialectical negation to amity, and is therefore seen by King as violent, whatever form it takes. Nonviolence, then, is the practice of neighborly love, leading to the creation of the beloved community as the shelter of Being.

Again in 1957, in "Advice for Living," King posits that love creates the conditions for human freedom by building the bonds between members of a community to form the beloved community (King 1994d, 280). As a creative force of redemption, love is related to divine creativity, and therefore to the good. As such, love is also a constituent part of justice. For King, justice is impossible without love, which allows human beings to recognize each other as such, which is to say, as God's creation. Love is the recognition of divine goodness as the beloved community, and thus the rectification of social estrangement, or sin. In this respect, love and justice are one. All violence, then, is unjust, as it stands against God's creativity as an affront to the beloved community. For Heidegger, however, this love is expressed inwardly, as a relationship between self and Being Itself, in Tillich's terms, and between the individual and divine love, in King's. Yet King mobilizes this concept for social engagement through the definition of being as the beloved community, where violence vandalizes the World House, in which all peoples live without the order of Being's preference.

Affirming the redemptive, creative character of nonviolence in "My Trip to the Land of Gandhi" (1959), King briefly outlines three possibilities for oppressed communities. The first, and worst, course of action is inaction. For King, this leads to "moral and spiritual suicide," by which he means complete alienation from divine salvation (King 1986, 54). The path of inaction in the face of segregation's oppression leads to eternal damnation. The second is violent resistance, which prolongs the state of alienation from grace, which King understands as freedom, the being of human being. Violent resistance means not eternal damnation but rather self-estrangement through the rejection of divine creativity and, ultimately, the beloved community. The third course of action is nonviolence, and this path ends with the beloved community's realization in existential freedom.

Of the three options, inaction is the worst, as it leads to eternal damnation through unpardonable offense, "suicide," which while here moral and spiritual is nevertheless mortal, hence King's intentionally inflammatory use of the term. For King, existence precedes essence just as death gives meaning to eternal life, and not the reverse.

For this reason, King believes, as a "brotherly" society, the beloved community is premised on reconciliation. This concedes an initial estrangement, which King associates with sin. Sin is the rejection of God's love experienced in the creative force of human freedom. In other words, it is a priori the condition of human existence. The recognition of Being as a shared, divinely created, beloved humanity provides this experience, which is that of the good. Because of this, the rejection of reconciliation is unjust, and the unreconciled community is premised on injustice. Damnation is the eternal state of injustice, or Nonbeing. As the goal of human redemption and salvation, the "ultimate end" to which King refers is the eschatological end of history as human unity in Being on earth. The "creation of the beloved community" is an earthly kingdom come. The social responsibility of all human beings is the facilitation of this end through the fight against Nonbeing (sin, violence, unreconciled death), making King's social theory of nonviolence also an idealist philosophy of history.[17]

That said, for King the idea that "nonviolence is absolute commitment to the way of love" does not mean love in any historically experiential sense. Indeed, he is quite specific about the nature of the love conceptualized. It is a Hegelian dialectical grasp of the existence of another human being in which the self loses itself completely, only to recover the self as other. King does not consider this selfish, or self-love; rather, he sees it as the recognition of common human being between two otherwise alienated individuals. This "pouring out" to the other is the same act of love human being performs in the face of the Other. Human love, then, is divine in the sense that it involves the same surrender to the recognition in which human being is defined. Nonviolence allows this emptying out or "Clearing" to occur. Violence can be defined as any idea or action that prevents the Clearing from taking place.[18]

When King insist that "at the center of nonviolence stands the principle of love," he indicates dialectically that violence is the principle of hate, and that nonviolence and violence are acts of spirit as much as they are physical acts (King 1994f, 324). Violence can equally be a thought as well as a use of physical force. In either instance, the spirit is obstructed from achieving dialectical recognition of the self as other, and the freedom of the other to be the self. For King, freedom means freedom from hate, the origin of all unfreedom. The recognition of unfreedom is the precondition for the experience of freedom. This recognition is redemption. The recognition of the other as the self's freedom is the redemption of the self through Being Itself.

Referencing Amos 5.21–24 in his 1963 memorial service for the victims of the terrorist attack on the Sixteenth Street Baptist Church, King sees the self being poured into the other, allowing justice to roll "down like waters and righteousness like a mighty stream" (King 1994f, 475). The fluidity of the self is that of justice, and indeed the self's movement toward the other is also that of justice. This means that justice is the act of self-surrender that opens the way to redemption as freedom's recognition. Injustice, then, is an act of hate, by which is meant any act that prevents the outpouring of the self in the justness of its movement. Justice is the facilitation of being's recognition in Being, as King could have phrased it in his dissertation. Justice begins with nonviolence, which is self-surrender to love as openness to the other's being, which is also that of the self. Doing justice to this openness, the self is emptied into the other, in redemptive recognition of their shared being, which is human freedom. This freedom is divine creativity as human possibility in history, and the "infinite hope" for union with God in eternity.

Because the stakes of earthy love are eternal, no institution or law preventing its earthly realization can be considered lawful. Indeed, the legal and the lawful can stand in the way of love and justice. Faith in the eternal is knowledge of the divine law of love. Any earthly law opposed to love's movement toward human unity and humanity's union with God is unlawful in eternal eyes and must be opposed by nonviolence. Only this form of opposition avoids doing further violence and increasing the scope of injustice. Love, then, is always right, and any law that does not flow from love must be opposed with nonviolence, for the sake of human salvation. This also means that all acts of lawmaking and of law's preservation that divide individuals from each other are a priori violent. As all states unify only to divine humanity more thoroughly, all laws supporting the state's existence, including its foundational laws, are violent. Divine violence is never retributive, as it embraces the whole of humanity, even when its immediate effect is to divide it. Divine violence always ultimately seeks to create paths to freedom through unity, even when it appears to engender disunity and cause destruction. This form of destruction is creative, clearing a space for Being Itself in existence.

All members of the beloved community have realized their freedom in God's love through a return to unity with the Creator. This return signifies both the end of history and its beginning, for King believes that while God's act of creation places humanity in the World House, nevertheless sin divides human beings in their home. Because being is made from God's creative act of love, sin can be said to separate being into beings. As dialectically apposite to unified, or "true" being, sin must therefore be "false" being, or simply "Nonbeing." Dialectical antagonism is sin, or Nonbeing, attempting to keep beings apart, or segregated, and eventually to absorb them entirely. Because it is opposed to being, Nonbeing results in unfreedom and an absence of peace. To oppose the unifying power of God's creative love is to reject peace and human freedom, with world-historical consequences.

Each relationship, then, contains the manifest antagonism of Nonbeing, and possible redemption from segregation through creative freedom. Humanity achieves redemptive unification through creative acts in recognition of God's love. Each individual act reflects a choice between being and Nonbeing, freedom and unfreedom, and justice and injustice. The last dialectical pair mentioned presents a unique problem in the history of the House. Unlike any other dialectical relation in the House, that of justice and injustice places moral value on each human act. Justice is done when an act advances human understanding and recognition, bringing two antagonists closer to unification in God's love. Injustice occurs each time an act drives two dialectical partners further apart, perpetuating unfreedom and misery. Justice negates injustice through just acts; acts of vengeance are unjust because, as isolated acts, they promote human division. Retributive acts are unjust; acts of love and friendship alone "redress" wrongs, by promoting human unity and freedom. King articulated these Heideggerian ideas in a spiritual way meant to reach a popular audience, so that they could do the widest good. The ideas themselves, however, originate with King's doctoral study in philosophy and allow him to correlate his theological universalism with the spiritual concerns of a socially conscious Christianity.[19]

3 Black *power* as Nonviolence

I. King's Correlations

KING'S EFFECTIVENESS AS A theologian and social activist lies in part with his ability to reach consensus through correlative terminological replacement. For this reason, the extent to which he uses supernatural terms literally rather than euphemistically is subject to debate. Fairclough writes:

> In sermons, for example, he frequently likened nonviolence to a kind of supranatural power—a "Soul Force" that could defeat physical force. Of course, such descriptions were not meant to be taken literally: King was simplifying complex ideas and communicating them in a way that black Southerners—poorly educated, politically inexperienced, but imbued with a deep religious sensibility—could grasp easily. (Fairclough 1986, 4)

Although they may not have been meant literally, these terms still signified something that was intended to be understood critically, and therefore more than euphemistically. The supernatural power of nonviolence—be it Gandhi's satyagraha or "soul force," or Tillich's "Being Itself"—is not identified strictly as a rhetorical device; its various names are philosophically correlative. As such, they play a significant role in a wider conceptual scheme that *was* meant literally, for the purposes of coalition building. With such terms, King cogently introduces a simplified philosophical concept with which his audience would not already be familiar, in order to create philosophical consensus.

King's ability to do this was singular among Civil Rights leaders and other public figures engaged in Black freedom and liberation movements in the 1950s and 1960s. Therefore while, as Kennedy has written, "it would be erroneous to conflate, without qualification, his career and the history of the [Civil Rights] Movement," nevertheless, King's contribution to communication within the movement is exceptional, particularly as he can simplify complex ideas and use them in this form to find conceptual common ground between seemingly incompatible points of view. This enables him to serve "as a conciliatory element in a diverse social movement" (Carson 2005a, 4). King's ability, Carson continues, "grew out of his unique combination of opposing qualities: on the one hand, his cosmopolitan awareness of the modern currents of theological and political thought, and, on the other hand, his lifetime of experiences in the black Baptist church, the largest African American religious denomination. Few other black leaders of his time possessed both advanced academic training in his case, a doctorate in systematic theology from Boston University and deep roots in a particular black community" (Carson 2005a, 4). Indeed, Carson concludes that the "most remarkable aspect of King's leadership, therefore, was his ability to express the broader significance of a freedom struggle that had many leaders. As the southern black protests of the 1960s became more massive and radical, his leadership was repeatedly tested as he sought to convince national political leaders to give in to black demands for civil rights reform and convince black militants to remain nonviolent" (Carson 2005a, 4).[1] King's talent for creating coalitions based on complex ideas expressed with an appealing clarity lending itself to diverse appropriation affected leaders as ideologically different from nonviolence as Malcolm X.

The relation between King's thought and that of Malcolm X provides an example of the correlative nature of King's rhetoric.[2] King's nonviolence can appeal even to staunch enemies of its fundamental principles due to the plasticity of its philosophical basis and the pliancy of its terms.[3] Because of this and, as Lewis Baldwin notes, "despite their differences, organizationally and ideologically, Malcolm and Martin displayed a genuine love and respect for each other which is seldom mentioned in the literature about both men" (Baldwin 1986, 395). In fact, the two leaders identified the same source and proposed a "common solution" to racial injustice. Removing "separatism" from the realm of possibility, King's definition of Black *power* becomes like Malcolm's.

As Carson writes elsewhere, "Martin would witness the destructive internal conflicts that disrupted African American political life in the years after Malcolm's assassination. More than Martin could have known in 1965, Malcolm's death signaled the beginning of bitter battles involving proponents of the ideological alternatives the two men represented" (Carson 2005b, 25). After 1965, King begins to speak positively more publicly about democratic socialism, in a bid to offer a different, more materially oriented means by which to bridge widening differences with Black radical groups. Although, as Kazin has written, King's "vision for a new America was closer to the dream of Eugene Debs than to a racially tolerant version of Cold War liberalism," it was not socialist enough to satisfy the Black Panther Party and other militant Black liberation groups (Kazin 2009, 987). Part of the reason for this is the lateness with which King privileges democratic socialism in his public thought. Even though, as Sturm remarks, "King's democratic socialism was rooted in his formative experience of the black religious tradition and was manifested from his student days at Crozer Theological Seminary forward," it was not manifest in his speeches and written work until the final years of his life (Sturm 1990, 79).[4] Yet these late gestures toward democratic socialism were still not enough to draw King from the political mainstream. As Fairclough writes: "True, King adopted a much more radical stance during the last two years of his life, but he never seemed to wander very far from the political mainstream. To the student radicals of the 'New Left,' as well as to the angry advocates of 'Black Power,' King remained a staid, unexciting figure, the ineffectual exponent of an outdated brand of liberalism" (Fairclough 1983, 117). Indeed, King "condemned advocates of Black Power because the slogan 'gives priority to race precisely at a time when the impact of automation and other forces have made the economic question fundamental for blacks and whites alike'" (Willhelm 1979, 11). Furthermore, the differences between King and Black Power leaders were not always ideologically substantive but rather concerned leadership style. SNCC rejected him in part because he "or his cohorts had 'grandstanded,' 'hogged' the stage, and took the spotlight when the cameras were rolling and did not share the glory with the SNCC troops or the local leaders who had prepared the ground that made these history-making events possible. Some of us in SNCC mockingly referred to Dr. King as 'De Lawd' and looked down our noses at him and most preachers, who we often cast as 'Uncle Toms' because of the roles many of them had traditionally played in the South as 'spokesmen' for the race" (Simmons 2008, 192–193).

That said, "De Lawd" did not consider himself above "issues of violence and legacy" and the demands of Black Power leaders and their constituents. The belief that King disdained engagement of this sort is a misconception that in turn extends to Black Power. Williams has noted that

> King's engagement of the issues of violence and legacy are instructive when one considers the long dominant interpretation of the civil rights movement and its

relationship to the Black Power movement. Lauded for their sustained commitment to nonviolence, organizations such as King's Southern Christian Leadership Conference (SCLC) and the National Association for the Advancement of Colored People (NAACP) have received privileged attention. Long dismissed as little more than an angry reaction to the slow pace of progress associated with the civil rights movement, groups and individuals associated with the Black Power "phase" of the movement stand accused as "prophets of rage" whose lack of a moral center and violent posturing helped to curtail the civil rights era. Perhaps no group is more closely identified with this legacy than the Black Panther Party (BPP). Founded in Oakland, California, in 1966, the BPP rose to prominence as the most radical of the black militant organizations. (Williams 1997, 16)

As Williams indicates, this conception of the Panthers is largely erroneous, and in part the product of their persecution. Recent historiography has attempted to provide a more accurate picture of the BPP, focusing on the movement in terms of human rights rather than violence. As the self-fashioned heirs to Malcolm X, the Panthers accepted his understanding of self-defense as well as his more nuanced views of Black liberation developed after his break with the Nation of Islam (Robinson 2001, 8–9). Malcolm X set an example for the Panthers, both before and after his pilgrimage to Mecca. Furthermore, they believed that Malcolm intended to set an example for Black revolutionaries, and it was their primary debt to his legacy to do so as well. Indeed, Huey P. Newton saw the BPP as the Black political avant-garde's heir to Malcolm X, and believed "black revolutionaries have to set an example" (Lynd 1969, 69).

At times, the interplay between academic, avant-garde, and organic intellectualism failed, giving the false impression that Newton knew little about the history and thought particular to the community he tried to liberate, concentrating instead on "foreign" models (Henderson 1997, 188). As Assata Shakur puts it, the Panthers "talked about intercommunalism but still really believed that the Civil War was fought to free the slaves. A whole lot of them barely understood any kind of history, Black, African or otherwise. . . . That was the main reason many Party members, in my opinion, underestimated the need to unite with other Black organizations and to struggle around various community issues" (Shakur 2001, 221). Yet intercommunalism may have been Newton's most important philosophical-political innovation (Anderson 2012, 253). "Intercommunalism" arose from the belief that nation-states no longer existed and that marginalized communities sharing bonds of social, economic, and racial oppression formed their own sovereign political network. The concept was not ignorant of African American history and philosophy; rather, it privileged a global cultural coalition instead, where no one tradition could take priority. As Abron notes, the "Black Panther Intercommunal News Service was dedicated to presenting and analyzing similarities and connections between global oppressed communities" (Abron 1986, 35).

Williams describes well the move from Black Nationalism to intercommunalism: "While nationalism often is defined as loyalty to a native country, with black nationalism, the nation can consist of the black people who live in a particular country, as in the United States. Black nationalism also can be defined as a desire for a separate geographical nation within a country, or as a feeling of community with other blacks in the world—an extension of pan-Africanism. Still, black Americans who exported black nationalisms not only sought community with other blacks in the world but also supported and sought kinship with other ethnic groups engaged in similar struggles like the Cubans, Vietnamese, and Korean" (Williams 1997, 13). Although intercommunalism rejected the nation-state as anything more than a fiction, the BPP nevertheless can be considered a revolutionary nationalist movement. As Harris writes:

> Revolutionary Nationalists believe that there can be no separate racial peace with the oppressor. Instead, alliances are to made with Third World peoples, and later, after careful scrutiny, with white radicals. Within these working relationships, the black laboring or underclass would compose a leadership vanguard, and eventually, through revolutionary struggle, the downtrodden would eliminate or reduce social class distinctions, banish neo-colonial imperialists from the globe and usher in an era of unprecedented gains for humanity. This philosophy, although international in scope, is Afrocentric in its promotion of black Americans as the liberating vanguard. (Harris 2001, 164)

While all this is true, it does not tell the whole story of the BPP. Indeed, the state of BPP studies is still evolving, having gone from relative obscurity two decades ago to becoming part of what Joseph calls "Black Power Studies." According to Joseph, "'Black Power Studies' places the history of the era within the broader context of American and African American history at the local, national, and international level" (Joseph 2008, 8).[5] Joseph writes elsewhere, "Black Power came to be defined as the cutting edge of black activism, a movement whose militancy contrasted with the more measured tone of the civil rights movement and seemed to signal a break from past modes of black activism. Black Power echoed through America as a bold call for African American liberation" (Joseph 2009c, 755). Yet for Joseph, and Black Power studies generally, the "meaning of the term 'black power' remains contested." Joseph rightly calls for a reconceptualization of black power, as "Black Power Studies both builds on and stands out in contrast to previous stages. Most notably, the new works 'reperiodize' black liberation struggles by examining the ways in which black radicals influenced black politics during the 'heroic period' of the Civil Rights movement. In studying the Black Power movement as a two-decade struggle for black liberation (1954–1975), these recent studies are contributing to the reconceptualization of conventional civil rights narratives" (Joseph 2008, 9–10). It is also important to note that the BPP shared elements of radical political form presented in racially diverse groups active in the Bay Area going back to the 1940s (Bae 2017, 700).[6]

Although a revolutionary nationalist organization inspired by the Bay Area's interracial history of radicalism and premised on intercommunalism, the BPP still shares some basic goals and assumptions with black nationalist groups. As Valls puts it,

> black nationalists argued for changes in both policy and in attitude toward racial concentration. The attitudinal change they urged combated the dominant view among whites (but also shared by some African Americans) that any geographic or institutional clustering of African Americans should be viewed negatively, as a reflection of American society's failure to achieve an integrated and color-blind society. To the contrary, they argued that such racial clustering is often valued by African Americans, and quite reasonably so. The problem of racial justice in the United States is the terms on which that clustering took place, and the maldistribution of resources associated with it. The policy change that follows from this perspective is that public policy should support black institutions and communities rather than undermine them in the service of integration. (Valls 2010, 479)

Valls's analysis is exemplary, underscoring Black nationalism's material objectives, including policy change, a reconfigured understanding of justice, accompanied by economic reform and institutional reorganization. That said, neither Valls nor other commentators address the conception of race driving Black nationalist critical theory and social critique. It would not be accurate to say the BPP, as an example of either Black or revolutionary nationalism, embraced a fully contingent understanding of racial difference. Indeed, Newton's Platonism suggests otherwise. Even as an example of culture-based organizing, the BPP still cannot be viewed as anti-essentialist regarding racial ontology. According to Laing, African American culture-based organizing includes:

> (a) a definition of the target community, (b) a definition of community problems, (c) empowering oration, (d) antiracist hegemony focus, and (e) strategies that challenged existing power relationships. (Laing 2009, 635)

The "definition of the target community" implies race without specifying its meaning. The term "community problems" suggests that leaving the community's scalar dimensions would assuage the individual's concerns, and that "antiracist" hegemony can be achieved strictly in the physical basis of community. Any strategies conceived to challenge "existing power relationships" would be communal interventions that maintain race while in practice are anti-racist yet hegemonic. In other words, without racial essentialism, intercommunalism is insufficient as a political philosophical concept, playing instead as critical theoretical sleight of hand.[7]

For this reason, the BPP, as a "community-control movement [with] Black Nationalist origins, flew in the face of desegregation efforts, and instead pondered radical solutions that made conservatives, and even liberals, anxious" (Williamson 2005, 152). Furthermore, as Calloway puts it, "Newton and Seale recognized the importance of naming the enemy in the struggle" (Calloway 1977, 61). That is, there was as much to be gained politically by maintaining racial division as by coalition building in the manner of King. Because all contingent forms of inequality could at least in principle be overcome, permanent racial division could be seen as legitimate only insofar as all racial types were essentially different. For this reason, in Black Panther Party philosophy, and for Huey P. Newton specifically, racial types are eternal, Platonic forms shaping the whole of life.

II. Newton's Republic

Plato's *Republic* shapes Newton's relationship to literacy entirely. By his own account, Newton was functionally illiterate until his senior year of high school, and the chapter "Reading" in his autobiography, *Revolutionary Suicide* (originally published in 1973), speaks eloquently to the decisive role the *Republic* plays in remedying this:

> Then I told how, under the influence of my brother Melvin, I had taught myself to read by going again and again through Plato's *Republic*. I tried to explain what a deep impression Plato's allegory of the cave had made on me and how the prisoners in that cave were a symbol of the Black man's predicament in this country. It was a seminal experience in my life, I explained, for it had started me thinking and reading and trying to find a way to liberate Black people. Then I told of meeting Bobby Seale at Oakland City College and how the Black Panther Party grew out of our talks. (Newton 1995, 248)

Without much explanation for the choice of reading matter beyond wanting to participate in the intellectual discussions taking place around him, Newton tells how he began to read Plato's *Republic* in order to become literate under his own tutelage. He bought this text along with a dictionary and memorized passages while looking up all the words he did not know. Much like Malcolm X, Huey Newton is an autodidact who reads Western philosophy to achieve literacy as a means of engaging in learned dispute. Unlike Malcolm X, however, Newton has a passion for literature and poetry. Indeed, it is while he is recounting his attempts to read poetry that Newton mentions his selection of Plato as teacher and guide. This association of Plato with poetry is odd, given the *Republic*'s negative attitude toward poets. Fully cognizant of this tension, Newton makes the remark as a way of distancing himself from the transition between poetry and political philosophy in the evolution of his thought.

This development may be caused by Newton's extensive reading of Plato's *Republic*. The work returns several times in *Revolutionary Suicide*, and the allegory of the cave seems to have been of particular interest to Newton as an autodidact, pedagogue, and philosopher.[8] While in prison, Newton incorporated it into his "street philosophy," in which the cave was the penitentiary and the light revolutionary consciousness:

> I told [the other inmates] about the allegory of the cave from Plato's *Republic*, and they enjoyed it. We called it the story of the cave prisoners. In the cave allegory Plato describes the plight of the prisoners in a cave who receive their impression of the outside world from shadows projected on the wall by the fire at the mouth of the cave. One of the prisoners is freed and gets a view of the outside world—objective reality. He returns to the cave to tell the others that the scenes they observe on the wall are not reality but only a distorted reflection of it. The prisoners tell the liberated man he is crazy, and he cannot convince them. He tried

> to take one of them outside, but the prisoner is terrified at the thought of facing something new. When he is dragged outside the cave anyway, he sees the sun and is blinded by it. The allegory seemed very appropriate to our own situation in society. We, too, were in prison and needed to be liberated in order to distinguish between truth and the falsehoods imposed on us. (Newton 1995, 359–360)

Just as the cave's prisoners would refuse to believe the truth of the world above, many of Newton's fellow inmates found him to be crazy and even developed animosity toward the philosopher who tried to bring Plato to the street without altering ancient Greek philosophy substantively to suit the new environment. Indeed, Newton would repeat the allegory of the cave and his other attempts to impart Platonic philosophy to all who would listen, including and especially members of the Black Panther Party. Newton, who had read the *Republic* some eight or nine times by his own count, transformed the allegory of the cave into the emblematic account of the intellectual journey undergone by the liberated mind.

Demonized by the media and criminalized by police, Newton spent most of his adult life imprisoned, literally reproducing the scene of Plato's cave (Austin 1979, 3). The terms of his incarceration were extraordinary. Allowed visits from only ten individuals, nine of whom had to be family members, Newton was effectively cut off from the world. Perhaps because of the similarities between his condition and that of Plato's prisoners, as Blake recalls, Newton

> often returned to one of his fondest memories—discussing Plato's "Allegory of the Cave" with the brothers on the block. To Newton, Plato's tale of prisoners in a dungeon with their reality limited to shadows on the wall was a parable about the ghettoes in which many Black people lived. He recalled sharing this parable with street brothers as they debated the conditions of the community. To Newton, they were all like the occupants of Plato's cave, and he sought to use the parable to enlighten them about their circumstances. (Blake 2012, 242)

Newton "was well known for having repeatedly reread, and street-lectured upon, the Republic" (Vandiver 2016, 768). Fashioning himself a modern-day Socrates, Newton would have had to make his street and prison lectures on Plato's cave easily acceptable to his target audience (Sowers 2017, 26). Using "dropout mentality," or "epistemological privilege," Newton offered the "perspective of oppressed and marginalized people" to provide "a more accurate view of social conditions than that of the ruling group who often gazes upon a world in ways that legitimate their power" (Hughey 2007, 220).[9] In his Platonic scheme, white power's gaze limited that of Black Power, as a means of social and economic control. Delivering this message using Plato to talismanic effect, he and Seale tried to recruit among the Black community's most marginalized members (Williams 1998, 8). Using Platonism to frame the bleak material circumstances of racially marginalized existence, Newton was able to incorporate further philosophical content in his street lectures, using Plato as the starting point.

Plato's allegory of the cave, then, provides the Black Panther Party with a metaphysics of race and power:

> Everywhere I went in 1967 I was vehemently attacked by Black students for this position; few could present opposing objective evidence to support their criticisms. The reaction was emotional: all white people were devils; they wanted nothing to do with them. I agreed that some white people could act like devils, but we could not blind ourselves to a common humanity. More important was how to control the situation to our advantage. These questions would not be answered overnight, or in a decade, and time and again the students and I went for hours, getting nowhere. We talked right past each other. The racism that dominated their lives had come between us, and rational analysis was the victim. When I left San Francisco that afternoon, I reflected that many of the students who were supposedly learning how to analyze and understand phenomena were in fact caught up in the same predicament as the prisoners in Plato's cave allegory. Even though they were in college, they were still prisoners in the cave of exploitation and racism that Black people have been subjected to for centuries. Far from preparing them to deal with reality, college kept their intellects in chains. That afternoon I felt even more strongly that the Party would have to develop a program to implement Point 5 of our program, a true education for our people. (Newton 1995, 181–182)

Newton uses the story as a type of hermeneutic for interpreting the exploitation and gradual elimination of African Americans in the United States. In particular, he sees Plato's dark vision of enshrouded humanity as the perfect image of and narrative for "the Black Man." In this way, Newton's reading of the cave allegory traces the cognitive and epistemological effects of race ideology on Black men in America. Self-perception is skewed to such an extent that when Newton encounters Black students resistant to his message on college campuses, he perceives them solely through the lens of Plato's cave narrative. In reaction, Newton begins to formulate and modify the points of the program through which the Black Panther Party intends to offer racially normative principles for all African Americans.

From the *ontological* perspective, the philosophical inspiration for these principles is Plato's allegory of the cave, read to speak to Black being. "Negroes" live in the cave, enchained and unaware of the truth in the sun's light. Through proper pedagogical guidance, "Negroes" become Black men, or superior beings who reach the surface to perceive the true world of forms. In other words, Newton's use of Plato to measure the wages of American racism begins by articulating the compromised duality of the African American mind. W. E. B. Du Bois's Hegelian double consciousness as the "Negro" mind is then respectfully superseded by the ideologically enlightened, superior Black mind. The tactical advantage to this elaboration of double consciousness lay in Newton's inversion of the interracial master-slave dialectic. For Newton, Blacks are the naturally aristocratic, spiritually essential, intellectually absolute masters of truth.

Newton's gesture toward a Platonic ontology of race and power suggests intellectual and physical superiority as moral value and spiritual substance. While the spirit itself had ostensibly little to do with Christian attainment, it nevertheless linked body materialism with a metaphysics of racial presence that determined Blackness as manifestly superior to all other categorical expressions of race. Newton's achievements as an autodidact mirrored those of other Black subjects, indicating superior intellectual ability among those conforming to his physical ideal. Cultural values decisive for racial identification could be seen in Newton's portrait, which represented the characteristics all African Americans were meant to embrace by nature. The image of the leader Newton presents is the highest Platonic form of the African American racial type, and represents the moral, spiritual, and physical apex of human being.

Because Black being is separate and superior to whiteness, Newton rejects social and political activism premised on or striding toward interracial cooperation. Indeed, in *Seize the Time: The Story of the Black Panther Party and Huey P. Newton* (1970), Seale recounts the first time he and Newton met. On this occasion ("one particular day"), Newton expresses his "black nationalist philosophy" in part as the rejection of the NAACP, Civil Rights legislature, and Martin Luther King, Jr.'s program of nonviolence. Seale writes:

> I met Huey P. Newton in the early Sixties, during the Cuban blockade when there were numerous street rallies going on around Merritt Junior College in West

Oakland. One particular day there was a lot of discussion about black people and the blockade against Cuba. People were out in front of the college, in the streets, grouped up in bunches of 200, 250, what have you. Huey was holding down a crowd of about 250 people and I was one of the participants. After he held the conversation down to what in those days they called "shooting everybody down"— that means rapping off information and throwing facts—people would ask Huey a question or refer to something he said. They tried to shoot Huey down by citing some passage in a book concerning the subject matter being discussed, and before they knew it, Huey whipped out a copy of *Black Bourgeoisie* by E. Franklin Frazier and showed him what page, what paragraph, and corrected the person.

I guess I had the idea that I was supposed to ask questions in college, so I walked over to Huey and asked the brother, weren't all these civil rights laws the NAACP was trying to get for us doing us some good? And he shot me down too, just like he shot a whole lot of other people down. He said, it's all a waste of money, black people don't have anything in this country that is for them. He went on to say that the laws already on the books weren't even serving them in the first place, and what's the use of making more laws when what was needed was to enforce the present laws? So all the money that the people were giving to Martin Luther King and the rest who were supposed to put these laws on the books for black people, was a waste of the black people's money. I was ready to accept that when he started citing many more facts to back up his point of view. Huey always brings out basic, practical things; that's the way he talks to you, that's the way he explains things to you. He gets to a point where you can't get around, so you have to face things. (Seale 1970, 13–14)

Intermittently refuting members of the audience with passages from Frazier's book, Seale's Newton expands on his own idea that it is a waste of money for African Americans to donate to Martin Luther King, Jr.'s movement or any Civil Rights organization whose goal is the creation of new laws or the alteration of current laws. According to Seale's account, Newton believed these laws do not benefit African Americans, whose condition can only be improved outside the law and by a rule of their own devising. This means that for Newton not only has Civil Rights legislation failed; it is also a priori unlawful, insofar as it does not achieve its purported goals, serving instead to accomplish the opposite. This would also indicate that for Newton a higher law or legal form must exist, and it is to this law or form that African Americans need be beholden. Ultimately,

Newton's Platonic model of oppression could not dispense with racial essentialism without collapsing in on itself as a race-neutral form of community control, or worse, a version of King's nonviolence. For Newton, Seale, and the Black Panther Party generally, "by any means necessary" means obeying the higher law of hierarchically valued racial type. Violence as self-defense protects the eternal formal order as much as any individual or group.[10]

III. King's Eros

While King's thought also held eternal value above historically contingent legality, Newton and Seale could not accept his refusal to identify ontological affiliation by racially typological modes of being that privilege particularity in erotic attachment above love's universal filiation. King's avowed source for the definitions he uses for eros, agape, and philia is the Greek language, as used in Platonic philosophy. For example, in *Stride Toward Freedom* King elucidates his belief that love is nonviolent resistance as "understanding, redemptive goodwill." To prove this, King shows how the "Greek language comes to our aid. There are three words for love in the Greek New Testament. First, there is eros. In Platonic philosophy eros meant the yearning of the soul for the realm of the divine. It has come now to mean a sort of aesthetic or romantic love" (King 2010b, 125). King also mentions philia as a type of love, defining it as "intimate affection between personal friends. Philia denotes a sort of reciprocal love; the person loves because he is loved" (King 2010b, 125). Because philia depends on being loved to love, it cannot be the type of love King has in mind for nonviolent resistance, which requires loving those who do not return love. This also indicates that King's definition of personal friendship is selfish, in the sense that giving love depends on receiving it, creating a paradox of affection in which love can have no origin specific to the affected subjects. If the condition for loving is to be loved, then loving cannot begin with any one subject. As King presents it, philia begins with an object or disposition external to the loving subjects. Philia is determined originally by an object outside of the loving subject, either as the love of another subject or as the misidentification of the love that originally gives rise to the (false) recognition that one is loved.

The problem of love's origin is solved in agape. For King, "*agape* means understanding, redeeming goodwill for all men. It is an overflowing love which is purely spontaneous, unmotivated, groundless, and creative. It is not set in motion by any quality or function of its object. It is the love of God operating in the human heart" (King 2010b, 125). By this definition, love begins outside the subject, as its precondition. In other words, unselfish, disinterested love does not originate in human being. The "love" that begins in human being is a desire, and is therefore always intentional and instrumental, to varying degrees. Because it does not arise from human being—which, in a fallen state, is therefore tainted by original sin—agape retains the purity of its divine source, at least in its originality. It is "unmotivated, groundless, and creative" because its source is divine, and it is as a result without desire or justification, alive to infinite possibility.

The fact of King's total commitment to the concept of agape is not lost on commentators or the public, nor could it be. King spoke or wrote numerous times about agape and its meaning for nonviolence, often using the same formulation. He believed agape was "understanding goodwill for all men" that "affirms the other unconditionally. It is agape that suffers and forgives." Indeed, King was certain that the "basic and only adequate symbol for God's love is agape." Agape, therefore, "seeks nothing in return. It is a redemptive love. It is a love of God working within men. And so when men move to the point of agape, they love not because the individuals are so wealthful to them, not because it's anything they like so much about the individuals, but they love them because God loves them. They love them because they are wealthful to God, and this is the meaning of agape" (King 1994b, 327). King thus asserts that when "we rise to love on the agape level we love men not because we like them, not because their attitudes and ways appeal to us, but because God loves you" (King 1994c, 459). As Carson points out, here King very closely follows Harry Emerson Fosdick, who writes, "*Agape* means nothing sentimental or primarily emotional at all; it means understanding, redeeming, creative good will" (quoted in King 1994f, 459).

King also often insisted that agape is "more than eros." This does not mean that King was "basically silent" on eros. It would be incorrect to assume, as Martha Nussbaum has, that "as for erotic love and sexual desire . . . King is basically silent. He wants to make sure people understand that the agape he is talking about is not the same as eros or philia, but he never disparages those attitudes or urges their removal" (Nussbaum 2018, 125). Far from being "basically silent" on eros, King regularly mentions it in relation to agape. More importantly, King consistently defined agape through eros, providing a place for both in his philosophy of nonviolence. As Nussbaum seems to realize, eros is not a fully debased form of love in King's thought. Yet to insist he mentions eros solely to dismiss it and thereby distinguish agape alone is also and inevitably to grant that King has a concept of eros. This would also concede that eros performs more work in King's thought than merely to distinguish agape as a concept. Because she cannot see the extensive task eros accomplishes in King's thought, Nussbaum cannot perceive the depth of King's intervention in the Western metaphysical tradition. To fail to understand King on eros (and philia as well) is to fail to do full justice to King's ontology. What follows is an attempt to pay King his due as a vital philosopher of eros *as* civilization.

King writes in his dissertation, "We can see that the first point of divergence between the philosopher and the theologian is found in their cognitive attitude." To support this assertion, King footnotes Paul Tillich's claim in *Systematic Theology*: "The first point of divergence is a difference in the cognitive attitude of the philosopher and the theologian. Although driven by the philosophical erōs, the philosopher tries to maintain a detached objectivity toward being and its structures. The philosopher seeks to maintain a detached objectivity toward being" (King 1994b, 366). Citing this passage in Tillich obliquely, Harris Wofford suggests in a 1956 letter to King that "objectivity toward being" becomes impossible with eros present. That is, eros separates philosophy from theology, with the latter motivated by passion rather than reason (King 1994b, 226). Presumably, Wofford had reason to believe his reference to Tillich would resonate with King, along with the suggestion of his "stigmata" and the agape King is able somehow to "radiate." In an awkward ending, Wofford compliments King's take on eros while inadvertently introducing a sexual context both to King's radiant stigmata and to the Wofford letter itself. Ultimately however, Wofford, taking his Tillich reference for granted, makes the point that King is a spiritual philosopher rather than an erotic theologian. King himself distinguishes Christian love from the Greeks' philosophical definitions, and from the Greek understanding of eros. This, however, does not disagree with Wofford's reference to Tillich but rather reinforces the idea of a Christian philosophy unfettered from the Greek philosophical terms used to conceptualize individual relationships to God. In other words, King's reading of the Greek words for love is bound to a concept of individual selfishness as opposed to devotion to community above the self.

King does not reject the Greek terms in principle; indeed, he sees them as the authoritative source for philosophical and theological concepts of love. Rather, he disdains definitions of love focused on the individual above the community. The individual is lower in meaning than the community, King writes, citing Tillich, and eros "is the movement of that which is lower in power and meaning to that which is higher" (King 1994b, 486). As King continues, still citing Tillich, "All love, except *agape*, is dependent on contingent characteristics which change and are partial, such as repulsion and attraction, passion and sympathy" (King 1994b, 441). Calling it "a sort of esthetic or romantic love" at the 1957 Conference on Christian Faith and Human Relations in Nashville, King presents eros as subject to contingency and therefore as subjective, whereas agape is objective and true universally. King makes this clear in the dissertation by expressing eros's limitations in symbolic representation: "*Eros* cannot properly symbolize God's love, because God in his eternity transcends the fulfillment and non-fulfillment of reality" (King 1994b, 441). Limited in symbolic function by the contingency of its state, eros cannot express God's eternity and is therefore intended for lower functions.

Yet during the Prayer Pilgrimage for Freedom, King again describes eros as "a sort of aesthetic, romantic love," once more leaving open the possibility that it inspires more than its strict definitional parameters would allow. Listing yet again Greek forms of love, King clarifies in a sermon delivered at Ebenezer Baptist Church that eros

> is another type of love which is real love, and we're moving on up now into genuine, meaningful, profound love. It is explained through the Greek word eros. Plato used to use that word a great deal in his dialogues as a sort of yearning of the soul for the realm of the divine. But now we see it as romantic love, and there is something beautiful about romantic love. When it reaches its height there is nothing more beautiful in all the world. A romantic love rises above utilitarian love in the sense that it does have a degree of altruism, for a person who really loves with romantic love will die for the object of his love. A person who is really engaged in true romantic love will do anything to satisfy the object of that love, the great love. (King 1994f, 439)

Eros is "real love" as "a sort of yearning of the soul for the realm of the divine." Citing Plato as the source of eros's revelation, King believes "romantic love rises above utilitarian love" in its intuition of divinity in Plato's philosophy. Although philosophy requires objectivity for its identity, nevertheless eros insinuates itself in philosophical thought to direct objective reflections toward God. The yearning for God in philosophy gives universal meaning, and therefore communal value, to philosophical speculation. Indeed, the fusion of philosophy and theology as the Platonic yearning for the divine found in "erotic" moments of love is most apparent to King in literature's philosophic content. To makes his point, King often refers to Poe's "Annabel Lee" and Shakespeare's *Romeo and Juliet*, stressing the eternal, and thus objective, aspect of some erotic expression. Although fictional, the loves Shakespeare and Poe describe show the human potential for transcending the self through eternity in erotic love. Literature can pose the possibility of erotic love that is similar in scope to agape, which is "understanding, creative, redemptive goodwill for all men" (King 2000 48). In other words, although eros in its highest form is situated in literature, it is not creative; this power belongs to agape alone. For King, creativity, or divine spontaneity, reveals the objective, eternal bonds between subjects in beloved community.

While still Greek, King's conception also comes from his reading of Anders Nygren's *Agape and Eros*, as can be seen in a student paper titled "A View of the Cross Possessing Biblical and Spiritual Justification." In it, King cites Nygren approvingly on God's love as "spontaneous in contrast to all activity with a eudemonistic motive. The divine love is purely spontaneous and unceasing in character. God does not allow his love to be determined or limited by man's worth or worthlessness" (King 1994a, 267–268). In fact, in an address delivered at the American Baptist Assembly American Home Mission Agencies Conference, King insists on the Greek conception: "The Greek helps us out a great deal. It talks about love in several senses. It talks about eros. And eros is a significant type of love, eros is a sign of aesthetic love. Plato talks about this love a great deal in his dialogue with Phaedrus. It is, it boils down to a romantic love. It is craving for something, and it has with it a bit of affection, an affectionate feeling" (King 1994b, 327). Plato again guides King's presentation of eros, which focuses this time on the *Phaedrus*. For King reading Plato, eros is aesthetic, insofar as "it is craving for something" and so combines affection and feeling, or carnality and spirit. In this sense, King perceives romantic relationships that strive for eternity as "erotically" aesthetic because they exist only in literature.

The Greek is also authoritative regarding eros's affective range as an aesthetic phenomenon. For, King explains, "the Greek comes out with something higher, something that is strong, something that is more powerful than eros or any other type of love. It talks about agape, and agape is understanding goodwill for all men. Agape seeks nothing in return. It is a redemptive love. It is a love of God working within men" (King 1994b, 327). King is direct in his formulation in "Facing the Challenge of a New Age": "I mean understanding goodwill. The

Greek language comes to our aid at this point. The Greek language has three words for love. First it speaks of love in terms of Eros. Plato used this word quite frequently in his dialogues. Eros is a type of esthetic love. Now it has come to mean a sort of romantic love. I guess Shakespeare was thinking in terms of Eros when he said 'Love is not love which alters when it alteration finds, or bends with the remover to remove.' It is an ever fixed mark that looks on tempest and is never shaken. It is a star to every wandering bark.... This is Eros" (King 1994b, 458). Here King indirectly cites Fosdick, who writes in *On Being Fit to Live With* (1947): "Love in the New Testament is not a sentimental and affectionate emotion as we so commonly interpret it. There are three words in Greek for love, three words that we have to translate by our one word, love. Eros—'erotic' comes from it—that is one.... Philia—that is another Greek word. It meant intimate personal affectionateness and friendship.... But the great Christian word for love is something else: agape.... [A]gape means nothing sentimental or primarily emotional at all; it means understanding, redeeming, creative good will" (Fosdick 1947, 6-7). While King's words follow Fosdick's basic logic and sentence structure, King has made an important alteration: he has added Shakespeare to the reference. Beginning in Plato's dialogues, King transforms eros into an aesthetic phenomenon insofar as only through literary example can it be explained *in the philosophical sense he means*, as the sensuous striving toward eternal love. King even recites Shakespeare from memory at the NAACPs 1957 Emancipation Day Rally, joking afterward with the audience, "Now you see I remember that. I remember that. [applause] Now my wife can tell you that I know that because I used to quote it to her when we were courting. [laughter] That's eros. That's eros. Eros is significant" (King 1994d, 81).

Eros is a common, "significant" experience that nevertheless does not create community. As King says in a 1957 sermon delivered at Dexter Avenue Baptist Church, Montgomery, Alabama: "Everybody has experienced eros in all of its beauty when you find some individual that is attractive to you and that you pour out all of your like and your love on that individual. That is eros, you see, and it's a powerful, beautiful love that is given to us through all of the beauty of literature; we read about it" (King 2000, 48). As early as 1957's "Nonviolence and Racial Justice," King states plainly: "In Platonic philosophy eros meant the yearning of the soul for the realm of the divine. It has come now to mean a sort of aesthetic or romantic love" (King 1994d, 121). For King, Platonic eros is the sensuous yearning after God that in modern, presumably secularized philosophy has seemingly come to signify either aesthetic *or* romantic love. Yet the either/or King appears to offer is meant to connote indifference of choice. Aesthetic love and romantic love are the same love, which can be expressed as aesthetic or romantic. Modern philosophy presents eros as an inseparable either/or, whereby ideal, eternal love can be portrayed poetically or as the goodwill of lovers invested in a fantasy of spiritual carnality. King's use of the word "romantic" is novel, insofar as its aestheticization recalls that of early German Romanticism more than Christian views of carnality.[11] It is eros without eros, because for King any evangelical understanding of love, including loving one's enemy, cannot involve passion. True Christian love is philosophical, reflective, and communal, yet still dialectically erotic. It is agape enhanced by the negation of eros; as such, it can render justice only in dialectical tension with eros, and as indicative of Being-in-love.[12]

Because of this, King can thus insist, in his NAACP Emancipation Day speech and elsewhere, that "when we talk about loving those who oppose you, we're not talking about eros" (King 1994d, 81). For, King states, "I will never love some people like I love my wife or like I love my personal friends. It is agape that we are talking about now and it is this type of love, my friends, which I think is the solution to all of the problems that we confront in the South and all over the world. It is this love of God, which we find expressed throughout our Christian faith, this love of God working in the lives of men" (King 1994d, 82). Although King appears to be reading Plato as a Christian philosopher before the fact, he makes a strong distinction between eros's development as a philosophical principle, beginning with Plato, and agape as a concept that began with Plato yet was Christianized by Saint Paul. King writes: "In [Nygren's] book, *Agape and Eros*, he is primarily concerned with the contrast between two kinds of love, easily confused in modern languages, but clearly distinguished in Greek: the 'love' (Eros) of which Plato speaks in his Symposium and the 'love' (Agape) of which St. Paul speaks in the 13th Chapter of I Corinthians. In these two words he finds the Ground-motives of Greek religion and original Christianity concretely expresses" (King 1994b,127). Referencing this time Plato's *Symposium* as authoritative (as opposed to his *Phaedrus*), King leaves eros conceptually fixed in metaphysical thought while suggesting Paul can translate agape theologically due to the word's lexical meaning.

Studying Nygren closely, King writes further, "As Nygren set out to contrast these two Greek words he finds that Eros loves in proportion to the value of the object. By the pursuit of value in its objects, Platonic love is led up and away from the world, on wings of aspiration, beyond all transient things and persons to the realm of the Ideas. Agape as described in the Gospels and Epistles, is 'spontaneous and uncaused,' 'indifferent to human merit,' and creates value in those upon whom it is bestowed out of pure generosity" (King 1994b, 127). In tracing eros's philosophical lineage, King follows Horton's *Contemporary Continental Theology*, citing his text extensively in the footnotes. In one footnote, King quotes Horton to show that "the union of Eros with Agape began with St. Augustine. It was his Neo-Platonism, with its double motion, form God to man as well as from man to God that made it possible to unite Platonic love with Christian love in the new composite idea of charity. The union was carried to perfection in the teaching of St. Thomas Aquinas; but his work was soon undone by Luther (who went back to primitive Christian Agape) and the Renaissance (which went back to Platonic Eros). Liberal Protestantism is not the heir of Luther, but of the Renaissance" (King 1994b, 128). King believes eros and agape are "easily confused in modern languages" in large part due to Neoplatonism's elision of their conceptual differences in Greek.

In another footnote, King points out Horton's argument that "it is Eros, not Agape, that loves in proportion to the value of its object. By the pursuit of value in its object, Platonic love is led up and away from the world, on wings of aspiration, beyond all transient things and persons to the realm of the Ideas. Agape, as described in the Gospels and Epistles, is 'spontaneous and "uncaused,' 'indifferent to human merit,' and 'creates' value in those upon whom it is bestowed out of pure generosity. It flows down from God into this transient, sinful world; those whom it touches become conscious of their own utter unworthiness; they are impelled to forgive and love their enemies, not because they are inherently lovable, but because the God of grace imparts worth to them by the act of loving them" (King 1994b, 127). Essentially, King views Platonic eros as a false form of agape, misconstrued by modern philosophy, misrepresented aesthetically in literature, and ultimately falsely posited as the highest form of love. Opposed to this, King seeks to recuperate the truth of agape for philosophy and theology by sharply distinguishing between the two. Understanding that philosophy and theology are entwined, King recalls that the philosopher's disposition is more objective than the theologian's, linking the philosopher more closely to agape, which rejects all forms of "subjectivism." Seemingly paradoxically, King embraces philosophy as more systematically theological even than systematic theology, where systematicity ensures objectivity over erotic subjectivism.

IV. King's Platonism

King models his argument on Heidegger's systematic deconstruction of metaphysical systems and structures since Plato. Where Heidegger sees being obscured by the Platonic logos, King witnesses eros's conceptual infiltration and obfuscation of agape. For King, agape is the spiritual manifestation of Being Itself, or what I refer to as Being-in-love, and nonviolence is its social expression. King's nonviolence returns thought to Being-in-love by restoring agape's conceptual integrity in Western metaphysics. King, then, is not making an intervention in theology, which already recalls agape in its original Greek intent yet has no sufficient social use of it. As King sees it, activism that seeks the widest appeal (universal love) is philosophically oriented—rather than primarily directed by Christian theology—in order to accommodate different understandings of spirit. King seeks to recuperate agape for philosophy, and therefore for a theory of universal social action. In other words, nonviolence is a communal philosophy of negative revelation and not a ritual of individual transcendence. As King ad-libbed in his "Montgomery Story," told to the forty-seventh annual NAACP convention: "And if there is a victory in Montgomery, it will not be a victory merely for fifty thousand Negroes, but it will be a victory for justice [applause], a victory for democracy [applause], and a victory for good will. This is at bottom the meaning of Christian love, and we are trying to follow that. It is that high type of love that I have talked about so often. The Greeks talked of so many types of love. But we are not talking about eros in Montgomery, we are talking about agape" (King 1994b, 232). Agape, in Montgomery as elsewhere, is a philosophical principle obscured by eros in philosophy and made socially ineffectual by individual-driven spiritualism in theology.

Like Heidegger, King wants to bring thought back to an awareness of thinking that perhaps is not pre-Socratic but rather may have been possible before Plato. King sees eros, like Heidegger's being, as the basis for the deconstruction of Western metaphysics. Agape as Being-in-love and expressed socially in nonviolence aligns for King with Tillich's Being Itself, which Tillich in turn takes from Heidegger's description of the general characterization of Plato's *Phaedrus* embedded in his wider 1924–1925 seminar on *The Sophist*. Heidegger states that Socrates's "concern is to expose the basic determination of the existence of man, precisely the concern of the second part of the dialogue, and human Dasein is seen specifically in its basic comportment to beings pure and simple. And the love Socrates speaks of, both the natural and the purified, is nothing else than the urge toward Being itself."[13]

This type of love is the ontological condition of Heidegger's "being-in-the-world"; its expression or frustration details humanity's soteriological history. For King, humanity's eschatological end is the formation of the beloved community, in which all have been recognized in divine love individually and collectively.[14] Because "*agape* makes no distinction between friend and enemy," the soteriological end of history cannot be reached through any form of love originating with human being. Having no existence in God, eros and philia form social bonds that have their origin in Nonbeing alienated from Being Itself. Therefore, they are self-contradictory, as their exclusive desire for one object excludes another object, and in so doing denies the excluded object's worthiness of love. Divine love sees all as worthy and seeks to bring all human beings together in the recognition of this worthiness, which King sees as the only path to salvation.

Because *agape* is redemption and salvation, each subject needs the other. If there is no other subject to love, salvation is not possible for a human being, as the redemptive act of recognition becomes impossible. To be saved by divine love requires someone to recognize another as infinitely worthy of love, and to be recognized in the same way. The refusal to recognize the being of another acknowledges the power of Nonbeing, or sin, which rejects Being Itself, or divine love. For this reason, King concludes that, since "the white man's personality is greatly distorted by segregation, and his soul is greatly scarred, he needs the love of the Negro. The Negro must love the white man, because the white man needs his love to remove his tensions, insecurities, and fears" (King 2010b, 126). The "white man" needs to be recognized and "redeemed" in divine love by the "Negro" for his salvation. Desegregation and the end of racism are matters of "white redemption," which makes agape of cosmic importance.

"In the final analysis," King writes, "*agape* means a recognition of the fact that all life is interrelated" (King 2010B, 127). That said, not all of life's interrelated parts perform a reciprocal function. Agape as the "recognition" of interrelatedness does not oblige each subject to view this connected state in the same way. "White redemption" occurs when "the Negro" receives "the enemy" as a friend. As the highest form of recognition, agape redeems those filled with hate, which for King is sin, or Nonbeing. In the process, the oppressed community is not "redeemed" by the oppressor's recognition of interrelatedness; rather, the oppressed are saved by experiencing divine love as finite beings defined in their historicity by sin, or Nonbeing. African Americans redeem white Americans through love, and by loving are redeemed by God. Oppressed communities, then, constitute the beloved community in its historical form.[15] As such, they are tasked with the cosmic mission of awakening consciousness to Tillich's Heideggerian Being Itself by loving the enemy and in turn being loved by God. Nonviolent resistance is a global form of missionary work in oppressor communities, and it has both theological and philosophical implications.

King defined agape many times in his speeches and writings, usually relating the concept back to its meaning in philosophy. King's synthetic account is deeply indebted to Plato as well as to Heideggerian philosophical aspects of Tillich's theology, among others. As with Tillich, King's investment in Plato's philosophy, and metaphysics generally, enhances rather than negates his intellectual investment in existentialism. The combination of *Existenzphilosophie* and Heidegger's fundamental ontology provides a platform for King's understated Platonism, particularly in his theologically oriented reflections. Indeed, the addition of Heidegger's critique of metaphysics to King's ontological synthesis of race and Platonic eros allows King to produce a powerful social critique, for Heidegger's rejection of Platonic formal essentialism leads to King's anti-essentialist conception of Being Itself as God's racially inclusive, egalitarian, universal love. Whereas Newton exploits Platonic forms to produce a racial ontology of singularity and power, King counters this essentialism with Heidegger's deconstruction of the Platonic tradition.

Chronicling much of his intellectual journey through this tradition in "Pilgrimage to Nonviolence"—including studying Heidegger—King concludes the account with a presentation of the basic tenets of his philosophy of nonviolence. Nonviolence is "passive physically, but strongly active spiritually. It is not passive nonresistance to evil; it is active nonviolent resistance to evil" (King 2010b, 123). Nonviolent resistance acts against evil and is for King the only way to combat evil. Evil, then, is violence. For King, all evil is violent, and all violence is evil. Passive, nonviolent resistance is action without evil. This leads to a "second basic fact that characterizes nonviolence," which "is that it does not seek to defeat or humiliate the opponent, but to win his friendship and understanding" (King 2010b, 106). Because all evil is violence, all violence forecloses on friendship. Thinking dialectically, King concludes that nonviolence is the good, which in turn is friendship. For this reason, a "third characteristic of this method is that the attack is directed against forces of evil rather than against persons who happen to be doing the evil" (King 2010b, 123). The act of passive nonviolent resistance is directed against evil. Nonviolent resistance cannot be directed against any one person, group, or institution; otherwise it becomes a personal act of retribution, and is violent. Instead, nonviolence moves against evil itself, which, avoiding the principle of contradiction, cannot negate itself, making nonviolent resistance forceful yet good.

To maintain this posture, it is essential that the protestor observe King's fourth rule of nonviolent resistance: "a willingness to accept suffering without retaliation, to accept blows from the opponent without striking back" (King 2010b, 124). Retaliation of any sort is an evil act, compromising the integrity of the good with an act of enmity rather than amity. This brings King to his fifth point, that "nonviolent resistance . . . avoids not only external physical violence but also internal violence of spirit. The nonviolent resister not only refuses to shoot his opponent, but he also refuses to hate him. At the center of nonviolence stands the principle of love" (King 2010b, 124). As an act of friendship, nonviolent resistance reflects the spiritual state of its practitioner. Feeling the love of friendship for the "enemy," the protestor is spiritually equipped to withstand evil violence in order to realize the greater good in God's love. Because of these divine stakes, a "sixth basic fact about nonviolent resistance is that it is based on the conviction that the universe is on the side of justice" (King 2010b, 111). Love as justice is a cosmic fact to which nonviolence bears witness.

In raising nonviolence to the degree of cosmic ontology, King recognizes and rejects the extent to which violence could be construed as negative ontology. Premising collective singularity on radical human difference, violence as ontology posits antagonism according to the measure and degree of its identification. In Newton's case, race determines the divisive ground of social conflict. King counters this with a philosophy of irreducible human equality governed by love's universal commensurability in Being Itself, or God. In essence, King rejects Newton's version of Platonism as domination (Black Power), in favor of a gnostic deconstruction of the Platonic principles he accepts as the basis of Western metaphysics and theology.

More invested in the Platonic metaphysical tradition than in Heidegger's attempted destruction of it, Newton conceives of Blackness as truth beyond contractual racist division. He takes from Plato's allegory of the cave the basic structure in which truth is hidden from Blacks as they labor relentlessly in the shadows. The nature of truth is a matter not of human equality but rather of power in inequality, and the truth of Blackness is the power to control social relations and political decisions in caste society to the greatest beneficial effect for all. In other words, Newton uses Plato to envision Black racial essence as power.

Newton's revision of Plato refuses to grant transcendence to Being that fails to recognize race as the primary ontological category of Western metaphysics. Because of this, Newton would argue, philosophers may avoid racist biologism when discussing the human condition, yet they cannot escape a concept of race that names essential difference. In Newton's racial ontology, difference is essential, even if the substance of those differences is not. Racial difference decides the legitimate use of power in society.

Rejecting Being as power, King's African American ontology is not racially essentialist; it is a form of historical materialism given ontological meaning through a universal understanding of human dignity. There is no racial ontology, there is only ontology, the meaning of which is revealed most authentically in the historical-material matrix of African American life. In this respect, King suggests that, ontologically, all human beings experience some degree of African America's anguish, yet only African America fully experiences the effects of Nonbeing's imposition. African American philosophy, then, is world-historical; its methods, analyses, and conclusions impart ontotheological truth.

King, then, is unable to conceptualize philosophically African American being as singularity without recourse to a version of Newton's highly differentiated racial essentialism. His solution to the problem of African American ontology is to go further into metaphysics to arrive at theology. He accepts Being, or God's love, as the condition for all things, or the *ens realissimus*. In so doing, he moves beyond race as the final arbiter of social being to posit universal community premised on unconditional love, or the beloved community. Premised on hate, racism is the negation of human being's self-recognition in true Being, which knows no race. The task of African American philosophy is the destruction of racism through the recognition of community without race. King lays the groundwork for this project in his dissertation, which cannot be called the product of a juvenile phase in his intellectual development, but rather is *the ontological basis for his categorical rejection of racial essentialism*. In it, King looks to revise Heidegger, not to posit the Being of Blackness; or Being as Blackness; or Black being or any qualification of Being or being with being Black, etc. Rather, King appropriates Heideggerian philosophy to show that Being has no authentic, essential stake in race. Blackness, like whiteness, is a product of reifying Nonbeing, and therefore inessential. This ontological project, of course, does not deny the specificity of African American suffering; quite the opposite, for it seeks to establish the ground for true peace and justice.

4 Gnosticism and Nonviolence

I. King's Classical Thought

IN A 1964 INTERVIEW, Eric Voegelin sums up well the debt King's "Letter" owes to concepts of peace and justice in classical thought:

> The problematic of the institutionalization of certain ideas that were developed by philosophy still plays a large role today. In the contemporary Negro revolution in America, one of the Negro leaders used the formula "Peace is not the absence of violence; peace is the presence of justice." I do not know whether he invented it, but it is in any case brilliant. Here you have the substance of the classical formula of justice captured in one sentence. (Voegelin et al. 2004, 157)

For Voegelin, the line from King's "Letter" captures the epitome of classical thought on justice.[1]

It is interesting that Voegelin, among the émigré philosophers, should have seen this in King's thought. Unlike Arendt, Marcuse, Jonas, Löwith, and to some extent Strauss, he had not been trained in or influenced by Heidegger in 1920s Germany. In fact, Voegelin claimed he was largely unfamiliar with Heidegger's work, since his philosophically formative years were spent visiting the United States in the 1920s (Maier and Cockerill 2000, 721).[2] As Voegelin states in his *Autobiographical Reflections* (2011), "He [Heidegger] did not impress me at all with *Sein und Zeit*, because in the meanwhile, with John Dewey at Columbia and with Whitehead at Harvard, I was acquainted with English and American commonsense philosophy" (quoted in Gerolin 2015, 635).[3]

These philosophical differences helped Voegelin to develop a political philosophy very different from Heidegger's, at least in relation to the National Socialist thought Heidegger presented in his 1933 National Socialist *Rektorrede*.[4] In *Political Religions* (1938), Voegelin identifies National Socialism with organized religion rather than with a cult, describing a highly differentiated and structured system of belief that expresses its faith in the state. This "leviathan," however, is premised on the *Volksgeist* as embodied in the charismatic ruler and articulated in all state administrative and social functions. The total state as *ens realissimum* is the result of "modernity without restraint," or humanism that replaces the concept of God as "the most real being" with that of "man." As Voegelin writes, "The inner-worldly religiosity experienced by the collective body—be it humanity, the people, the class, the race, or the state—as the *realissimum* is the abandonment of God; and some Christian thinkers, therefore, refuse—even with regard to language—to put the inner-worldly political religion on the same level with the spiritual religion of Christianity" (Voegelin 2000, 71).

For Voegelin, "humanity, the people, the class, the race, or the state" amount to the same conceptual proof of divinity, in the Kantian sense of *ens realissimum*, insofar as they may be interchangeable as the most real being defining existential reality, depending on the contingent, qualifying needs of the body politic. "Some Christian thinkers" reject political religion based on *ens realissimum* usurping the place of God as the conceptual limit in the ontological definition of all things. They see National Socialism as a form of "humanism" in the sense that, as a product of secular modernity, it sets humanity as a collective political project, or the state, above God as the apolitical ground of being, or Being itself.[5] Racial realism, thus, is race as *ens realissimum*, the beginning and end of all being, expressed collectively in the political religion of the state. Heidegger's racial realism avoids this sense of humanism, in that Being is not race even though Heidegger's Being *prefers* a people, their language, their culture and their nation over all others. In short, Being in later Heidegger is an ontological *preference* that makes race the most existentially real qualification of being. The basis of National Socialism as political religion is racist ontological *preferring*, in reaction to which race is constructed; racism, then, is a "humanism" of the "spirit." This is the sense of race—not as essential but rather as the product of an essential racism—with which King grapples in Heidegger's thought, and in which Being is a *preference rather than substance*.

In theorizing political religion, Voegelin was following "Christian thinker" (and subject of King's dissertation) Paul Tillich on National Socialism as political religion. Tillich used the term "political religion" to describe "disturbing affinities among Nazi ideology, Christian antisemitism, and anti-Marxism, [and to address] the way in which Nazi ideologues and theologians attempted to synthesize Christian theology and racial ideas, opting for a 'positive Christianity' purified from its Judaic roots" (Varshizky 2019, 253). Beginning in 1926 with a map of Germany that depicted the dissemination of radical religious ideas by political affiliation, Tillich went on, in 1929, to describe the National Socialist as a "romantic-conservative" religious type (Neddens 2012, 322–323). Although Tillich was one of the first to develop this idea, Voegelin expanded and popularized the concept of "political religion," publishing an essay with this title in the United States in 1938 (Neddens 2012, 310–311). Through concepts of "political religion" and Christian socialism, both Voegelin and Tillich left indelible traces in American political thought, including in King's.

Framing his concept of beloved community within a Pauline sense of universalism, King's "Letter" appeals for justice provoked by action born from "purification":

> As in so many past experiences, our hopes had been blasted, and the shadow of deep disappointment settled upon us. We had no alternative except to prepare for direct action, whereby we would present our very bodies as a means of laying our case before the conscience of the local and the national community. Mindful of the difficulties involved, we decided to undertake a process of self-purification. We began a series of workshops on nonviolence, and we repeatedly asked ourselves: "Are you able to accept blows without retaliating?" "Are you able to endure the ordeal of jail?" We decided to schedule our direct-action program for the Easter season, realizing that except for Christmas, this is the main shopping period of the year. Knowing that a strong economic-withdrawal program would be the by-product of direct action, we felt that this would be the best time to bring pressure to bear on the merchants for the needed change. (King 2011, 88)[6]

After good-faith negotiations on the part of the aggrieved and considering the clear determination of injustice by any Christian standard, King decides to proceed with nonviolent protest in Birmingham. He chooses the Easter holiday for the time to commence the action not for religious reasons but rather because this period is a high shopping season, and the protest will cause maximum economic distress. In this way, King hopes to force good-faith negotiations from the white community leadership, leading to social and political concessions and the amelioration of the oppressive conditions of African American life in Birmingham.

To achieve this, King also depends on the spectacle of police violence playing on televisions in living rooms across the nation and the world, viewers witnessing the visual evidence of Southern racism's lawless, and lawful, brutality.[7] King, then, has the means to instigate the dissemination of images of injustice across America in an instant, in solicitation of a unified national judgment against what was previously a regional or local concern. The national spectacle of southern racial injustice, as weighed in the private sphere of the living room, appeals to universal Christian justice as a private matter. King reasons that while Jim Crow is not the law of the land, it is nevertheless supported by social attitudes stronger than any decision of the United States Supreme Court. Because of this, King brings the private sphere legislating southern life into all American households, to include all forms of private adjudication.[8] In this way, King creates a public sphere in private space through the spectacle of violence. His sense of "peace" echoes that of classical thought, insofar as it insists peace is achieved in the presence of justice rather than the absence of violence.

Voegelin, then, has not misread King's "Letter," perceiving clearly that King does not intend secular justice to be done without violence. In the "Letter," and citing classical sources, King indicates that nonviolent protest is not meant to contain violence in society. Quite the opposite, for it is meant to unleash both the practical and productive forces of law within a society by refusing to participate in its required functions. As King writes powerfully in the "Letter," addressing clergy and others who accuse him of fomenting violence in Birmingham:

> In your statement you asserted that our actions, even though peaceful, must be condemned because they precipitate violence. But can this assertion be logically made? Isn't this like condemning the robbed man because his possession of money precipitated the evil act of robbery? Isn't this like condemning Socrates because his unswerving commitment to truth and his philosophical delvings precipitated the misguided popular mind to make him drink the hemlock? Isn't this like condemning Jesus because His unique God-consciousness and never-ceasing devotion to His will precipitated the evil act of crucifixion? We must come to see, as federal courts have consistently affirmed, that it is immoral to urge an individual to withdraw his efforts to gain his basic constitutional rights because the quest precipitates violence. Society must protect the robbed and punish the robber. (King 2011, 97)

In the scene of civil disobedience, both opposing parties are mandated by the state to engage in violent altercation to maintain the integrity of the state itself, as premised on the coercive force of law. Nonviolent protest imposes a type of "general strike" on the requirement to commit violence and consolidate the conditions for the state of emergency required for state legitimacy.

Nonviolent protest refuses to engage the state according to the norms on which its legal authority rests. In effect, nonviolence rejects self-legitimating state sovereignty, submitting instead to the divine law of God's love. For King, nonviolent protest is the pure means by which to acknowledge the higher authority of God's law in secular society. This acknowledgment invalidates the state's claims to sovereign power over all its subjects, despite the imperfect application of positive law. In other words, nonviolent protest is not merely a morally superior means to positive ends and intended to maintain the current state in altered form. Rather, King's mode of civil disobedience is eschatological, advancing the historical realization of the City of God through beloved community.

In any specific instance nonviolence is used, its final phase, good-faith negotiation, can only be arrived at through the eschatological crisis produced by its previous phases. As nonviolent protest's legal and, as Benjamin would suggest, moral contradictions come into evermore intensifying conflict, two competing notions of legal right, the natural and the positive, emerge. Natural law is the positive instance of divine law, while positive law in the absence of nature is represented in police violence. State and police violence are both ungodly and unnatural.

In light of this theopolitical background, King identifies with Socrates:

> I have earnestly opposed violent tension, but there is a type of constructive, nonviolent tension which is necessary for growth. Just as Socrates felt that it was necessary to create a tension in the mind so that individuals could rise from the bondage of myths and half-truths to the unfettered realm of creative analysis and objective appraisal, so must we see the need for nonviolent gadflies to create the kind of tension in society that will help men rise from the dark depths of prejudice and racism to the majestic heights of understanding and brotherhood. (King 2011, 89)

Socrates' introduction into King's discussion provides an enhanced correlative field by which to imagine the tension created by nonviolent protest. For King, Socrates suffers the death penalty because of his "extremist" opposition to philosophically inconsistent institutional structures. Socrates's self-sacrifice defends the universality of his philosophical position as it stands before its unethical elaboration as inimical to public reason.[9] This generalized sense of martyrdom allows King to correlate Socrates with Paul, using them interchangeably along with the rest of his "extremists" as correlative proxies for his own position.[10] Likening himself to Socratic extremists in this way, King perforce correlates the regimes against which the extremist agitates with the United States.[11] From this perspective, there is no defense for defending Birmingham, because it is yet another existential manifestation of sinful Nonbeing. Within this historical frame, Nonbeing names sinful American segregation in all its Christian theological aspects.

King thus does not differentiate between Socratic, Pauline, and Lutheran extremisms and his own, applied for the sake of universal justice within contingent historical circumstances. This amalgam of extremists presents Being-in-love's sovereign agency in history as ecstatic yet affective and eschatological purposive. This Gnostic sense of justice authorizes a civil disobedience that seeks to make and enforce no new law that is not legitimated from beyond legality, in God's love. Likewise, those laws that stand apart from or in opposition to this love are illegitimate and subject to nonviolent challenge. However, as Benjamin might insist, the localized use of force in this way, be it violent or nonviolent, would merely articulate the prevailing social order using a different ideological language. From this perspective, because of its racial focus King's Gnosticism would risk advancing a false universalism, thereby usurping divine prerogative and betraying itself as another form of humanism. To examine this possible contradiction, an account of the interwar German debate surrounding Gnostic sovereignty, in which Benjamin's essay acts as a key early intervention, will help clarify King's political theology.

II. Racial Gnosis

As van den Broek defines it, Gnosis is "the existential certainty that the core of my being comes from the divine world of light and must return to it but is held captive in the material world in which it has become entrapped. Gnosis is the liberating insight into mankind's origin, present situation and destination. It is a religious worldview which easily could (and can) attach itself to existing religious and philosophical traditions, thereby reinterpreting and reshaping them" (van den Broek 2014, 231). That is, Gnosis posits two central ideas. First, the divine and human spheres are dualistic, and second, they are joined solely by knowledge of this duality. In the Christian Gnosis, spirit and nature, as Ferdinand Christian

Baur theorized in his *Die christliche Gnosis* (1835), united in the figure of Christ (Ledger-Lomas 2014, 446). Messianic knowledge gives eschatological meaning to history in the Gnostic union of nature and spirit. In this sense, Gnosticism is as much a form of historicism as it is a theory of revelation.

Indeed, as Wolfe maintains, "the crisis of historicism, the rise of existentialism, and the surge of political religions" were the dominant forces shaping interregnum political theology and metaphysics (Wolfe 2019, 55). Feldman further shows that, beginning at least with Heidegger's lectures on Plato's Doctrine of Truth, an unsettling "revolutionary Gnosis" "starts to emerge . . . [as] an ominous sense of mission to liberate an enslaved community through redemptive higher knowledge. Moreover, this form of revolutionary gnosis is one that assumes an increasingly explicit and contemporaneous political content" (Feldman 2005, 183).[12] Heidegger's student Hans Jonas described his teacher's Gnosticism after the Second World War as nihilistic "paganism" that perfectly captures National Socialist philosophic belief (Cahana 2018, 158).[13] Differing slightly from Heidegger, Paul Tillich saw Gnosis in Platonic eros, which he read through New Testament Greek as "cognitive, sexual, and mystical union at the same time" (Tillich 1966, 96–97).

This general conception of Gnosis does not align with what Driver takes to be Tillich's belief that "God's action is a work effected in and through all the dimensions of life, and not, as Gnosticism would have it, simply a work of Divine Mind acting on the human mind" (Driver 1965, 30). Alternatively, Macquarrie rightly point out that Tillich "ascribes the difficulties of culture, especially of the functions of *theoria* and knowing, to the 'estrangement between subject and object,' and the longing for 'reunion.'" Macquarrie goes on to criticize this aspect of Tillich's thought, noting, "Gnosis or religious knowledge may be a desire for reunion with being, but scarcely episteme" (Macquarrie 1964 , 358). In other words, Macquarrie corrects Driver, who has misread Tillich's lack of success theorizing Gnosis as the idea's absence in his thought. The confusion in Tillich's theology derives from an ambiguous account of God's temporality in history.[14] "In . . . Tillichian theology," Scaer clarifies, "God is there and not there at the same time. In His immanence God is transcendent. In the gnosis concept, God is removed as a kind of 'Wholly Other,' but He is present in multiple situations through the emanations. It is doubtful whether Tillichian thought is any less fanciful than crass Gnosticism with its multiple aeons. Both gnosis and modern approaches are destructive of the historical claim of Christianity, which makes for itself an exclusive claim in the area of revelation" (Scaer 1975, 339). The destruction of Christianity's historical claim is exactly what Heidegger Gnostic ontotheology presupposed.

For Heidegger, ontotheology identified God with Being, obscuring the truth of Being through metaphysical-theological determination. The "critique of the identification of God with Being, an identification which literally 'goes without saying' for centuries, is the crucial step in the attempt to overcome metaphysics" (Godzieba 1995, 5). Heidegger attacks the union of metaphysics and theology he posits, again as early as his lectures on Plato's Doctrine of Truth, where he sees the fusion of religion and metaphysics occurring for the first time as ontology in Plato's doctrine of the ideas (Thomson 2000, 313–314). As Schrijvers succinctly puts it, "For Heidegger, ontotheology is, like metaphysics, essentially a forgetting of being" (Schrijvers 2006, 302). This ontotheological "forgetting" originates with Plato. Of course, Heidegger's use of ontotheology is very different from Kant's original intention in coining the word, with which, as Rubenstein reminds us, he meant "the philosophical effort to prove God's existence a priori, as distinct from 'cosmotheology,' which endeavors to prove God's existence a posteriori" (Rubenstein 2008, 728). Heidegger would of course include Kant's definition of ontotheology within the preexisting history of metaphysics as an example of the ontotheology he seeks to destroy. The combination of Greek philosophy and biblical theology has also been referred to as Christian humanism, a designation Heidegger would also accept, with wider affinity and application, in his "Letter on Humanism," which Arendt so admired (Ingraffia 1999, 497).[15]

Arendt was in a strong position to recognize and appreciate the "Letter's" eschatological Gnosticism and ontotheological critique. Heidegger's former student and lover, Arendt also studied eschatology with Bultmann at Marburg, eventually forming the opinion that eschatology sacrificed history for the eternal, debasing the political in the process (Lasater 2019, 167).[16] Heidegger himself, while against theology as a science, nevertheless saw, at least in his later work, Gnosis as a means by which to recover the thinking of Being. As Wolfe writes, "Heidegger responded to the crisis of philosophy and history in the post-war period not by resolving but by embracing the tension between trajectory and end: the world, he concluded, simply was one in which things were or appeared oriented towards an end but could not reach or find fulfilment in that end" (Wolfe 2019, 67). In the context, it might suffice to reintroduce Feldman's analysis, given earlier:

Thus, for example, Heidegger's meditations on Hölderlin become political exhortations for a future that finally overcomes the baleful legacy of Socratic humanism. For this German poet takes centre stage in Heidegger's later work as (in his view) *the first gnostic* to mourn the loss of the spiritual in a constantly unfolding Greek tragedy on the withdrawal of Being. Although this play nearly reached a triumphant climax under National Socialism, what seemed a final curtain signaled only an interval. (Feldman 2005, 193, italics added)

In structure, Heidegger developed an anti-historicist hermeneutic of negative transcendence like the one Karl Barth proposed in his groundbreaking 1918 reading of Saint Paul's epistle to the Romans. Barth's 1918 work served as the dominant influence in the debate over method in theology in Germany for years, shaping the thought of the theologians King studied closely. "In contrast to historical-critical readings that had sought to liberate the early Christian texts from some of their mythical-naïve elements," Keedus observes, "Barth insisted on the essential link between the 'unfamiliarity' or even 'transcendence' of these original sources, and the content of the Christian revelation. When one seeks to translate these sources into contemporary language in order to adapt these to the tastes of our supposedly more rational and enlightened age, one only risks adding specifically modern layers of miscomprehension between the reader and the text" (Keedus 2014, 310). This produced a form of anti-historicist reading that eschewed historical contingency for eschatological narrative in which transcendent spirit elaborated its destiny clandestinely. The historicity of spirit can be seen in its orientation toward an established, spiritual end rather than in the interpretation of contingent historical facts.

Barth and Heidegger attempt a hermeneutic approach that was very appealing to Bultmann (Albrecht 2019, 540). Following Barth, and Adolf von Harnack, interpretation in the theological-cultural crisis of the interregnum was particularly attentive to Saint Paul for these reasons of hermetical methodology. The *Wiederentdeckung* (rediscovery) of Paul's theology helped interwar theologians address the dichotomy of human existence between the Law and life, and its expression in the double character of God—that is, the God of Law and the God of eternal grace in salvation. In this context, as Schmidt explains, "Paul becomes, as it were, the theological metonymy of cultural crisis, insofar as the gnostic interrelation in the dialectic of nomos and pneuma presents imminent danger, an aspect of this dialectic that Harnack's 1921 *Untersuchung über Marcion* apparently also interprets as an expression of the real gnostic danger of modern culture and cultural critique" (Schmidt 1998, 80).[17] The similarity between Harnack's study of Marcion and Barth's tireless insistence on God's radical Otherness to the fallen character of human being was already noted in contemporary reviews of his *Römerbrief* (Buch 2012, 179). Indeed, van der Heiden writes, "Barthian themes, as developed in *Der Römerbrief*, go to the heart of the contemporary philosophical interest as the particular importance of the crisis of the present form of the world, and the combination of this crisis and this otherness in a dialectics of suspension and transformation" (van der Heiden 2016, 54).[18]

Bultmann's reading of Paul's critique of the Law plays an important role in the theorization of Being in the Christian existentialism in which King's thought is steeped. As Congdon notes, for Bultmann the "community, as the bearer of the *kerygma*, is included within the event that it proclaims" (Congdon 2014, 1). As opposed to the Jewish community, which is trapped by the Law, the Christian community stands before salvation, dependent on God's grace alone. Because authentic human being depends on God's grace alone for salvation, "according to Bultmann, Paul has a biased view of Jews because [he believes] they understand themselves as a means toward the creation of 'works of the law' for God's favor and approval, seeking their καύχημα [boasting glory] instead of being humble in the knowledge of their creation by, and dependence on the grace of God, and in this humbleness to give Him glory" (Hammann 2012, 61).[19] The rejection of the Law as καύχημα in favor of the glory of recognizing God's creative power within speaks to the anti-humanism and anti-Semitism also current in mid-twentieth-century German thought. The division between secular law and divine law becomes that of world and spirit, where the two are radically divided, as in Gnosticism.

The Gnostic separation of spirit and body is resolved only in the chiasmic unity of apocalypse in which the two become one while remaining conceptually distinct. Yet the rejection of Law as before or instead of God's grace in salvation produced a skepticism of eschatology that lent support to Gnostic readings of history. For this reason, eschatology and Gnosis were related themes in interwar German theology and philosophy, with eschatology's perceived failure acting as impetus to Gnosticism's revival. As Buch puts it, "These are the two factors that, like no other, have given the decisive impetus for the dogmatization of Christianity.... The failure of eschatology and a competing answer to the problems it poses: Gnosis" (Buch 2012, 347).[20]

In this vein, Hans Jonas—another of Heidegger's (and Bultmann's) émigré ex-students whose theological philosophy exerted great influence in the United States while King was on his pilgrimage to nonviolence—theorized Gnosis in part to see Paul in a more problematic light. Persecuting Jewish being by providing a new structure for human subjectivity in which the followers of Christ were categorically superior to all other peoples, Paul engages not in meontology but rather in hierarchical ontology (Lazier 2008, 160). Jonas wrote the dissertation that became *Gnosis und spätantiker Geist* (1924), under the direction of Bultmann and Heidegger, and as a contribution to the growing interwar interest in Gnosticism. For Jonas, Gnosis is as much a cultural as religious force, powerful enough to qualify the second century as the "Age of Gnosticism" and embody "the spirit of late antiquity" (Brenner 1999, 52). "For Jonas," Brenner writes, "the essence of this religion was the alienation from the cosmos, a concept which never left Western culture and was most recently expressed by the philosophy of existentialism. Jonas, it should be noted, was then under the influence of both Heidegger and Spengler and identified himself as an existentialist" (Brenner 1999, 52). The Heideggerian aspect of Jonas's idea of Gnosticism is clear. While the Age of Gnosticism may be long over, the structure of its cosmological thought continues to exert its force throughout the history of "Western culture." Gnostic dualism in "Western culture" alienates being from divinity, which is present yet obscured in human existence. Philosophy and theology overcome Gnostic dualism by destroying the tradition of its thought in "Western culture," which, as a Spenglerian project, would have the potential to reverse the West's decline by returning "Western culture" to the source of its authenticity.

Jonas's existentialism finds pathways leading back to pre-Gnostic thought in the everydayness of human existence conditioned by its sustained experience of finitude, much in the same way Dasein is conscious of its relation to Being in being's orientation toward death. For Jonas, Bultmann, and other highly influential theologian-philosophers grappling in the interwar period with what they identified as "Gnosis," Gnosticism does not exclusively mean historically specific movements in late antiquity that were identified as heresies by the early church. Rather, "Gnosis" names a dualistic form of spiritualism imported by "Western culture" from "the Orient" well before the second century A.D., and which shapes Greek philosophy and pre-Christian rabbinical thought (Wilson 1974, 180). In other words, for Jonas, Gnosticism influenced the rise and development of Platonism, acting as the documentary source for Heidegger's Hellenic origin for being's alienation from Being.

As Bultmann put it, Gnosis was a "religious movement of pre-Christian origin, invading the West from the Orient as a competitor of Christianity" (quoted in Wilson 1974, 178). Bultmann suggests that while Gnosis is pre-Christian, it does not "invade the West" until the Christian era. He means, however, that Gnosis drives the Hellenization of Christianity in the second century A.D., situating Gnosticism in Greek thought well before Christianity's appearance as "the spirit of late antiquity" understood as the totality of Hellenic culture. As part of "the East," Hellenism spearheads the Gnostic invasion of Christianity. The theorization and historicization of a pre-Christian Jewish Gnosticism were more difficult than the appropriation of Hellenism for Heideggerian theology. Acknowledging the difficulty of adapting dualism to monotheistic belief, Scholem looked to Merkabah mysticism and Shiur Komah, to mixed results (Brenner 1999, 55–59).[21] The salient point for Jonas and Bultmann is that Scholem identified Jewish Gnosticism as a product of Jewish Hellenization in the second century B.C., confirming their belief that Gnosticism was strong enough in Hellenic culture by this time to catalyze and normalize dualistic thought even in systems of belief in which it would have originally been heretical.[22]

Bultmann ultimately tries to read Gnosis in the New Testament through a demythologizing historicism. This was not the case for some theologians, who, taking their methodological cue from Karl Barth's anti-historicism, read scripture formally and understood revealed truth as without historical mediation. This is not to say that Barth's reading of Romans was anti-Semitic; rather, it is to say that its anti-historicism allowed it to be used for contemporary anti-Semitic ends with little resistance. Jonas saw a similar tendency and flaw in Heidegger's philosophy. Although Jonas condemned Heidegger and his philosophy after the war, most notably in "Heidegger and Theology" (1964), the structure of his philosophical understanding of Gnosticism remained indebted to his teacher.

Jonas's early work on Gnosticism was part of a wider "theological revolt against liberalism and the expression of a deep sense of opposition between the fallen world and divine transcendence" brought on by rapidly increasing rationalization and reification in society and culture and the devastation of the First World War (Hershkowitz 2017, 349). As a response to trauma, "Gnosis offered a negative view of human existence with a glimmer of redemption and was therefore fitting for the general mood both in academia and outside of it" (Feller 2013, 378). Feller provides a valuable summary of interwar Gnosticism's basic tenets:

> 1) Dualism: a strict separation between a good, transcendent God and the world that is considered to be evil by its nature and governed by a tyrant force different from the true God (Demiurge). 2) The person and his redemption stand at the center of the teaching: against the existence of this world, there is said to be a possibility of redemption through Gnosis, mystic knowledge that transcends the limits of this world and its dualism. In most cases this knowledge is considered limited only to a predestined selected group, i.e., members of the Gnostic sect. 3) Central to research during the Weimar period was the mythos of the "primal man" (*Urmensch*), someone who is said to be perfect and able to redeem others from the existence of the evil world. (Feller 2013, 377–378)

Bultmann, Jonas, and other Marburg theologians turned alternatively to Paul and Gnosis to aid in their project of demythologizing theology (Hammann 2012, 208). Their concern over Gnosis was not part of a movement to mystify existence but rather was presented as a form of realist political theology. Indeed, the political theology of the interregnum can be seen as an attempt to overcome a mystical interpretation of Gnosis with realism (Paipais 2016, 1603). This aspect of Gnosis appears prominently in the work of Blumenberg, Scholem, and Jonas (Hotam 2007, 592). As Cahana has written, "Jonas's study of Gnosticism was able to demonstrate that existentialism is not just morally flawed (by nihilist ethics), but, no less importantly, it is philosophically flawed. Gnosticism, according to Jonas, was able to lay bare both the hidden metaphysical premises of an apparently nonmetaphysical philosophy as well as its internal discontinuity" (Cahana 2018, 166). In this respect, Jonas seems to suggest that "*Being and Time* can be read as an existentialized [i.e., *historicized*], jargoned description of the gnostic myth" (Cahana 2018, 169).

In Eric Voegelin's view, the apex of philosophical Gnosticism is reached in Hegel's conception of history, which Voegelin understood as secularized theodicy encouraged and legitimated in the development of totalitarianism (Woessner 2011, 94).[23] Voegelin's account provides a clear line of development from Gnosticism's beginnings in Christian late antiquity, through the Middle Ages and the modern period, and culminating in Nazism and Communism (Eccel 2015, 40).[24] From the historicist perspective in Voegelin's thought, his view of King's statement on violence and justice would include a historicized understanding of Gnosis. Along with Jonas, Voegelin viewed Nazism as "modern Gnosis," where the modern aspect of Gnostic thought describes the creation of political religion facilitating revolutionary transfiguration to achieve a state of perfection as revealed in Gnostic experience (Varshizky 2012, 314). As Varshizky shows, in Voegelin's and Jonas's accounts "the Gnostic model is used as a metaphysical infrastructure for formulating a racist, secular eschatology, through a conceptual transfiguration of the transcendental god into an immanent manifestation of the race-soul" (Varshizky 2012, 315). Varshizky points out that, as conceptualized by Nazi race theorist Alfred Rosenberg, race "is not a mere physiological or biological datum but constitutes a spiritual and metaphysical essence that gains its strength by virtue of a 'cosmic imperative.' This essence, identified as 'race-soul' (*Rassenseele*), constitutes the internal and concealed essence from which the physiological manifestations of the race emanate" (Varshizky 2012, 319–320). For Rosenberg, racial "wholeness" overcame the "splitting" that races endured in modern reification.

Racial Gnosis provided a secularized eschatological model for the chiastic racial union of spirit and nature (Varshizky 2012, 274). For Voegelin, political religion "thus designated a sacralization of the political community, which was accomplished through appropriating Christianity's symbolic forms and resulted in the foundation of collective life on the belief in a higher reality, whether humanity, a people, a class, a race or the state" (Burrin 1997, 323–324). In Nazism as political religion, history culminates in racial apotheosis. Voegelin referred to this sacralizing politics as the "fallacious immanentization of the Christian eschaton" with, in Nazism, the racial spirit, leading to the "realized eschatology" of "political Gnosticism" (Webb 2005, 66). In other words, as Raeder notes, Voegelin's concept of political Gnosticism identifies "the transfiguration of human nature through human action in history . . . to build a terrestrial paradise endowed with the meaning and salvational qualities of the Christian eschaton" (Raeder 2007, 352).[25]

Through this secularizing process, "the transcendent Christian end of history was transformed into a mundane 'End of History' to be realized in the immanent future" (Raeder 2007, 352). Despite Gnosticism's appearance in Christianity in the second century A.D., Voegelin believes that Plato is already aware of it and the danger it poses to the polis (Morales and Molas 2017, 46). Yet, as he states in his late *Autobiographical Reflections* (1973), "Since my first applications of Gnosticism to modern phenomena in *The New Science of Politics* and in 1959 in my study on *Science, Politics, and Gnosticism*, I have had to revise my position. The application of the category of Gnosticism to modern ideology, of course, stands. In a more complete analysis, however, there are other factors to be considered in addition. One of these factors is the metastatic apocalypse deriving directly from the Israelite prophets, via Paul, and forming a permanent strand in Christian sectarian movements right up to the Renaissance. . . . I found, furthermore, that neither the apocalyptic nor the Gnostic strand completely accounts for the process of immanentization. This factor has independent origins in the revival of neo-Platonism in Florence in the late fifteenth century" (Voegelin 2011, 66–67).[26] Although itself not derived from a Gnostic source, Neoplatonism furnishes Gnosticism with the "process of immanentization," or the mechanism by which Gnosis pervades and conquers wholistic thought to create a false eschatology of secular transcendence as the "End of History." The Gnostic "process of immanentization" Voegelin theorizes would be the essentialization of race King rejects in separatist historicism, including the power-oriented eschatology implicit in Newton's racialized allegory of the cave.[27]

5 Divine Nonviolence

I. King's Political Theology

ESCHATOLOGICAL MESSIANISM PLAYS critical roles in King's own philosophy. "Justice too long delayed is justice denied" and "an unjust law is not law at all" become the operative axiomatic expressions guiding the eschatological-messianic logic of King's "Letter." Each maxim helps to establish the fact that justice above all is paramount in considering the validity of civil disobedience and the extent to which it can be considered an infraction against the legal order and the cause of a fracture in a just society. King's first quote comes from a renowned jurist, and the second is from Saint Augustine. Both axioms understand the situation of revolt as one sanctioned not by positive law but rather by those precepts of a higher power. In the case of Augustine, deference is justly paid to divine law over that of the state, and in the instance of Supreme Court justice, King wishes to posit the priority of federal law over that of the states, whose local judicial rulings are vacated by the authority of the high court. In a sense, in setting these very similar quotes near each other, King runs the risk of achieving a contradictory rhetorical end. For in so doing, his text aligns the Supreme Court with divine law, and state law with its imperfect positive expression. In other words, King allows for the possibility of divine political order on earth and without need of police. Indeed, the existence of the police indicates the state's failure qua state.

King writes:

> A just law is a man-made code that squares with the moral law or the law of God. An unjust law is a code that is out of harmony with the moral law. To put it in the terms of St. Thomas Aquinas: An unjust law is a human law that is not rooted in eternal law and natural law. Any law that uplifts human personality is

just. Any law that degrades human personality is unjust. All segregation statutes are unjust because segregation distorts the soul and damages the personality. It gives the segregator a false sense of superiority and the segregated a false sense of inferiority. Segregation, to use the terminology of the Jewish philosopher Martin Buber, substitutes an "I-it" relationship for an "I-thou" relationship and ends up relegating persons to the status of things. Hence segregation is not only politically, economically and sociologically unsound, it is morally wrong and sinful. Paul Tillich has said that sin is separation. Is not segregation an existential expression of man's tragic separation, his awful estrangement, his terrible sinfulness? Thus it is that I can urge men to obey the 1954 decision of the Supreme Court, for it is morally right; and I can urge them to disobey segregation ordinances, for they are morally wrong. (King 2011 , 93)

Citing Aquinas indirectly, King insists that any just manifestation of positive law must correspond to its expression in and as natural law, where nature reflects the moral order as decreed by God in His essence. The unjust law does not attain to that of natural law and is therefore immoral in the eyes of God, thus circumventing the opportunity for human beings to raise themselves to the highest possible level of moral perfection possible within the divine precepts God sets forth in His being and as elaborated historically in positive law. This means, of course, that in seeking to correct unjust and therefore immoral governance, King's nonviolent protests are the articulation of natural law amending its falsified expression in and as positive law. Nonviolent protest is a direct manifestation of natural law as divine morality and, in its example as redefining legal intervention, the instantiation of universal salvation's possibility from within a corrupt system of positive law.[28] It leads inexorably to revolution.

King places the onus of revolution on divine law made manifest in collective nonviolent action. Unlike Benjamin's general strike, which operates as a systemic response to the state's discursive contradictions, nonviolence receives divine sanction and is the product of the ontological drive for oneness of Being. Segregation divides that which seeks unity naturally, whereas the general strike culminates in the apotheosis of class division. Unable to imagine racial conflict of world-historical importance, Benjamin sees class conflict as eschatologically motivated. As the general strike eliminates class conflict through extreme amplification, it resolves epistemological-critical contradictions in eschatological history without addressing disparity in racial difference. Race is simply not a factor in Benjamin's legal theory, whereas it is the substance of King's. Race promotes Nonbeing through segregation. The segregated state is "humanist," insofar as it reject's God's law for "man's."

King's "Letter" then reminds the clergy of Tillich's belief that forced separation is sinfulness and therefore inimical to Christian ethics. In situating his argument among Christianity's ethical theologians and philosophers, King effectively embeds the problem of segregation in Christian discussions of law and legality, preferring early Christian opinion on the matter. For at this time in the eschatological history of the church, Christianity still occupies a revolutionary insurgent position vis-à-vis the Roman world of late antiquity. It is in this situation that it founds its philosophy of law in practices of civil disobedience and conformity to nonviolence in submission to divine law above the positive law. Because of this delimitation of subject scope and definition, King is then able to give a succinct definition of the just and the unjust that is in complete conformity to the contemporary situation of segregation in the South. In this way, civil disobedience is authorized by divine law as elaborated in Christian morality, theologically expressed by foundational and current ecclesiastical authorities as the moral authority of the minority to regulate that of the majority. In other words, within the context of Christian morality, King's civil disobedience is not a positive legal matter, as the agitators here act within the limits of positive law. Rather, using terms such as "spiritual things," "peace-loving," "redemption," "happiness," and "revolutionary," nonviolence addresses the moral deficiency of a political theology that denies Gnostic duality and the superiority of divine law to that of the state.

In his afterword to Benjamin's "Critique of Violence," Herbert Marcuse excuses, with a combination of bitterness, nostalgia, and admiration, the thinker's use of terms such as "spiritual things," "peace-loving," "redemption," "happiness," and "revolutionary" (Marcuse 2014, 123). Singling out these particular words and phrases will seem odd to anyone familiar with Benjamin's text, which, while certainly invested in the general ideas these terms convey and the technical aspects of their use in philosophy, nevertheless does not provide a critique of violence for the sake of nonviolence. Indeed, Marcuse wrote the afterword shortly after finishing *One-Dimensional Man* (1964), and just a few months after John F. Kennedy's assassination. Eager to show the renewed relevancy of Benjamin's essay in the wake of Kennedy's assassination—and no doubt sensitive to Malcolm X's murder on February 21, 1965—Marcuse is also at pains from the beginning of his afterword to dissociate the "Critique of Violence" from any of King's key phrases, for fear of radical misunderstanding. As this chapter shows, Benjamin's and King's critiques of violence agree on the political nature of violence generally, and on the legal character of police violence. Their philosophies of nonviolence, however, differ in ontological terms that have to do with racial realism and the essence of class conflict.

While it goes without saying that King has a philosophy of nonviolence, the same cannot be easily said for Benjamin. Yet his critique of violence, aside from relying on a history of philosophical violence to critique, assumes its dialectical negation for the purposes of critique. Marcuse is eager to point out that the violence Benjamin refers to is not that which is "criticized everywhere" nor that which is "employed (or attempted) by those below against those above," to distance any reading of Benjamin from an association with nonviolence, and particularly the most current, popular version of it in 1960s America and Germany (Marcuse 2014, 124). Marcuse prefers that Benjamin's essay consider "pure," undialectical violence, which challenges the order of violence on which state sovereignty and law rests without positing nonviolent resistance. For Benjamin, as Marcuse reads him, true justice would be a state of nonviolence, initiated by the messianic presence of the truly just sovereign in history. This messianism rejects nonviolence as mere "civil disobedience," announcing instead the complete termination of the known order of sovereign power.

For Marcuse, nonviolence in Benjamin is the radical redemption of history, in the full material sense of justice in fully liberated humanity. The perpetual peace begun by messianic intervention in history institutes a period of happiness in which attendance to the spirit understood as the mediating factor in human deliberation, as opposed to force, offers the revolutionary path forward for Benjamin's troubled present. Marcuse emphasizes that the world in which Benjamin wrote the essay, just as the Second World War began, is not that of 1964, as Marcuse writes from the United States. Benjamin's language can no longer apply to the futurity of events and is validated instead in the ruins of the past. To preserve the ontological integrity of Benjamin's essay, Marcuse condemns any racialized reading of it with King as anachronistic.

Obviously concerned to consign the brunt of Benjamin's politics to the past, Marcuse, like Arendt after him in 1968, assiduously avoids articulating the racial politics of publishing Benjamin in 1964.[1] Without question, Marcuse's decision to publish Benjamin's "Critique of Violence" as a freestanding volume in 1964

Germany, as well as Arendt's later choice to exclude the essay from a 1968 English edition of Benjamin's essays, were probably taken with the essay's potentially illuminating and possibly damaging reflection of current events in mind.[2] The 1968 volume's publication coincided with King's April 4 assassination, the shooting of Rudi Dutschke on April 11, and Robert Kennedy's killing on June 6.[3] Indeed, 1968 saw no shortage of political violence. Neither Marcuse nor Arendt would have read Benjamin's essay, then, as an anachronistic relic from the past that uses an archaic language that no one outside the initiated will understand. The ruse of "anachronism" is just that. They understood clearly and unequivocally how alive Benjamin's essay was to the racial violence of the 1960s. In other words, Benjamin is as much King's contemporary in the 1960s as he was Arendt's in the 1920s, if not more so. His "Critique of Violence" shapes how Marcuse and Arendt approach violence in relation to King's obvious intervention in public opinion. And Benjamin's 1921 "Critique of Violence" can be used to understand better King's nonviolence of the 1950s and 1960s.[4]

Like Benjamin, King looks to political theology to ascertain the epistemological order of justice in which a particular community finds itself situated. For King, the measure of injustice the distressed population is permitted to conceive of in its situation, relative to the basic set of civil rights, is established not by United States law but rather by nonviolence as "divine violence." In the "Letter from a Birmingham Jail," King tacitly suggests God's law is represented in scripture and exegetically understood by the evangelicals and subsequent church fathers. Understanding that his critics are clergy, King assumes, as did Martin Luther before him, that a pervasive form of worldly corruption has overtaken the contemporary ecclesiastical establishment, obscuring the preeminent legal authority of God's word.

King expresses the logic of divine sovereignty when referencing Martin Buber's I-Thou in his "Letter." For King, Buber condemns the instrumental relationship between self and other as indicative of the subject's self-objectification. Through Buber, King equates segregative instrumentality with slavery's objectification of personhood and concomitant reification of justice. Yet as King points out, the Constitution of the United States guarantees a positive I-Thou relationship. Indeed, citing the First Amendment, King reminds the clergy of the right to free and peaceable assembly as the articulation of democratic equality's potential to exist, and that nonviolence increases the probability of its arrival. King thus establishes in the "Letter" a claim to a higher sense of normative order, where the Constitution elaborates the basic precepts of natural law as sanctioned by God. Here, the just law is that which conforms to the moral sense of justice contained in divine precept, as interpreted by the church fathers and as reiterated by the most morally sensitive contemporary theologians. This sense of justice entails the belief that any law that does not conform to divine precept no longer retains positive legitimacy and *must be* the target of civil disobedience. From King's point of view, nonviolent civil disobedience is not illegal even in a positive sense, as the Constitution originates in divinely inspired natural law. The separation of church and state, however, occludes this, imposing a Gnostic theological framework on American politics and jurisprudence whereby the Constitution's positive legitimacy *can* be called into question. That said, King does not seek the reunification of church and state, as this might infringe on democratic rights. Instead, he posits the natural law of human dignity as correlative intermediary between church and state. In this way, King envisions a Gnostic political theology legitimated by normative democratic praxis rather than by dictatorship authorized by the state of exception. King would reject as sinful humanism any political theology embracing a dictator as *eschaton* embodying the absolute ideal of human being. The dictator would in fact be the *katechon*, the one who restrains the apocalyptic forces of history, connecting the sacred and secular in sovereign dictatorship while simultaneously holding them apart. In this way, the dictator offers salvation in history, from history, serving the sinful forces of separation and preventing the chiastic unity of eschatological beloved community. In this respect, King would see the *katechon* as antichrist.

II. Pauline Contradictions

This view of political theology would be strongly at odds with Carl Schmitt's. "For Schmitt," Tertpstra writes,

> the *katechon* is a 'bridge' between the paralyzing effect of eschatology and political power. Thus, Schmitt adheres to a traditional and established reading of the Bible, accommodating it to the historical situation. Secondly, and in line with the idea of the *katechon*, Schmitt favours all power that restrains lawlessness and anarchy, in short, which prevents civil war. He is on the side of State and Church and spiritually invested in the authorities instituted by God. Thirdly, Schmitt coined the term 'political theology' in its modern sense, that is, political categories, which are always polemical concepts, cannot be grasped other than as secularized theological

concepts. Finally, Schmitt knew very well the political impact of the history of religious ideas even in the modern age. Clearly, there were enough overlapping themes to facilitate a conversation between the two men, despite their venomous enmity. (Terpstra 2009, 193)[5]

Schmitt thus adopts a Pauline understanding of *katechon* as "the defensive power to ward off the antichrist," where the antichrist is history itself (Terpstra 2009, 193).

In contradistinction to Schmitt, Taubes's Paul

> represents a promising intellectual position, avoiding both the dangerous implications of messianism (the violence or self-destruction of a people following a charismatic person) and the irresponsible flight from this world to purely inner, personal salvation (the Gnostic position). Although Taubes assents to the Gnostic move, he does not follow it completely, and considers that this is also Paul's position. The spiritual protest against 'the world as it is' adopts a political form without taking part in the usual political practices. Already in Taubes' earliest work, Paul is the spiritual leader who operates in the transition from apocalypticism to Gnosticism. (Terpstra 2009, 190)

As Styfhals points out, "like Carl Schmitt, Taubes is, for example, interested in the different continuities between the concepts of theology and secular politics. From a political perspective, the apocalypse would be the ultimate state of exception that overcomes liberal normativity's static lawfulness" (Styfhals 2015, 208).[6] That said, Taubes arrives at a very different political outcome. In fact, Taubes presents Schmitt, along with Karl Barth, "zealots of the Absolute and the Decision," agreeing with Blumenberg and Kelsen on secularization and political theology, yet ultimately investing in the apocalyptic experience of world politics of nihilism he believed present in Benjamin's work (Mehring 1996, 244).[7]

Reading Paul in Benjamin, Taubes conceived messianism as a productive internalization of Gnosticism, like what Voegelin condemned (Vatter 2019, 475). The historical problem of "realist political theology," as Benjamin shows in the *Origin of German Tragic Drama*, "Critique of Violence," and elsewhere, the state of exception or any claim of "urgency can be perpetually invoked for political purposes without this urgency losing its persuasiveness even when the catastrophe never fully materializes. [For] Benjamin, this peculiarity of the discourse of perpetual urgency is reinforced by remnants of Christian eschatology that haunt concepts of agency in history and politics and animate the theological-political discourse that foregrounds sovereignty and decision" (Thiem 2013, 296).[8] While Christian theology in general "permeates the whole of Benjamin's oeuvre," eschatology holds a place of privilege in his philosophy (Naishtat 2019, 94). Benjamin, however, attempts to avoid strict Gnostic dualism through the introduction of a temporal model of rupture that negotiates pantheism and radical dualism. Benjamin sees clearly, as Agamben writes, "[i]f we push to the limit the paradigm of the separate substance, we have the Gnosis, with its God foreign to the world and creation; if we follow to the end the paradigm of immanence, we have pantheism. Between these two extremes, the idea of order tries to think a difficult balance, which Christian theology is always in the process of losing and which it must at each turn regain" (Agamben 2011, 87).[9] No doubt perceiving early "the political implications of the burgeoning fascination with Gnosticism," Benjamin attempts to overcome this tendency by setting it within a materialist historical model and there allowing the idea to destroy itself (Mendes-Flohr 2019, 72). Unlike "Gnostic" contemporary theologians and philosophers who "tended to shift the ground of eschatology from revelation to the inner logic of a system," Benjamin reversed the field and formulated "the ground of eschatology" within the system, only from within which revelation became possible (Wolfe 2019, 55). In this way, Benjamin intervened in the rise of eschatology as a reaction to philosophies positing "weak Messianic power."

Against progressivist politics, Benjamin proposes a "weak Messianic power" "in which each day is lived as the day of judgment on which the Messiah comes" (Kroeker 2005, 40). Beyond historicity, this "Messianic time" has its historical equivalent in the state of exception. As Kroeker writes, "It will bring into view the violent and destructive foundation of this sovereignty by remembering another sovereignty: a messianic sovereignty that reorders the secular on completely different terms" (Kroeker 2005, 40–41). Messianic time's interruption in history suspends all action, all being in the eternally present *Jetztzeit*. Benjamin's interrogation of messianic power can be considered a meontology, or philosophy of Nonbeing, which is how Jacob Taubes has described it, in connection with the apocalyptic messianism of Saint Paul (Kroeker 2005, 40). Taubes famously compared Benjamin's messianism with Saint Paul's, seeing them as bookends to a single tradition premised on pneuma, or the personal spirit unifying the community of Christ's followers, and separating them from all other communities essentially (Mehring 1996, 244). Pneuma is the power that transforms the

Christian community into God's Volk (Mehring 1996, 242). Taubes's focus on Nonbeing puts the ends of his argument at odds with Heidegger's ontology, causing Negri to speculate that Taubes's meontology led him to exclude the interwar philosopher of Being from his work in preference for Rosenzweig, Schmitt, and Benjamin (Negri 2010, 38–39).

Yet Heidegger's sense of Parousia in Saint Paul accords well with Benjamin's *Jetztzeit*, at least structurally, insofar as the attentiveness to the Second Coming in Paul and other early Christian thinkers is a structuring principle for temporality rather than one historical event among all others (Vaughan 1995, 150).[10] Heidegger thinks of this event as Kairos, or the structural awareness of the state of exception as the historicity of Being (Forgone 367).[11] Taubes's inclusion of an account of Heidegger might have undermined his understanding of Benjamin, as Benjamin's conception of messianism is material and historical, rather than personal and spiritual. Like Bultmann's reading of Paul, Benjamin considers soma over pneuma (Neugebauer 1959, 292–293). Like King's combination of Paul Tillich and Heidegger, Bultmann unites Saint Paul and Heidegger to formulate a theology of Being premised on Dasein's personal interrogation of spirit as how God is encountered in history as veiled Being (Landmesser 2013, 14).

Heidegger's own reading of Paul falls along similar lines, with the important distinction that Being is not the Christian God as conceived in the history of metaphysics, which occluded the philosophical insights of both Paul and presocratic thinkers (Popkes 2006, 269). As Stanley points out, "Heidegger believes that the patristic Augustinian 22 reading of Paul's letter is a classic example of Christianity's misunderstanding of the primordial Christianity Paul was trying to express in opposition to Greek thinking" (Stanley 2007, 43). Following Luther rather than Augustine, Heidegger follows an meontological approach to Paul, concentrating on historicity and hiddenness instead of properly soteriological speculation (Armitage 2014, 576). Vedder observes that, for Heidegger, "the truth of Christianity is to be found not in the dogma or the doctrine of the two separate worlds, but rather in Christian life experience. What is lived (note the transitive sense of the verb "to live" here) in Christian religiosity is temporality or historicality" (Vedder 2009, 161). As McManus shows, in his early reflections on Parousia in Saint Paul, "Heidegger asks us to reflect on what it is to 'be prepared for' and not to be 'overtaken by' this event; and his remarks do indeed suggest . . . a sense in which the concern of those who 'talk of peace and security'—with when the parousia is to happen—shows them to be 'unprepared' for that event and in a way that the 'children of light' aren't" (McManus 2013, 149). In this sense, Heidegger does not view Paul from an anti-historicist perspective, as does Barth. Rather, he reads him in a way like Bultmann, whose historicism demythologizes, or deconstructs the tradition in which the Pauline text is embedded. King, who studied Bultmann's work, reflects Bultmann's mediation of Heidegger and Saint Paul in his dissertation.

Benjamin's Paul differs from Bultmann's, and presumably King's, in the important sense that, whereas Bultmann's Paul rejects violence as both means and end of redemption, Benjamin's allows for the most extreme forms of violence in eventual negation of secular law and political order through nullifying divine violence (Mack 2000, 418). As Greenberg notes, "despite the resemblance that Taubes identified with Paul, Benjamin said nothing about the individual salvation of the soul, and was concerned only with the end of collective law and violence" (Greenberg 2008, 330). Paul's focus on pneuma places the emphasis on spiritual salvation as opposed to worldly revolution, leading him to propose a "politics of peace" (Campbell 2013, 129). Yet for Benjamin *and* King, messianic time as radical state of exception is the realization in historical time of revolution as idea, or "thought." The material realization of this "thought" indicates the extent to which, for Benjamin and King, the reflective structure of historicity is categorically other than that of the Messiah reflected, whereas for Saint Paul it derives from God and is, therefore, a messianic inflection of divine spirit (Kavka 2020, 21).

Agamben has famously read Benjamin's messianism in relation to the Schmittian state of exception in "Critique of Violence," as well as his "Pauline" messianism both through Taubes and through a series of Benjamin excerpts Agamben not unproblematically sees as secret quotes of Paul (Britt 2010, 271–272). Although Agamben's sense that Schmitt constantly attempts to contain the sovereignty of messianic force in "a judicial context," while Benjamin seeks to situate it outside the law entirely may be overstated, nevertheless his reading of Benjamin's messianism with Taubes, Schmitt, and Paul remains formidable (de Wilde 2011, 366–367). In Agamben, as Loose writes, "The Messianic has always been proclaimed as the coming, and that remains also today what it has always been. The profession of Creed notwithstanding, it is, as for Walter Benjamin . . . nothing other than the lasting profession of the coming times in the present: *ho nun kairos* is *il tempo che resta*, the time that remains in every present time. . . . The event is always advent, to come, *avenir, avenement*. Messianic time is the paradigm of every historical time" (Loose 2009, 139). Yet this formulation is as much Heidegger's as it is Benjamin's, if not more so. As Birmingham writes, "[f] or Benjamin, human beings can live only in the void between the past and the future. Benjamin, he argues, captures perfectly this living in the void with the 'particularly felicitous image' of Klee's angel of history caught facing backward and being blown toward the future" (Birmingham 2014, 107). Living in the void between past and future, human being understands its temporal predicament eschatologically either in terms of political theology or otherworldly salvation.

That said, Heidegger's form of historicism presents challenges to reading his version of Saint Paul with Benjamin's, or King's. Insofar as Benjamin's Paul echoes many of Heidegger's philosophical concerns, Benjamin would reject tout court both Heidegger's structuring of these issues and his methodological approach. Beatrice Hanssen finds it "remarkable . . . that Benjamin's own disclaimers regarding his so-called Heideggerian ethos have failed to stop several commentators, critics and interested readers from constructing sometimes problematic analogies and parallels between the writings of these two thinkers" (Hanssen 73–74). Yet Rebecca Comay believes "a posthumous encounter" between Benjamin and Heidegger "is both necessary and urgent today" (Comay 1992, 139). While never having met and, in Benjamin's case, openly hostile to the other's philosophy, nevertheless, Comay insists, "Benjamin articulates in an exemplary fashion two strands of the ontotheological (or rather, onto-thee-technological) tradition that remain at once both most susceptible and yet most recalcitrant to Heidegger's diagnosis of 'metaphysics' (also most recalcitrant to each other). I mean Marxism and Judaism" (Comay 1992, 139). According to Comay, "Benjamin promises to provide a kind of historical concretion or focus to Heidegger's thinking-both a date and a place-a focus which . . . might bring out some of the practical resources still latent (despite everything) in the Heideggerian system" (Comay 1992, 139–140). On firmer historical ground, Hanssen is more sanguine about the potential virtue in arranging "a posthumous encounter" between the two philosophers. She writes: "Benjamin's growing uneasiness with, and political aversion to, Heidegger's 'philosophy of being' motivated him to distinguish his own emerging theory of the dialectical image from the flawed historicity of Heideggerian philosophy, as is evident in a cryptic note of *The Arcades Project*. Moreover, in a 1930 letter to Scholem, Benjamin reported that, together with his Marxist playwright-friend Bertolt Brecht, he planned to convene a critical reading group, whose sole purpose was to demolish Heidegger's thought. Although this group to all appearances never materialized, Benjamin's reference to the planned meeting leaves no doubts as to his political view of Heidegger" (Hanssen 2005, 73). These two readings of a dialectically productive encounter between Benjamin and Heidegger's philosophies are not diametrically opposed. Both Hanssen and Comay agree that Benjamin historicizes what Heidegger leaves more abstract. For Hanssen, Benjamin and Heidegger cease to be discussing the same matters once historical reality articulates the issue as an objective, material process in the world. Heidegger's more abstract, ahistorical formulation of philosophical problems leaves them as potentialities without the capability to produce historical consequence in themselves. In other words, Benjamin engages in historically grounded philosophical ideology critique, while Heidegger philosophy manufactures ideology.[12] As opposed to Heidegger and, to some extent Bultmann, Benjamin has a more nuanced, materialist reading of Paul that seeks to dislodge him from ideological tradition to present his epistles in a more radical setting—something Heidegger's philosophy only claims to do (Lamarche 2001, 37).

In this sense, Benjamin's "Critique of Violence" evinces Pauline thought more than any of Heidegger's works:

> Like his predecessor and likely source of inspiration in this argument, Immanuel Kant... Benjamin draws attention to the absence of any serious meditation on the symbolic function of the written law in the traditional critique of law as norm and invites us to consider the specific function of the law's writtenness as distinct from whatever content it might communicate. Significantly, both authors appeal to the commandments of the Hebrew Decalogue to illustrate the indispensable role of the written law in resisting the lure of the imaginary and the blind submission to power it encourages. This focus on the commandment form is especially provocative with respect to Paul's polemic, since for Paul the commandment is not just one example among others of the defect in the written law, but absolutely exemplary of the problems internal to the written law as a distorting mediation. Paul is careful to specify that the holy commandment is not the law of sin. Nevertheless, he asserts that the law of sin 'finds opportunity in the commandment': 'I should not have known what it is to covet if the law had not said, 'you shall not covet' [Romans 7: 7]. In prohibiting, the law incites transgression by offering up to the imagination an object of desire. The commandment is thus the vehicle through which sin and death insinuate themselves into the Jewish law, perverting or derailing our quest for the purely spiritual law of God. In short, Paul understands the

commandment as nothing more than a representation of divine law, corrupted by the mediation of the letter, which consigns it either to a rote normativity devoid of spiritual meaning or to a transgressive seduction by the imagination. (McNulty 2007, 36–7)

Benjamin revises Paul to account for the mediation of writing in divine Commandments. This prior form of mediation accounts for the normative struggle specified by the translation of divine commandment into the historicity of positive law as police violence.

III. Love's Extremist

The same holds true for King, who claims that, like Paul to Macedonia, he has been called to Birmingham to break the law. Arrested there by design in 1963 for demonstrating against a state court injunction and writing from a Birmingham prison on scraps of paper including bath tissue, King authors a missive to clergy who have condemned his presence in the city as a provocation to violence: "So I, along with several members of my staff, am here because I was invited here. I am here because I have organizational ties here. But more basically, I am in Birmingham because injustice is here. Just as the eighth-century prophets left their little villages and carried their "thus saith the Lord" far beyond the boundaries of their hometowns; and just as the Apostle Paul left his little village of Tarsus and carried the gospel of Jesus Christ to practically every hamlet and city of the Greco-Roman world, I too am compelled to carry the gospel of freedom beyond my particular hometown. Like Paul, I must constantly respond to the Macedonian call for aid." The fight against injustice calls for extremism, in God's name. King admits he "gradually gained a bit of satisfaction from being considered an extremist. Was not Jesus an extremist in love?—"Love your enemies, bless them that curse you, pray for them that despitefully use you." Was not Amos an extremist for justice?—"Let justice roll down like waters and righteousness like a mighty stream." Was not Paul an extremist for the gospel of Jesus Christ?—"I bear in my body the marks of the Lord Jesus." Was not Martin Luther an extremist?—"Here I stand; I can do no other so help me God." Was not John Bunyan an extremist?—"I will stay in jail to the end of my days before I make a mockery of my conscience." Was not Abraham Lincoln an extremist?—"This nation cannot survive half slave and half free." Was not Thomas Jefferson an extremist?—"We hold these truths to be self-evident, that all men are created equal." So the question is not whether we will be extremist, but what kind of extremists we will be. Will we be extremists for hate, or will we be extremists for love? Will we be extremists for the preservation of injustice, or will we be extremists for the cause of justice?" (King 2011, 100–101). King is an extremist in love. This means, agape solicits reconciliation, forgiveness, and beloved community; yet eros provokes the extremism necessary for Kairos as police violence. As the provocation of unlawful police violence, eros is essential to King's philosophy of social action and revolutionary political change.

Indeed, the "Pauline" aspects of King's "Letter from a Birmingham Jail" attempt to redress police violence by inviting communities in distress into God's grace through teaching the eschatological specificity and contingent sociopolitical properties of divine law. Ultimately, in aligning and identifying himself with Paul while writing from prison, where the question of law and legality in relation to political theology and the gospel has become manifestly obvious, King seeks to have his mission understood in concert with Paul's conception and presentation of the law not to the Macedonians, per se, but rather to the Romans. He writes: "Injustice anywhere is a threat to justice everywhere. We are caught in an inescapable network of mutuality, tied in a single garment of destiny. Whatever affects one directly, affects all indirectly. Never again can we afford to live with the narrow, provincial 'outside agitator' idea. Anyone who lives inside the United States can never be considered an outsider anywhere within its bounds" (King 2011, 87).[15]

Paul's conception of the law as universally applicable in accordance with the proliferation of Christian faith—as opposed to the restricted province of those born into it by special covenant with God—advances a notion of Christian universality in social activism that rejects the label of "outside agitator." For King as for Paul, there can be no identification of an outside to injustice. For wherever injustice abounds, King insists, the entire legitimacy of justice falls under attack. One local injustice, if allowed to stand, dismantles the entire understanding of justice as authentic and valid in all situations. In this respect, King is writing not only about the idea of Christian justice in relation to the political-theological applicability of divine law and grace—thus justifying his presence everywhere by deconstructing the supposition that he could ever be an outsider anywhere, as the conception of Christian law and justice advanced by Paul rejects this possibility on the grounds of the faith's universality. He is also addressing the positivistic legal objection that the sovereignty in whose name King agitates, that of the federal government and the Supreme Court, exceeds its reach as it seeks to intervene in a matter over which the clergy believe that the individual state has authority through the specificity of force of custom.[16] King's concern for universal justice is a political theological matter involving police violence in the name of states' rights in the face of federal decree. In other words, King comes to Birmingham to combat an individual state's improper yet sovereign use of police violence. "Injustice" in Birmingham names the local exercise of police violence, in a manner contrary to both federal law and divine law, as Kairos, the moment of decision.

Indeed, both King's and Benjamin's conceptions of police violence culminate in Kairos, or what Agamben refers to as "the time that remains": the event in preparation for Gnostic revelation as the end of history. As political theology, Kairos calls for a critique of violence that, instead of condemning violence and being done with it, sees violence as the engine of political economy and reconceptualizing it as how to end politics in toto. As Agamben writes in a very early essay sent, by way of introducing himself, to Hannah Arendt,

> The exigency of rethinking violence is not a question of scale; it is a question of violence's increasingly ambiguous relation to politics. Thus, this critique diverges from Benjamin's exposition of violence's relation to law and justice, seeking instead to determine its relation to politics, and in so doing, to uncover the question of violence in and for itself. In other words, we aim to determine the limits—if such limits exist—that separate violence from the sphere of human culture in its broadest sense. These limits will allow us to address the question of the only violence that might still exist on a human scale: revolutionary violence. (Agamben 2009, 104)

Agamben's short cover letter to the essay informs Arendt of their mutual acquaintance, Dominique Fourcade, with whom he attended Heidegger's 1966 and 1968 seminars in Provence. His early essay about Benjamin and violence is very much a product of these seminars.

For Benjamin, and for King as well, a form of violence exercised within the reciprocal order of legal means and ends could provide the basis for an experience of justice outside of the very system of violence in which it occurs. Benjamin writes:

> Among all the forms of violence permitted by both natural law and positive law there is not one that is free of the gravely problematic nature . . . of all legal violence. Since, however, every conceivable solution to human problems, not to speak of deliverance from the confines of all the world-historical conditions of existence obtaining hitherto, remains impossible if violence is totally excluded in principle, the question necessarily arises as to other kinds of violence than all those envisaged by legal theory. It is at the same time the question of the truth of the basic dogma common to both theories: Just ends can be attained by justified means, justified means used for just ends. How would it be, therefore, if all the violence imposed by fate, using justified means, were of itself in irreconcilable conflict with just ends, and if at the same time a different kind of violence came into view that certainly could be either the justified or the unjustified means to those ends, but was not related to them as means at all but in some different way? (Benjamin 1986, 293)

Benjamin wishes to convert these basic philosophical premises into legal-epistemological claims to recuperate or reinitialize a critique of violence that accounts for "a different kind of violence." This other violence would exclude a logic of means as related in any justifiable way to the ends of justice, as embodied in the juridical-theoretical form of the modern state. It would not, however, be nonviolent protest and pacifism. Here state violence is brought to bear on a form of resistance and disruption that resembles that of the strike in its refusal to perform a duty, yet which nevertheless intervenes in the sphere of legal action, where its goal is the preservation of the state. However, nonviolent civil disobedience as an "unnatural" or supernatural (i.e., divine) form of sovereignty would, like the general strike, suspend all law-preserving violence and in effect end the state. King's nonviolent protest, for example, aims to perpetrate divine nonviolence and bring in the name of sovereign beloved community. All forms of violence—including nonviolent protest that does not have the radical aim of ushering in the end of history through Gnostic revelation—are "natural," meaning they are either law-making or law-preserving. Divine nonviolence (or divine violence, in Benjamin) exceeds this binary.

This means, of course, that as his opponents among the clergy suspected, King includes violence in his calculus of nonviolent civil disobedience as spatiotemporally removed from the local site of the protest. Such violence, however, transcends positive law, belonging instead to the eschatological-spiritual realm of divine prerogative. This form of violence, perpetrated by the purified soul resisting injustice, is sanctioned by God. The struggle for civil rights in America through nonviolent protest, then, can only be adjudicated in heaven, as it uses pure means to achieve just worldly ends. The subsidiary state violence it produces does not belong to its purified subjects, who submit to God as the chosen people of this time and place to advance the eschatological progress of divine justice as sacred temporality. Hence, nonviolent protest in the cause of racial justice in Birmingham and elsewhere is eschatologically necessary to bring about God's kingdom on earth, as the United States is the contemporary national site of positive law determined by Christian morality deemed the absolute subject of history. In this regard, all justice is racial in nature, or "natural," as indicated by the advanced soteriological-historical state of the United States' struggle to realize the City of God on earth.

IV. Benjamin and Police Violence

For Benjamin, ignominious forms of violence are those that can be either law-making or law-preserving. Police violence would be an example of ignominious force:

> The ignominy of such an authority, which is felt by few simply because its ordinances suffice only seldom for the crudest acts but are therefore allowed to rampage all the more blindly in the most vulnerable areas and against thinkers, from whom the state is not protected by law—this ignominy lies in the fact that in this authority the separation of lawmaking and law-preserving violence is suspended. If the first is required to prove its worth in victory, the second is subject to the restriction that it may not set itself new ends. Police violence is emancipated from both conditions. (Benjamin 1986, 286)

It is law-making in that it is a lethal legal intervention outside of the normal juridical process that would otherwise be mandatory for the use of deadly force by an agent of the state. The police, as potential perpetrator, must be seen as using ex facto legal and formal criminal means to meet de facto just ends to create and abolish a law pertaining directly to them. Once that dual action is completed, and after having been sanctioned, it disappears, becoming instead the occasion for justice without legal means. Using law-making violence to preserve existing laws, the police's function expires as the criminal event is retired by the judicial system. In turning a blind eye to or even authorizing unlawful police violence, this system admits its unwillingness to intervene where its authority is exercised unauthorized and exceptionally by a law-preserving agent.

As law-preserving violence, police violence presents a more accessible, recognizable, yet utterly ignominious expression of state violence, in which the law preserved is the one that comes into being with its preservation. Benjamin writes:

> It is lawmaking, for its characteristic function is not the promulgation of laws but the assertion of legal claims for any decree, and law-preserving, because it is at the disposal of these ends. The assertion that the ends of police violence are always identical or even connected to those of general law is entirely untrue. Rather, the "law" of the police really marks the point at which the state, whether from impotence or because of the immanent connections within any legal system, can no longer guarantee through the legal system the empirical ends that it desires at any price to attain. Therefore, the police intervene "for security reasons" in countless cases where no clear legal situation exists, when they are not merely, without the slightest relation to legal ends, accompanying the citizen as a brutal encumbrance through a life regulated by ordinances, or simply supervising him. (Benjamin 1986, 286–287)

Unable to preserve a preexisting law due to the law-making character of its force, police violence serves to preserve the power of the police in the service of, yet not as, the state.[17] In this way, as agents of the state, the police risk becoming an autonomous or at any rate unaccountable organization within the state itself. The danger of this occurring presents itself despite the fact that police autonomy is always relative to that of the state. The police in their law-making, law-preserving violence nevertheless depend on the existence of the state for the parameters of their action. Therefore, police violence does not threaten the state at its foundation and is not capable of foundational violence, for it ceases to exist with the state and is thus bound to the state's existence as an expression of state power in another, officially unsanctioned yet irreproachable form. Police violence is "unnatural," because it mirrors that of the state without official sanction, and yet it cannot be held accountable for any crime because it does not threaten the state in the least. The police are the state within the state, or the heart of the state, such that every state is a police state, making sanctioned and unsanctioned forms of violence recognizable ultimately solely through the lens of police violence itself.[18]

Benjamin will further condemn police violence by insisting that where this form of violence is tethered to monarchical power, it possesses a greater sense of connectedness to the reality in which it intervenes:

> Unlike law, which acknowledges in the "decision" determined by place and time a metaphysical category that gives it a claim to critical evaluation, a consideration of the police institution encounters nothing essential at all. Its power is formless, like its nowhere tangible, all-pervasive, ghostly presence in the life of civilized states. And though the police may, in particulars, everywhere appear the same, it cannot finally be denied that their spirit is less devastating where they represent, in absolute monarchy, the power of a ruler in which legislative and executive supremacy are united, than in democracies where their existence, elevated by no such relation, bears witness to the greatest conceivable degeneration of violence.
>
> All violence as a means is either lawmaking or law-preserving. If it lays claim to neither of these predicates, it forfeits all validity. (Benjamin 1986, 286–287)

For the name in which it performs its intervention, as separate from the people directly affected by this invasive, non-martial expression of lethal force, is not the legal entity invested with the authority on behalf of whom the police violently intercede. In this conception of police violence in relation to sovereignty, the sovereign is outside of such means and methods of law enforcement, and the police have no right to lay hands on him, in either their law-making or law-preserving capacity, precisely because police violence cannot decide between the two. Benjamin, like King, is unequivocal in his belief that where this distinction breaks down, violence is invalidated, not as violence, for it is still recognized as such by the state, but rather as legal violence. This other violence obtains in a legal contradiction made unavoidable by sovereignty's inherent ambivalence of nature. Benjamin, then, insists the sovereign is immune to this form of violence; in a democratic society, however, police violence usurps this immunity. Benjamin suggests that where dictatorial immunity does not apply and a state of exception has not been called, the police have no legal or moral right to act autonomously and without full legal consequences.[19] As King also realizes, in the buildup to and wake of *Pierson v. Ray* (1967), "qualified immunity" cannot exist outside the state of emergency.

Benjamin defines the parameters of his engagement in terms of law and justice, relegating the violence produced by a political cause such as police violence to the secondary status of event. Such actions are determined by law and justice negatively as excluded from their purview, which is that of morality. Law and justice decide the moral sphere and are thus the elements of moral philosophy that determine and contain all moral action, of which violence itself remains a part. Any action that resembles violence yet falls outside the dialectical purview of law and justice is not to be considered violence at all. This seems an impossibility except when it is understood that for Benjamin and King, virtually no human action falls outside of this socially interpretative frame, and the human itself is conceived through the institutional frame of moral action.

Benjamin thus describes what appears to be a contradiction in the legal situation, yet which is to him consistent with it. For Benjamin, "legal" means the practical application of the law. The law is guided by the epistemological logic that inhabits all manifestations and praxis-oriented enactments of its legal being. The legal cannot found or destroy a state; it merely performs its function as an expression of legality. The law, however, exists outside of the state, shaping its incarnations as historically contingent. This means that access to the law is granted both within the legal system, as a particular manifestation of the law's praxis-oriented expression, and outside of the legal apparatus, in the general sense of the form-giving concept of right. In this way, the ability to found and destroy states is possible only through an act of "violence" outside of the systematic representation and elaboration of the state as a legal apparatus. Benjamin's critique of violence, and King's, depends on this distinction.

Indeed, there is no legal contradiction because there are only legal facts as objects of legal determination, or legality. This continuum of legal substance is categorically different from that of law, which has no intended object other than the existence of the state itself. The uses of violence within legal means are non-contradictory even where the manifest violence is unsanctioned, in that it can still be recognized as violence by the legal order and determined as a legal means in itself. Here its illegality comes only where its use is unsanctioned, leaving any form of violence legal because it is recognizable yet deployed illegally. Illegality becomes an issue of timing rather than an issue of the quality of violence itself. Any violence concerning law as a foundational gesture, if recognized as violence, is a priori in agreement with the state, as it falls within its purview and field of recognition. This is not to say that such violence might not threaten the existence of the state in its current configuration and distribution of social forces, but rather that it does not seek to destroy those forces. The contradiction is present in legal ends, yet not in legal means. In the consideration of legal ends, destructive, indeed apocalyptic violence does not obtain, whereas in the analysis of legal means, all possible forms of violence are permissible under certain circumstances, insofar as violence is recognized by and relevant to considerations of legality as such.

Ultimately Benjamin, like King, posits that no nonviolent solution is possible in contractual agreements of any sort because the consequences of breach of contract always entail, at some point as a final measure, a violent solution. Likewise, the very legal structure and sense of law that give the "nonviolent" contract its language and sense, its judicial context, derive from both foundational and lawmaking violence. The contract as an extant legal entity owes its existence and status to the violence inherent in the law itself as its ontological basis. All legal transactions and entities are a priori engaged in violent means and ends, either directly or at some remove, by virtue of the nature of their legal representation as sanctionable or not by the state. The fact that the state can recognize an object or event in a legal sense and within its own parameters of legality, even if only to exceed those limits, determines said object or action in the context of both pure violence as origin and statutory violence as an event of legal intent.

Benjamin suggests that nonviolent means are possible in the pursuit of conflict resolution, yet it is important to understand the mode in which such procedures can be executed without falling into the legally recognizable patterns of sanctioned and unsanctioned strategies of decision in such matters of sociopolitical disagreement. Their applicability comes in disputes between private persons perceived as monads yet unalloyed reflections of the sociolegal totality, and not in direct conflict with or rectifying intervention in this totality itself, or in the state. No legal matter brought before the state can sustain or even present nonviolent intentions and applicability. However, such a situation may be achieved under certain circumstances within the private sphere, in which the state still exhibits invasive vigilance regarding the content of individual events, as civil law. However, the private sphere has insufficient capability to evaluate and police the full range of possible linguistic signification when parties speak outside of or around easily identifiable legal discursive semantic structures, of which Benjamin selects modes of sociolinguistic conduct as courtesy, kindness, deference, and so on. He is therefore not concerned with the social import of, say, respecting one's elders in language as well as deed, but rather with formal stylistic structures of expression that carry with them intensive social force, yet which are nonetheless beyond the pale of legal activity. Benjamin sees these exemplified in the exemplary conduct of the conference if no concerned party engages in deception. Language itself provides social spaces foreign to the legal logic of sanction and the sanctimonious: hence the need for persistent, abiding honesty, or Parrhesia, as King would think of it.[20] Benjamin thus identifies unalloyed legal aesthetics as appropriable tools for social conflict resolution without engaging law-making or law-preserving state power and the violent being of the state more generally.

The potential for fraud present in Parrhesia diminishes this nonviolent solution to conflict, which, because it relies on the private sphere to achieve its resolution, cannot be influenced directly by state intervention. Yet the legal restriction against fraud does seek to control, to some extent, the nature of private discursive negotiation in conflict resolution. This occurs to the point where certain legal freedoms, or liberties with and within the law, must be granted to maintain a sense of order and containment in terms of the wider threat to the state in the face of fraud while simultaneously retaining the potential for nonviolent contractual agreement among private parties, thus avoiding deliberation at the juridical level of the state. Allowing any form of private contractual agreement, unseen by state oversight, may seem against the state's interests more generally. However, as in the case of the strike, which the state allows despite the apparent contradiction to self-interest, such forms of negotiation among citizens yet external to the state legal apparatus forestall the urgency of insurrectionary claims represented by the actions of the offended parties in seeking any resolution in the first place from within the state itself. In the state's allowance of external or even directly opposed actions to escape its legal scrutiny, it plays for time in devising better, less divisive solutions to the threats it faces, instigating a process by which "pure" violence can take place.

So-called pure violence is any action that speaks to the eradication of the entire state system in all its political configurations, and thus to the end of politics construed in oppositional or violent terms. Pure violence is, then, nonviolent, in conventional legal terms. The state as Benjamin construes it, in its ontological basis as a legal or constitutional entity, demands violent conflict to exercise its being as law. The political organization of any given state elaborates its being as a legal entity defined by violent challenges to its basic structure, positing as its existential condition the antagonistic friend/enemy dichotomy of the political that Carl Schmitt theorizes. Benjamin, however, seeks an anarchistic solution to this otherwise intractable binary by destroying the distinction in the private sphere. Here friend and enemy are not stable positions in the social adumbration of private relations mediated by a sense of language itself as objective, or without intention, and pure, regarding legal means and ends. Indeed, language that avoids mendacity is pure precisely because the law has no use for it. Such language already exists outside the state, available to private citizens who can, in their honesty, speak a language the state cannot understand.[21]

Benjamin goes on to state the unavoidable material fact of his presentation—namely, that all forms of legal action are to some extent implicated in violence. This provokes the question of violence outside this dichotomous logic of state ontology and historical expression, in which violent action, while still engaged in the a priori horizon of all statehood, does not require the logic of its means and its ends to coincide in justice. In other words, Benjamin seeks an unjust form of violence that would escape this causal binary logic that leads exclusively to its own undoing. Benjamin thus searches for a form of violent means for their own sake and for themselves, as well as violent ends that fulfill their requirements within the conceptual, critical adjudication of their contained, completed event. This would be a violence that retroactively reimagines its otherwise unalloyed means as meeting the standards of its expressive form of justice. This could only mean violence prescribed by God's law and not that of the state. These events are laws unto themselves and possess their own form of justice. As amoral modes of action belong to no political cause, they form no part of a social system of representation. To distinguish them terminologically and conceptually, they can be said to be moments of divine violence.[22] For King, they would be moments of divine nonviolence.

For Benjamin, violence is not enacted by God, being "divine" only by virtue of its origin beyond human intention despite its creation and containment within sociopolitical constructs. Divine violence, then, is neither an act of nature nor an act of God; it is an autonomous effect of political systems that eradicates all systematicity, both in specificity and as general concepts. This form of violence could be considered "nonviolence" from a physical and a spiritual point of view. Indeed, "pure" nonviolence is a form of ultraviolence in that it vehemently rejects the basis of civil society; it is a violence in purified passivity that is so extreme it exceeds any existentially qualitative evaluation. It is the (non)violence of universal inaction, as if suddenly all things ceased to perform their being, instead of ceasing to be. Benjamin's divine violence is King's divine nonviolence as the performative embrace of Nonbeing in dialectical negation. Thus, for Benjamin and King, the violence of ends and means does not exist except as Nonbeing, and divine violence is recognizable only as nonviolence. Their critique of nonviolence embedded in their critique of violence embraces divine (non)violence as the absolute negation of law-making, law-preserving police violence and the violence of the unjust state in its unlawful state of exception.

Agamben's conception of the state of exception in his work on "Critique of Violence," and most notably on Adam Smith, does not take into sufficient account that once "a state of emergency is installed, the police can purportedly legitimately use violence to secure the market order. In other words, the sovereign of political theology responsible for defending the social order in times of unrest surreptitiously reappears in liberal governmentality to back up the economic theology of the free market when the latter lacks popular support" (Christiaens 2021, 68). Because of this oversight, Agamben does not adequately account for the fact that "in suspending the law, the state of exception does not also suspend the violence that creates and maintains law, but rather makes it available for appropriation by revolutionary groups, dictators, the police, and so forth" (Morgan 2007, 60). While Agamben is certainly aware that the state of exception legitimately reassigns the force of law to otherwise illegitimate agents such as revolutionary groups and dictators, he does not account for the police as a revolutionary group or a form of dictatorship unto itself, as its own, constant state of exception. As Britt remarks, Agamben "ascribes a concept of indefinite deferral to Benjamin's messianism, one that has no immediate political significance (without the help of Schmitt)" (Britt 2010, 268).[23] Yet when considered together with his critique of police violence, Benjamin's messianism uses "indefinite deferral" as a convenient description for the immediate, inexpressibly devastating effects of police violence right now. For Benjamin, the police act as if in a state of exception decided not by the sovereign but rather by the system of violence of which they are a part. Their power is immediate and subversive, both against the state and in deadly collusion with raw, inhuman power.

Against both sources of police violence, divine violence ends coercive violence demanded by law, and violence as its own law. It is thus not the case that Benjamin's divine violence makes "new forms of politics" possible (Cimino 2016, 111). As fundamental meontology, messianic divine violence in Benjamin ends all politics, for all time. Divine violence for Benjamin is the "messianic cessation of happening"; as such, it does not reinitiate "happening" (McKinney 2011, 502). This does not mean that reading Benjamin through Paul or vice versa is fundamentally incorrect. Indeed, as Kroeker notes, "for Benjamin, this weak messianic power accomplishes what Marx's proletariat revolution cannot. It hollows out the progressivist alienating, abstracting grip of the capitalist count from within, but with reference to the very sovereign power of creation—that is, redeeming love. For Paul, the *ekklesia*—those who are called out in the various callings—is precisely this classless society where all are freed by becoming slaves of the

Messiah" (Kroeker 2005, 51). Agamben's focus on law leads him to deemphasize the role total revolutionary liberation plays in Paul, and likewise in Benjamin (Svenungsson 2017, 68). For "weak messianic power" should not be understood as limited or bastardized messianism. It means instead messianic power acting in history as "redeeming love" that abolishes division between human beings to create beloved community.

V. King's State of Exception

In King's philosophy, a special place in the beloved community is reserved for African Americans because of the existential circumstances racial segregation creates (Baldwin 1986, 104). Because separation is the sin of Nonbeing, racism is the science of sin, and segregation its empirical experiment. The attempt to overcome segregation nonviolently undermines the essence of Nonbeing. In this sense, King's philosophy is as much a meontology in the vein of Benjamin and Heidegger as it is fundamental ontology reimagined. While "King's theology focused on the themes of justice, love, and hope, all grounded in the black church's faith in Jesus Christ," as Cone has firmly established, his meontology is grounded in Pauline eschatology seen in and as African American history (Cone 1986, 22). The personalism King encountered at Boston University among DeWolf, Brightman, and others "held that the human personality, i.e., all individual persons, was the ultimate intrinsic value in the world," and was for this reason "extremely attractive to King [because] it placed human equality, and respect for all human individuals, at the center of the social value system" (Garrow 1986, 12–13). However, personalism could not explain the larger metaphysical issues that interested King. He sought to honor personalism's approach while developing an anti-racist ontology that engaged with messianic concerns.

Indeed, King's reference to Isaiah 40 in the 1963 "Dream" speech—with which he "told how he longed for that day when the glory of the Lord shall appear, valleys would be exalted and mountains would be made low, a time when freedom will have come at last"—would not have been possible from the perspective of a strict personalism (Downing 1987, 20). Personalism is inadequate to understanding King both historically and philosophically. A 1991 *First Things* editorial captures the essence of the matter well: "Martin Luther King, Jr. is rightly honored as a hero in the telling of the American story—not because of his personal virtue but because he was the chosen instrument to advance a morally imperative change in our common life. His character was grievously flawed. He was, to borrow from Saint Paul, an 'earthen vessel'—a very earthen vessel. For believers this only underscores the truth that, as the Apostle says, 'the transcendent power belongs to God and not to us'" ("Theses" 1991, 7). To frame it theologically, Franklin reminds us that "King's eclectic Protestant understanding of human sinfulness and possibility undergirded his skepticism regarding overly optimistic proposals for social reform. Based on his personal experience and nurture in a black family and church, his encounters with racism and his formal education as a young adult, especially his reading of Augustine, Paul Tillich, and Reinhold Niebuhr, he was convinced that persons were created in God's image, but that that image was now distorted due to sin" (Franklin 1990, 68). King begins with an understanding of experience as personal, only to develop a concept of existential experience as universally distorted by Nonbeing. Personalism reaches the point of sin's universal obstruction, which must then be a matter for messianism.

As Black theologians after King who have embraced his messianism emphasize, liberation through racial unity saves all races. Through abject suffering, African America stands poised to redeem the world through beloved community (Garber 1975, 110). This was noticed in 1963 by King's commentators in the popular press as well. Calling him the "Apostle of Crisis," a reporter for the *Saturday Evening Post* remarked, "King endows this American struggle with qualities of messianic mission. A short man whose thick neck and heavy shoulders convey an impression of height and power, he can fill New York's cavernous Riverside Church with eloquence about 'the battering rams of historical necessity,' or set rural Negro Baptists in Georgia to clapping and shouting rhythmic responses when he says, 'The cloud is dark, but the sun is shining on the other side'" (Cleghorn 1963, 16). This messianism connects the "Apostle of Crisis" "with the Apostle Paul on matters of race and the new humanity," since King sees a humanity unified in Being to the point of the apocalyptic elision of all inessential difference (Waddell 2012, 51). For King, "the fierce urgency of now" is the messianic *Jetztzeit* meant to suspend "the myth of time," or the instrumental reason of the humanist tradition in the unity of Being (Simpson 2008, 59).

The idea that Benjamin rejects nonviolence as an ontologically valid mode of civil disobedience may seem to have little to offer practical struggles with police violence, and fly in the face of King's nonviolence, which has been the most effective means to bringing about legislative change in America. Yet, surprisingly,

King's and Benjamin's structural understanding of police violence as political mean is similar, despite reaching very different conclusions about divine violence as an end. Unlike Benjamin, however, who identifies the force of divine violence within the system itself as an aporetic effect inherent in provision for the state of exception, King acknowledges no structural capacity for the state of exception because, from the point of view of African Americans, the state always operates in the state of exception. The state of exception is African America's basic norm.

The appeal to God acknowledges the lack of universally applied legal norms in the United States. God provides the basis for all law, with police violence acting as the unholy upholding of Nonbeing. King's "general strike" is nonviolence as the rejection not of the state's sovereignty but rather of all human authority. This is not Benjamin's ultimate sense of divine violence, which is pure negation without recuperation in established doctrinal norms. King's "Letter" shares Benjamin's fundamental insights into the force of law and nature of police violence yet disagrees with his sense of divinity and human potential. In other words, King and Benjamin share the same structural views on state violence and transcendence, yet their ontologies are fundamentally opposed. King ascribes agency to human being through intentional surrender to divine authority, whereas Benjamin limits the power of the will in the face of discursive aporia structuring the rule of law. The reason King appeals to God rather than critical theory as a form of revelation has to do with African America's position within the constant state of exception. Benjamin's theory of law makes sense only in a society in which all citizens enjoy the same rights in the same way. For Benjamin, law's aporia exists in the concept of a Gnostic state of exception, which implies a stable normative state equally applicable to all. The Gnostic state of exception would suspend citizens' rights where otherwise they would be upheld. King points out that African Americans live in a constant state of exception.

This perpetual state of lawlessness is made evident in police violence, which makes the law by which African Americans live by preserving state and federal authority above God's sovereignty. For King, this is the result of "humanism." The authority police violence serves is anthropological, by which "humanism" assigns its own racial ontology as the measure of law's legitimacy and state sovereignty. King rejects this ontology, which he sees as an illegitimate form of humanist-driven sovereignty. For King, racist police violence is the result of the Gnostic "humanist" tradition—or "metaphysics since Plato," as Heidegger might put it—and cause for civil disobedience.

Conclusion
Eros as Nonviolence

AS MENTIONED EARLIER, King is not at all silent on eros. Indeed, erotic love is the dialectical opposite of agape, urging retribution as will to power. For King, eros is a negative emotion perverting reconciliatory agape by driving toward the sin of Nonbeing. Eros is *libido dominandi*, and King, along with Heidegger—and Adorno, who with Horkheimer called Plato "the philosopher of power"—would agree. For King, Adorno, and Heidegger, Plato's thought is the philosophical-historical source of this *libido dominandi*. Yet in the history of philosophy this term means something different to each thinker. For King, it is a history of segregation as sin and alienation from God's unifying love; for Adorno, it entails the creation of second nature as the means to dominate society; and for Heidegger, it is the obfuscation of existential truth. Yet whereas King and Adorno each respond positively to the question of Being—with King equating it with God's love and Adorno rejecting the question entirely—Heidegger refuses to name or renounce Being, leaving it an existential question. For Adorno, this ambivalence reinscribes Heidegger in the Platonic tradition he attempts to destroy (Hammer 2020, 474–475).

Specifically, Adorno argues that "εἶδος [eidos] (which is just the old Platonic name for essence), is reproduced in Heidegger's concept of being, in the notion of the separation of being from the entire realm of beings" (Adorno 2019, 190). Because of this, Heidegger "defends the claim that being itself hardly permits any other historical relationship to it than this sacrilegious approach and the forgetfulness of being which accompanies it. We are thus eventually driven to downright Gnostic speculations about the character of being itself, as if it were a sort of Evil Demon that has already destined human beings to mistake their own relationship to it" (Adorno 2019, 192). For Adorno, the gnostic structure of Being Heidegger posits is itself part of Plato's authoritarian Doctrine of Truth, irrespective of Being's ascriptive label of "eidos," "eros" or "libido." For, Adorno argues, in Heideggerian *Existenzphilosophie*, existence, which thereby declares itself to be the criterion of thinking, is already the lie of a self-appointed elite. Lacking anything beyond itself, anything to which it might open itself, it confers validity on its own decrees in an authoritarian way, just as, in political practice, the dictator confers validity on his own world-view. Through this reduction of thought to the thinker, the flow of thinking, through which alone it can become thinking at all, and in which alone subjectivity can live, is arrested. Subjectivity, precisely as the heavily trodden ground of truth, is objectified. All this can already be overheard in the word "personality." (Adorno 2019, 232)

Does Heidegger's reinscription of Platonic "truth" expose even the structural appropriation of his (and indeed any) "thinking of Being" to attack as authoritarianism? Paradoxically, would King's thought then be vulnerable to this criticism? The answer this question lies in a brief, proxy confrontation between Heidegger and King in the work of Heidegger's student Herbert Marcuse.

It is not surprising that many students were enthralled by Heidegger's "authoritarian pedagogy," as it conferred "validity on his own world-view." That said, it perhaps comes as a surprise that Heidegger's former student Marcuse would have remained invested in him personally and professionally after their apparent break in 1933, when Heidegger joins the National Socialist Party (Peterson 2005, 599). The troubling aspects of Heidegger's philosophy, considering his active political commitments, caused Marcuse and others to stop working with him, while continuing to influence their work. Indeed, in his attempt to reverse Heidegger's Platonic authoritarian thought, Marcuse maintains the conceptual structure of his former teacher's destruction of metaphysics while replacing Heidegger's terminology with Freud's (Janicaud 1969, 169–170).[1] This led Habermas to state in 1968 that Marcuse's psychoanalytic critical theory cannot be understood without seeing in it "the persistence of categories from *Being and Time* . . . in the concepts of Freudian drive theory out of which Marcuse develops a Marxian historical construct" (quoted in Sokolsky-Tifft 2020, 162). Hardly reproducing the philosophy of history presented in the Frankfurt School with which he is associated, Marcuse's thought continues to exhibit the influence of Heidegger's fundamental ontology. Marcuse's own understanding of his philosophy's relation to Heidegger's is that of an overcoming. Marcuse continued a long correspondence with his former teacher, even after Heidegger rationalized the Holocaust in their letters (Luft 1994, 488). He claims that he and other students were completely unaware of Heidegger's National Socialism until 1933, and that elements of Nazi thought became apparent "ex-post" in *Being and Time*'s morbid fascination with death. In a 1977 interview in which the subject comes up, Marcuse states:

> It is very good that you bring up the tremendous importance the notion of death has in his philosophy, because I believe that is a very good starting point for at least briefly discussing the famous question of whether Heidegger's Nazism was already noticeable in his philosophy prior to 1933. Neither in his lectures, nor in his seminars, nor personally, was there any hint of his sympathies for Nazism. So, his openly declared Nazism came as a complete surprise to us. From that point on, of course, we asked ourselves the question: did we overlook indications and anticipations in *Being and Time* and the related writings? And we made one interesting observation, ex-post (I want to stress that, ex-post, it is easy to make this observation): in *Being and Time* the essential characteristics of existence or Dasein . . . give a picture which plays well on the fears and frustrations of men and women in a repressive society—a joyless existence: overshadowed by death and anxiety; human material for the authoritarian personality. I see now in this philosophy, ex-post, a very powerful devaluation of life, a derogation of joy, of sensuousness, fulfillment. And we may have had the feeling of it at that time, but it became clear only after Heidegger's association to Nazism became known. (Quoted in Sokolsky-Trfft 2020, 163)

In this reading, Marcuse's championing of the pleasure principle as the drive to live negates any National Socialism in his teacher's philosophy. Despite Heidegger's refusal in his correspondence with him to acknowledge Nazi criminality, Marcuse still in 1977 cannot grasp Habermas's 1968 point that the categories of Heidegger's fundamental ontology are National Socialist in structure, and these categories have been replicated in Marcuse's reconfiguration of Freud and Marx. Oddly, Marcuse himself saw this in 1934, writing in "German Philosophy, 1871–1933":

> Heidegger's philosophy is wedded to the idea of an authentic existence that is realized through a firm willingness to die for one's own possibilities. It is here that Heidegger's existential analytic is transformed into a politics of heroic, racist realism . . . the characteristics of authentic existence—the resoluteness toward death, the decision, the risking of life, and the acceptance of destiny—become the fundamental categories of the racist worldview. (Marcuse 2005b: 161)

Heidegger's "racist realism" is clear in his politics of heroism, as are his "fundamental categories of the racial worldview [or world picture]."

Marcuse read Heidegger in 1934 in relation to Nazi racism and believed that his own Freudian Marxism had overcome it, even at the categorical level of fundamental ontology. Perhaps Marcuse's failure to overcome Heidegger's fundamental ontology led Adorno to remark that Marcuse was "hindered [only] by Judaism from being a fascist!" (quoted in Thomson 2000, 204–205). Chalking this up to "vicious intrigue," Thomson does not investigate the matter further and concentrates instead on Marcuse's de-Nazification activities in the immediate postwar period. His reading of Feenberg's book, like the book itself, does not question the political foundation of Marcuse's own philosophy in terms of Heidegger's National Socialism, despite granting that the early continuity between Marcuse's and Heidegger's philosophical categories persists. Indeed, Feenberg agrees with Habermas that Marcuse never abandoned the ontological categories of *Being and Time* yet does not perceive this as a problem (Scharff 2007, 91). Feenberg insists "Heidegger's thought had a continuing influence" on Marcuse (Feenberg 2013, 172). In particular, the two shared a similar attitude toward the reifying effects of technology as an example of the failed project of Enlightenment (Feenberg 2003, 39). From "a Heideggerian standpoint," Marcuse would seem to have merely substituted "sociology for ontology. Is there not a more fundamental ontological level shared by all these various types of Dasein? Marcuse would agree, but he argues that that fundamental level can only be described starting out from the concrete human situation that is characterized by the struggle for the necessities of life" (Feenberg 2013, 173). Richard Wolin sums up *Being and Time*'s category problem as it relates to Marcuse's search for an existential Marxism in the early 1930s. Wolin writes:

> *Being and Time* operates with a conceptual distinction between "ontological" ("existential") and "ontic" ("existentiell") planes of analysis. The former level refers to fundamental structures of human Being-in-the-world whose specification seems to be the main goal of Heidegger's 1927 work. The latter dimension refers to the concrete, "factical" actualization of the "existential" categories on the plane of everyday life-practice. It is this level that exists beyond the purview of "existential analysis" or "fundamental ontology" properly so-called. Yet, if this is the case, then the dimension of ontic life or everyday concretion would seem to fall beneath the threshold of Heidegger's ontological vision. And consequently, his

category of "historicity" would never be capable of accounting for the events of "real history." The dilemma is further compounded by the fact that Heidegger's existential analytic treats "everydayness" as such—and thus the sphere of "ontic life" in its entirety—as a manifestation of "inauthenticity." (Wolin 1991, 25-26)

"Yet," Smith writes, "instead of discarding the idea of historicity, Marcuse reaffirms it. In effect, he condemns his earlier approach to historicity as—a violation of the principle of historicity" (Smith 1992, 5-6). As Smith explains:

Adopting Heidegger's category of "thrownness" (*Geworfenheit*), Marcuse emphasized that Existence is "thrown" before us empirically. But Being, as necessity, is ulterior to Existence. Historicity, the "Being" of history, is thus the ontological ground of "thrown" Existence. This is wholly Heideggerian. But now Marcuse departs sharply from Heidegger to say (à la Lukács) that "historical necessity" is linked to revolution. For Marcuse, unlike Heidegger, Being is the Becoming of social transformation. (Smith 1992, 4)

Despite Heidegger's historicity being divorced from material history, and therefore from revolution's historical necessity, Marcuse doubles down on his fundamental ontology to establish a Heideggerian sense of historicity through Marx's philosophy of history. Marcuse's work for the de-Nazification commission did not alter his sense of fundamental ontology. As part of the de-Nazification commission, Marcuse formulated an ideology-based theory of anti-Semitism (Müller 2002, 154). Marcuse did not, however, read this back into the Heideggerian fundamental ontology grounding his postwar thought. He criticizes Heidegger not for lacking a social ontology, as Holman suggests, but rather for maintaining a sense of historicity that does not allow for communication between fundamental ontology and lived society (Holman 2012, 101).

This would also be the sense in which King perceives Heidegger's philosophy, and Arnold L. Farr has written that King's critical strategy of internal political critique was exactly that of Herbert Marcuse in the enormously popular *Eros and Civilization* (Farr 2009, 96). The argument, however, is hard to sustain beyond surface agreement between Marcuse and King, given that Marcuse was highly critical of nonviolence philosophies. For Marcuse, nonviolent resistance panders to unproductively narrow racial identification confined to and defined by a national context instead of embracing a numerically superior global, multiracial solidarity, thus excluding the oppressed from militarily supported political processes and hindering their preparedness for inevitable armed civil disobedience. He insists "that preaching nonviolence on principle reproduces the existing institutionalized violence. And in monopolistic industrial society this violence is concentrated to an unprecedented extent in the domination that penetrates the totality of society. In relation to this totality the right of liberation is in its immediate appearance a particular right. Thus, the conflict of violence appears as a clash between general and particular or public and private violence, and in this clash the private violence will be defeated until it can confront the existing public power as a new general interest" (Marcuse 2005, 62-63).

Here, Marcuse speaks indirectly yet obviously to the nonviolent protests embraced by the Civil Rights Movement and led by King. The critical theorist tacitly suggests that King's intervention is ultimately false in intent and execution, in that despite their refusal to commit violence, nonviolent protesters cannot recuse themselves from the cycle of force that lies at the heart of the legal system within which nonviolent protest is content to remain.[2] In other words, nonviolent protesters cannot escape the authority and force of law that they attempt to overturn. For they are unwilling to meet this law with the violence that authorizes its legitimate use, regardless of whether its application against nonviolent protest addresses the abstract or extralegal issues of inequality activists seek to arrest. This means that, despite the unlawful use of violence in the dominant social order's enforcement of extralegal racist policy, the attempt to redress the matter nonviolently meets resistance from the medium of political discourse to which it seeks to appeal yet in which it is unable to intervene. Without violence, activists and insurgents possess no legal means with which to penetrate the legal order itself.

Marcuse sees this defensive act of violence as representative and therefore as influential. While the student protest itself may not commit acts of directed violence, it nevertheless inspires such acts against the state in the form of attacks on either important institutions or individuals, themselves representing the structure of oppression preventing the realization of natural human freedom. Hence, Marcuse is very close to a theory of the partisan for the New Left, where violence, while not recommended for the purely representational student protest movement, is nevertheless necessary from individuals and associations unalloyed with yet inspired by the campus protests.[3] Much like King's nonviolent protests, then, Marcuse meant for violent confrontations between the state and protesters to take place. For Marcuse, violence creates a clearing in civilization's totalizing logos, revealing eros as veiled social Being. In this sense, Marcuse's ideology critique remains deeply indebted to the alienating doctrine of truth Heidegger identifies in Plato. King's, however, does not. His rejection of eros as the drive to essentialist separatism forms the negative dialectical basis for the positive appropriation of Being as Being-in-love. For King, Platonic eros is the necessary starting point for gnostic reconciliation within a transcended Heideggerian structure of Being. Marcuse does not escape this structure; he burrows further within it.

Martha Nussbaum, who, as noted earlier, suggests that King was silent on sexuality, would agree more with Marcuse about eros than with King, making it obvious why she cannot acknowledge King's brief yet definitive statements on erotic love. This refusal to do King justice, so to speak, extends to her highly attenuated yet impactful presentation of Malcolm X. Nussbaum understands Malcolm to have "urged people to reject King's nonviolent movement as a slavish compromise with white power" (Nussbaum 2018, 116). She thinks Malcolm believed that "to be revolutionary, anger has to remain 'hot,' meaning poised to engage in violent retributive aggression" (Nussbaum 2018, 116). Nussbaum takes the image of Malcolm X for that of Huey P. Newton, and in so doing perceives both incorrectly. Neither Malcolm nor Newton saw violence as revolutionary; they advocated armed self-defense. They rejected King's nonviolence because it disarmed a community under incessant, irrational, violent attack. Malcom and Newton were revolutionary, insofar as they believed Black self-reliance and self-defense would demand racial recognition, provoking fundamental social and political change in the United States. Their philosophies were revolutionary because they rejected retribution as beside the point.

In Nussbaum, Newton and the BPP are absent, and Malcolm is little more than a straw man with which she condemns Black Power as a retributive movement diametrically opposed to King's belief in nonviolence and racial forgiveness. Yet this two-dimensional approach to Black radical thought prevents Nussbaum from perceiving Black *power* in King's philosophy as well. Instead, she sees Black Power as driven by negative emotions, including the desire for racial retribution, and therefore as possessing a diminished capacity to judge civil rights according to intuitions of fairness, in conformity to an equanimous moral character. This understanding of Black Power informs Nussbaum's reflections on the programmatic study of Black culture in higher education. She writes in "African-American Studies":

> Many curricular problems have arisen as institutions try to include African Americans and their heritage. Among these, none is more difficult than the demand for an "Afrocentric"' curriculum. While the liberal cosmopolitan demands inclusive learning for all citizens, a more radical and more retributive approach to the legacy of racism is to demand a curriculum that is unbalanced in a direction opposite to that of earlier imbalances, Afrocentric where the old curriculum was Eurocentric. . . . Such a retributive approach has a limited place in the academy, when it prompts us to uncover prejudice that has been parading as objectivity. But it cannot be productive when it departs from the pursuit of truth and substitutes a new distortion for the old one. (Nussbaum 1997, 178)

She goes on to insist on King's vision of love in the World House as the curricular model for African American studies, citing how the president of Morehouse University used the idea of one of that institution's most distinguished graduates:

> Morehouse College, Spelman's brother institution, has recently initiated curricular changes that follow this same promising pattern. New President Walter Massey, a well-known scientist and scientific administrator, has taken as the motto of his administration "creating a world house at Morehouse": This goal, he argues, requires strengthening the offerings in African-American studies by insisting on a rigorous structure for the departmental major and in general by infusing new depth and excellence into the curriculum. But it also requires an emphasis on the interdependence of all the world's peoples and their need for mutual understanding. The "world house" theme, Massey continues, takes its inspiration from Morehouse alumnus Dr. Martin Luther King, Jr. (Nussbaum 1997, 179)[4]

Nussbaum regards any African American studies curriculum that does not embrace an interracial understanding of knowledge production, favoring racial exclusion and blame in instructed material, as retributive and therefore as epistemologically flawed. Furthermore, the curriculum would be inimical to King's message and his sense of critical freedom.

Nussbaum's idea of critical freedom is very close to that of bell hooks's concept practice of freedom, described earlier. In clarifying this concept, hooks has written that whereas the Civil Rights Movement "practice of freedom" is one of love and universalism, the Black Power movement's rejects these notions in favor of eroticism and racial particularity. Lamenting the disappearance of a revolutionary ideal in contemporary politics, hooks writes in "The Practice of Freedom":

> In this society, there is no powerful discourse on love emerging either from politically progressive radicals or from the Left. The absence of a sustained focus on love in progressive circles arises from a collective failure to acknowledge the needs of the spirit and an overdetermined emphasis on material concerns. Without love, our efforts to liberate ourselves and our world community from oppression and exploitation are doomed. As long as we refuse to address fully the place of love in struggles for liberation we will not be able to create a culture of conversion where there is a mass turning away from an ethic of domination.... Critically examining these blind spots, I conclude that many of us are motivated to move against domination solely when we feel our self-interest directly threatened. (hooks 1994, 243)

Condemning the selfish, materialist determination of love in contemporary culture, hooks looks instead to establish selfless love as a powerful basis for the recognition of human being-in-freedom in all of its diversity.

She believes "eros is a force that enhances our overall effort to be self-actualizing, that it can provide an epistemological grounding informing how we know what we know" (hooks 1994, 195). Here, hooks expresses an idea of eros as the phenomenological ground of all knowledge. Eros is more than erotic love; it is self-care awakened in desire for the self and actuated by desire. As "epistemological grounding," eros informs all experience and determines the nature of relationships as the basis for being-in-the-world. The practice of love, then, is that of freedom, insofar as Being-in-love establishes the self in the world as knowing subject conditioned by an openness to the other achieved in ethical awareness, or recognition, of shared humanity. In other words, love forms intersubjective bonds without susceptibility to instrumental objectification, whereby the self and other express mutual concern or desire for human compassion. In this way, the epistemological ground of "what we know" is also the ontological expression of beloved community.

Because the expressive ground of the operable community provides the epistemological ground of love's knowledge, eros can be said to be a political and pedagogical matter as much as it pertains to the private, emotional life of the subject. Like Nussbaum, hooks sees no clear separation between politics and the emotions. In this respect, teaching is the practice of freedom, in that it enacts the political-pedagogical love scene of self-care as the ethical recognition of both the other and the beloved community of others (Bauer 2000, 265). In this way, hooks appears to provide a synthesis of King's spiritual activism and

Heidegger's *Existenzphilosophie*. Yet hooks does not perceive King as some do, as a mystic prophet who "forged a global spiritual vision and social mystic consciousness rare in the history of the world" (Lanzetta 2018, 240). Her understanding of King is practical and profound, taking King to be a social philosopher of the highest order who grounded his thought in a political ontology of love. In this way, hooks elaborates "black feminist love-politics' insistence on transcending the self and producing new forms of political communities as a kind of affective politics" (Nash 2011, 3). Indeed, for hooks "the beloved community and the politics of love" offer means to "revolutionary action" as the emancipatory practice of freedom inherent in the pedagogical scene (Fitts 2011, 112). For hooks, "the practice of love and the practice of freedom are inextricably connected, and any liberatory project must be undertaken within the context of an ethics of love" (Monahan 2011, 102).

"Drawing strength from the life and work of Martin Luther King," hooks presents in her work reflections on the politics of love as Being-in-love and Dasein as a relation of self-care and the desire for beloved community. Addressing questions of Being Itself as a political project, hooks elaborates indirectly on the Heideggerian elements of King's philosophy in the practice of freedom (hooks 1993, 11).[5] Education, then, is not "a 'tool' to prepare students for global citizenship, to get them ready for the interlocking and interdependent world in which they live," as it is in Nussbaum (Grant 2012, 912). Rather, it is a weapon for revolutionary change. In this respect, two types of appropriation emerge in King's philosophical reception, that of perfection and that of destruction. In hooks's version of it, a vision of African American studies true to King's World House concept would be more focused on reparation than Nussbaum believes. Marcuse would also be guilty of superficially reading King not as an integrationist, which he was, but rather as one seeking to integrate within a perfected version of the existing political-legal order.[6]

However, as hooks points out in a 1993 joint interview with Cornel West, this political-legal order is upheld by white supremacy, and in "a white supremacist culture, isn't the most dangerous thing Black people can do is to begin to love ourselves?" (Hamilton 1993, 3). It is unclear whether Nussbaum considers Black self-love a political category or in any way a politically commensurable desire. Her 1997 defense of African American studies to be modeled according to what she takes to be King's critical freedom does not consider the history and progress of Black studies in the academy. Given the fact that "as of 2005, approximately 9 percent of all institutions of higher education in the United States have academic units offering African-American Studies degrees," it would appear that a different approach to the discipline than Nussbaum's would be in order (Rojas 2006, 2147). Indeed, the Black Campus movement, which provoked institutional change in higher education and led to the establishment of African American studies as a discipline, was a branch of Black Power, which Nussbaum sees as detrimental to the true goals of African American studies.[7] In 2004, Nussbaum wrote that unlike Rawls, who sought "a procedural justification for political principles," she "makes intuitive arguments about what a good outcome is, in the form of an account of a minimally decent and just society; political procedures would be defined in accordance with what promotes that outcome" (Nussbaum 2004 , 196–197). The problem, then, is a fundamental difference of opinion. King did not see American society as minimally decent and just; he believed American democracy had the potential to be decent and just. Closer to Marcuse than either would ever have allowed to be imagined, King held the strong belief that Black *power* was self-love as authentic civil disobedience. He saw Black *power* as love beyond the law, and believed Black *power* was justice.

Notes

Introduction: Ontology and Nonviolence

1. Most notably as Kwame Ture, with Charles V. Hamilton, in *Black Power: Politics of Liberation in America* (1967).

2. Part of what recent work on King decries is the popularization and neutralization of his radicalism. See Shelby and Terry 2018, and Rose 2019, discussed later.

3. My recent work, *Phenomenal Blackness* (2022), looks more closely at Black Power philosophies and the question of racial essentialism. *Black Fascisms* (2007) also examined the place of race in Black radicalism, when all other forms of political resistance failed, and a unique form of Black separatist authoritarianism presented a desperate alternative.

4. See Crawford and Lewis 2019; Rose 2019; Jahanbegloo 2018; Shelby and Terry 2018; Terry 2018a and 2018b; Birt 2012, and Ansbro 1982. See also Krishnamurthy 2015. For a much less recent understanding of King's political philosophy, see Walton 1971.

5. King's avowed, revolutionary anti-humanism will be discussed in detail later. It is important to note that, for King, revolutionary anti-humanism does not mean revolutionary inhumanism, in the sense it might in Fanon. On Fanon and revolutionary inhumanism, see Nesbitt 2013.

6. On class and race in the Civil Rights Movement, see Bloom 1987.

7. This longer history, however, ended with the start of a new history ushered in by the "Third World." In *Black Power*, Ture and Hamilton write: "Black Power means that black people see themselves as part of a new force, sometimes called the 'Third World'; that we see our struggle as closely related to liberation struggles around the world. We must hook up with these struggles" (Ture and Hamilton 1967, 107). If successful, doing so would start "a new history of Man, a history which will have regard to the sometimes prodigious theses which Europe has put forward, but which will also not forget Europe's crimes, of which the most horrible was committed in the heart of man, and consisted of the pathological tearing apart of his functions and the crumbling of his unity" (Ture and Hamilton 1967, 138).

8. Morgan provides a different take on Black Panther imagery, mostly ignoring its appropriation for the purpose of undermining the BPP's reputation and legacy. See Morgan 2019. On the BPP newspaper and revolutionary aesthetics, see Gaiter 2020. On BPP military aesthetics, see Ongiri 2020.

9. In other words, it obscures the "engines of the Black Power movement." For more on the powerful forces combining to form a complex, multifaceted concept of Black Power, see Conyers 2007.

10. Peniel Joseph has described "Black Power Studies" several times as the means to correct this impression and expand our understanding of this crucial history. See Joseph 2009b, 2008, 2006, and 2001, among others.

11. Farmer 2019, Spencer 2016, Joseph 2009b and 2006, Austin 2006, and Lazerow and Williams 2006 are notable recent studies embracing this diversity of thesis and approach.

12. This negative impression is in part due to a repressive political, legal, and pop cultural campaign to discredit the organization, run by U.S. law enforcement and beginning as early as 1966. See C. Jones 1988.

13. In 1956, *Ebony* magazine's Lerone Bennett can already write about the "King Plan for Freedom," situating King in the Black radical tradition from the Civil Rights leader's earliest interventions in the public sphere. See Bennett 1956. Kreiss sees the appropriation of "the master's tools" that led to the development of the BPP beginning in 1952 as part of a wider field of Black radical thought that would include most avant-garde and vanguard Black cultural production throughout the 1950s. See Kreiss 2008.

14. For the BPPs defensive theorization of the ghetto, see Tyner 2006.

15. King's dream was not the American dream. The "Dream" speech speaks of the American dream unfulfilled and describes a new vision of humanity beyond national specificity. See Colaiaco 1984 and Sundquist 2009.

16. This view of King, for example, would see the 1963 "Letter from a Birmingham Jail" as a manifesto, instead of a constitutively rhetorical essay or sermon. See Westbrook 2013.

17. On King's militant nonviolence, see Colaiaco 1988.

18. Although Boxill does not do this, the images of Malcolm X and King elsewhere reflexively represent the separatist and assimilationist positions, respectively, he describes. For a more reflective discussion, see Corlett 1995.

19. See Boxill 2003.

20. See also Boxill 1984.

21. See also Appiah 1985.

22. See also Yancy 2012a, 2012b.

23. For an account of "Afro-American Studies and the rise of African-American philosophy," see Henry 2006.

24. Sociological critique has been the dominant mode of inquiry in academic African American philosophy. See R. Jones 2004 on "imagining Black communities" in African American sociopolitical philosophy. For some contrast, see Lott 2020, and of course Lott and Pittman 2003.

25. Language occupies a central place in Heidegger's later philosophy, where it "houses" human being's "dwelling" (Malpas 2012, 20).

26. On Heidegger and "earth," see also Taminiaux 1989.

27. There is no shortage of King biographies and analyses, and to expect each one to

appear here is unrealistic. King studies is its own field and rich enough to accommodate a highly targeted presentation of research. While this book uses some biographical detail, it is concerned with presenting King's intervention in ontology from a philosophically imminent perspective. Biographies and other texts consulted for this that nevertheless do not receive direct treatment here are Joseph 2020; Parr 2018; Ling 2015; Wills 2011; Baldwin 2010; Frady 2006; Kirk 2005; Garrow 2001 and 1986; Moses 1998; Smith and Zepp 1974.

28. King's philosophical use of "freedom," for instance, was so ubiquitous as to have been unavoidable. For a detailed, data-driven, quantitative analysis of King's inescapable repetition of the word "freedom" in public discourse from 1955 to his death, see Miller and Turci 2006.

29. King's understanding of agape and eros's dialectic is derived directly from Tillich's discussion of the matter in *Morality and Beyond* (originally published in 1963). Tillich writes,

> Essential *libido* (toward food or sex, for example) is concretely directed to a particular object and is satisfied in the union with it, while existentially distorted *libido* is directed to the pleasure which may be derived from the relation to any encountered object. This drives existential *libido* boundlessly from object to object, while the essential *libido* is fulfilled if union with a particular object is achieved. This distinguishes the lover from the "Don Juan," and *agape*-directed *libido* from undirected *libido*. The moral imperative cannot be obeyed by a repression of *libido*, but only by the power of agape to control *libido* and to take it into itself as an element.
>
> *Eros* is a divine-human power. (Tillich 1995, 60–61)

For an analysis of Tillich's concept of "essential libido," see Irwin 1990.

Chapter One: Being and Nonviolence

1. It is, of course, understandable that King should have wanted to distance himself from Heidegger's thought publicly.

2. Several cultural theorists have relied on Heidegger in the past several years to elaborate Blackness and experience. While this study is not directly concerned with this avenue of speculative inquiry, it assumes these works asked the Heidegger question before undertaking a different sort of response. I am thinking of Fred Moten's work generally, and particularly Moten 2008 and 2007.

3. For his extensive writings on Heidegger and National Socialism, see Derrida 1989; Derrida 2016. On the Heidegger controversy, see Farías, Margolis, and Rockmore 1989; Faye 2009; Ott 1993; Rockmore 1992; Wolin 1993; and Young 1997.

4. On Heidegger and anti-Semitism, see Mitchell and Trawny 2017 and Trawny and Mitchell 2015.

5. For Heidegger, the essence of truth and that of freedom are the same, insofar as "freedom" signifies not freedom to do but rather freedom to be (Farber 1958, 526).

6. For an opposing view, see Soffer 1996, 548.

7. See also Karl Löwith's *Martin Heidegger and European Nihilism* (1995) for an equally damning portrait, here by a former student.

8. For Heidegger and Hitlerism's ontological racism, see McDonald 2010.

9. On the Black Notebooks generally, see Krell 2015.

10. For some key works in the critically wide-ranging Heidegger controversy, see Faye 2009; Sheehan 1992; Hérubel 1991; Farías, Margolis, and Rockmore 1989.

11. For a general account of the social sciences in Germany between 1933 and 1945, see Derks 1999.

12. As Blok points out, for Heidegger Platonism represents a "turning away from our earthly existence" (Blok 2011, 108). It is the origin of metaphysics (Warnek 1997, 70). As William Richardson puts it, "Metaphysics begins precisely at that moment when Being (at least as Heidegger conceives it) is forgotten, namely with Plato" (Richardson 1963, 273).

13. King also often named influences and intellectual inspirations in speeches and writings—a rhetorical device that placed him within various traditions. As Fulkerson shows, the practice has a "multiplicative ethical impact, since the auditor assumes they are a carefully chosen sample drawn from a much larger store of information" (Fulkerson 1979, 131).

14. On King, Rauschenbusch, and the "social gospel," see Rathbun 1968.

15. In this sense, King's "theology of social action" would have to be read as a philosophy of social action as well. On a contemporary's view of King's theology of social action, see Rathburn 1968.

16. David Levering Lewis writes in his 1970 biography of King that he "was troubled but not as profoundly as he may have supposed. Nietzsche was too shrilly atheistic and egocentric to maim him in his philosophic growth" (Lewis 2013, 35). This is a bold assessment that flies directly in the face of King's own testimony. Incredibly, in the same biography, Lewis also writes that King "lacked the comprehensive critical apparatus and the inspired vision that bless good philosophers" (Lewis 2013, 45). In fact, Lewis condemns King's desire to be a philosopher as "the venial intellectual arrogance of a young man who held a doctorate from one of the nation's better universities" (Lewis 2013, 44). It was "self-deception" and "self-mystification" (Lewis 2013, 45).

In direct rebuttal, Warren E. Steinkraus writes in 1973:

> Is there any connection between King the famed apostle of nonviolence and King the contemplative philosopher? The answer must be in the affirmative. He is probably the only professionally trained philosopher of this century who has had a world-wide impact on large numbers of ordinary citizens and in the halls of government. On a superficial level, King's debts to philosophy are obvious because his six books are full of references to philosophers and philosophic concepts. He knew his way around in the history of philosophy far better than in theology. (Steinkraus 1973, 93)

17. To be clear, this is King's reading of Gandhi, or rather his use of him. Enough work has been done on King and Gandhi to form a subfield in King studies. This book focuses on King and Tillich instead. For work on King and Gandhi, see Chakrabarty 2014.

18. See Gregg 1934.

Chapter Two: Nonbeing and Nonviolence

1. Tillich was very influential in 1950s and 1960s American philosophy, theology, and psychology. While it remains vital, his work is less well known now. For a study contemporary with Tillich, see Adams 1965. Tillich was even considered by some to have a philosophy of science. For this, see Cooper 1969. Tillich was also a close friend of Arendt's (his longtime secretary and mistress, Hilda Fränkel, was Arendt's best friend), and the two had friendly yet pointed political disagreements. On these, see Christophersen and Schulze 2002. Despite their differences and shaped by the same philosophical forces, Tillich and Arendt had more in common than perhaps they realized. The same holds true for Tillich's other philosophical interlocutors such as Horkheimer and Adorno, and opponents like Herbert Marcuse. On these relationships, see Danz 2018; Tillich et al. 2007; and Sturm 1994.

2. I have little to say about the charge of plagiarism brought against King by Theodore Pappas and others. My concern here is for King's useable knowledge. As this book demonstrates, the material in the dissertation is key to King's entire body of work, from reader in philosophy and theology to Civil Rights champion and martyr.

3. On Tillich's infusion of theology with metaphysics, see Schüssler 1995. See also Sturm 2016; O. Thomas 1996; and, for a view of an American contemporary, J. Thomas 1953.

4. On Tillich, King, and Kairos, see Earle 2017.

5. Watson has written that

> Hannah Arendt's observations about the pressures of past and future on any person in the "now" of a present moment are particularly apt for Martin Luther King, Jr. in Birmingham in April 1963. Caught in what he later in his "Dream" speech called the "fierce urgency of now," King wrote a document that was to transcend that "now" by both drawing on the richness of the past and looking toward the potentials of the future. Written, in part, as a response to a particular set of rhetorical exigencies, King's "Letter" also speaks directly and powerfully to larger cultural and political issues. King's ability to transcend the Birmingham of 1963 is because the "Letter" is a perfect example of kairos. Since King was the ideal rhetor at a critical moment to pen the "Letter," it transcends the Birmingham of 1963 to speak to the nation as a whole and to continue speaking to us, 40 years later. (Watson 2004, 1–2)

Regarding Kairos, it could be said that King creates the perfect moment of crisis for his "Letter."

6. King will have ignored the Marxism in Tillich's thought. On Tillich's Marxism, see Murphy 1984, 13. On Tillich's religious socialism, see Dorrien 2018.

7. The rhetoric of King's "Letter" is that of the Civil Rights Movement as a whole, featuring, as Patton writes, "the centrality of Kairos (rhetorical timing) and the blending of pathos (passion, authentic commitment, and alignment with audience values) are keys to both the micro and macro levels of the rhetoric of civil rights" (Patton 2004, 54). King also practiced "rhetorical distancing," or, as Osborn puts it, the attempt "to control how the participants in rhetorical transactions see themselves and the world that beckons them to action" (Osborn 2004, 33).

8. Time and eternity are central ideas in the "Letter." As Berry writes:

> King's "Letter" . . . achieves its distinctive and enduring rhetorical power because he was able to overcome in expressive form the historical, political, and deeply personal problem that inspired it—the problem of time. His argument develops three interrelated conceptions of time, which for expository convenience I label "sacred," "personal," and "patriotic" time. At the end of the "Letter," all three conceptions converge to affirm in a profound sense the timeliness not only of the demonstrations in Birmingham but of the civil rights revolution as a whole. King's challenge to his audience, both emotional and intellectual, is to achieve a new understanding of time and to fulfill its demands in a moment of crisis. (Berry 2005, 112)

King's "now-time" is crucial to the "Letter's" achievement and the rhetoric of civil rights. The "Letter's" Pauline "now-time" of philosophical crisis endows it with its "enduring rhetorical power," and led to King being dubbed "the apostle of crisis" in 1963. See Cleghorn 1963. See also Aeschliman 2005 for more on the enduring rhetorical and doctrinal qualities of the "Letter."

9. In this respect, King reproduces Tillich's "theology of correlation," which, according to Loomer, insists that theological method and content are "mutually determinative" (Loomer 1956, 150). For a general account of Tillich's method correlation, see Röbel 2017. For an idea of the enormous attention Tillich's book commanded at publication, see Macquarrie and Randall 1964 and Graf 2017.

10. The source of King's oratory influence is the communicative power and aesthetic beauty of his rhetorical brilliance, which in the moment could be taken for philosophical rigor, as perhaps was the case here. See Klein 1981, 30.

11. For a wider discussion of the place of God in King's moral reasoning, see Mikelson 1990.

12. We see this also in the 1954 sermon, "What Is Man?" (in King 1994f, 174-179).

13. For an authoritative account of Tillich's debt to Heidegger's fundamental ontology, see O'Meara 1968.

14. Dreisbach has written that the "core of Tillich's theological system is his doctrine of religious symbols. With this theory Tillich attempts to give a coherent and intelligible account of how the divine can become manifest to man" (Dreisbach 1975, 84).

15. As Demos maintains, God's infinity—understood as Being and time—is the basis of Tillich's theology (Demos 1958, 75).

16. For the source of this line, see Miller 1998, 6.

17. King said this in his April 15, 1960, "Statement to the Press at the Beginning of the Youth Leadership Conference."

18. "In his earlier writings," Schatzki writes, "the clearing is identical with human existence because the light that constitutes the clearing is human understanding, the lumen naturale in man. In his later writings, however, Heidegger no longer identifies the clearing with human understanding. The light in whose illumination things can manifest themselves to us is something distinct from human understanding and existence, and the latter are now viewed as that by which we apprehend (in Heidegger's language, are 'open for') this light and what appears in it" (Schatzki 1989, 80).

19. King's easily recognizable universalism was the key to his success. As Sabl writes, his "moral appeals for civil rights succeeded—and King himself became so venerated—because he used a form of democratic rhetoric that combined particularistic moral leadership with universalistic democratic appeals" (Sabl 1999, 33). These were general enough to engage with any iteration of democratic universalist theory.

Chapter Three: Black *power* as Nonviolence

1. From King's perspective, a breakdown in "communication" is tantamount to violence. See Benson 1970.

2. On this relationship and the "jeremiadic cry," see Bell 1993.

3. As Leff and Utley point out, King's rhetoric is simultaneously instrumental and constitutive, creating goal-oriented community identification rather than identifying essentialist group designations. See Leff and Utley 2004. See also Mott 1975. For King as an "identificatory conglomerate," see Worthington 2013.

4. Writing in 1968, Roberts suggests that King had no coherent theory of nonviolence before Montgomery (Roberts 1968, 228). The difficult inclusivity of King's nonviolence philosophy made recognizing it as a coherent, sustained metaphysical concept integral to King's thought problematic for contemporaries.

5. In this sense, Black Power studies could be said to begin with and instantly supplant Van Deburg's classic 1992 study.

6. The historiography of the Civil Rights Movement is also ongoing, attempting to draw an ever-wider picture of the era while placing greater emphasis on local interventions by little known groups. See Davis 2001.

7. This was in part intentional, as the BPP sought to broaden its appeal after 1968, diluting its race-based ideology and displacing its rhetoric of the gun. This led to a schism in the party, evident in the break between Newton and Eldridge Cleaver. For a contemporary account of the BPPs "rhetoric of the gun," see Courtright 1974. For a historical overview, see Finzsch 1999. For a firsthand, and first-person, documentary account of the BPP, see Foner 2014. See also Nesbitt 1972.

8. Revolutionary suicide is the willingness to die for one's revolutionary cause. It differs from nonviolence in that it seeks revolutionary change through self-defensive defiance rather than nonviolent disobedience out of love. For a good discussion of Newton's concept of revolutionary suicide, see Freer 2013.

9. See also Hughey 2005.

10. Joseph writes:

> Violence is crucial to understanding the Black Power years in the United States. The political rhetoric of Malcolm X and his forceful advocacy of self-defense and physical retaliation in the face of violence against civil rights workers set the stage for the movement's complicated relationship with violence. After Malcolm's death, both Stokely Carmichael and the Black Panther Party (originally the Black Panther Party for Self-Defense) deployed provocative rhetoric that threatened domestic racial upheavals in the face of continued economic misery and social injustice. By the late 1960s, with the proliferating civil disturbances and clashes between urban militants and law enforcement agencies, the Black Power era was to some extent contoured by violence. But while most Black Power organizations retained the right to self-defense, only a small number of groups, most notably the Black Panther Party, openly advocated proactive revolutionary violence. (Joseph 2009a, 1003)

11. According to Carson, King's aestheticized, romanticized carnality ultimately follows Harry Emerson Fosdick's understanding of sexual love in the Bible. Fosdick writes, "Love in the New Testament is not a sentimental and affectionate emotion as we so commonly interpret it" (King 1994c, 459n). In this context, as Carson is quick to note, "While the Greek language has three words for love, eros does not appear in the Greek New Testament" (in King 1994d, 121n).

12. On love and justice in King, see Beshai 2017.

13. On Heidegger and Platonic eros, see Gelven 1973; see also Rojcewicz 1997. On Heidegger's reading of the *Phaedrus* in his *Sophist* lectures, see Lier 2018 and Gonzalez 2015.

14. For King, this is both a spiritual and a material state occurring before the end of history. See Alsup 2009.

15. These include engaged in anti-colonial struggle. See Inwood 2009.

Chapter Four: Gnosticism and Nonviolence

1. King owes much of this thought on the "love-justice relationship" to Tillich. See Williams 2001.

2. For a brief overview of Voegelin and his thought, see Schmutz 2009. On Voegelin and the Continental tradition, see Trepanier and McGuire 2011. For Voegelin's "contribution to political science," see Trepanier 2018.

3. This may have also led Voegelin to hold very different views on Plato than did Heidegger and many of Heidegger's former students. That said, these views can to some

extent be seen as most complementary to Strauss's, in an interdisciplinary sense. See Pangle's essay on Strauss and Voegelin, particularly 232. For a narrative of Strauss's political development, from Weimar to America, see Armon 2010; Barber 2006; G. Smith 1997. For Strauss's critique of Heidegger, see O'Mahoney 2011 and S. Smith 1997. For readings of Strauss with Heidegger, see Velkey 2011, 2008; Ward 1987.

4. See Gontier 2013; Porter 2002; Baruzzi 2001; and Maier and Cockerill 2000.

5. In contradistinction, on the concept of the apolitical in German Jewish thought between the wars, see Gordon 2007.

6. I am thinking here of Badiou's *Saint Paul: The Foundation of Universalism* (originally published in 1997), which investigates how the

> paradoxical connection between a subject without identity and a law without support provides the foundation for the possibility of a universal teaching within history itself. Paul's unprecedented gesture consists in subtracting truth from the communitarian grasp, be it that of a people, a city, an empire, a territory, or a social class [one might add here "or a race"]. What is true (or just; they are the same in this case) cannot be reduced to any objective aggregate, either by its cause or by its destination. (Badiou 2003, 5)

However constitutive King's universalist rhetoric, it nevertheless remains instrumental as the sign of his representative exceptionality. In King, Parrhesia as self-revelation paves the path to universal justice.

7. The importance of the "image event" of Birmingham throws into relief the extent to which rhetoric for King is both literary and visual. Indeed, as Johnson writes: "The rhetorical problem is one of visibility: how to get the white moderate to see, quite literally, the actual fact of racism and thus realize the impossibility of laying hold of a moral and progressive identity in the face of the status quo brutality" (Johnson 2007, 2–3).

8. As Gaipa notes, "King . . . demonstrates the inherent instability of exclusive systems, finds liberating power in creative rhetorical play, and inverts center and margins to figure forth (from the inside out) a less hierarchical or dominating order" (Gaipa 2007, 281).

9. "Public reason" is here used in Rawls's sense. As Dyer and Stuart explain:

> The idea of public reason is based on the common-sense notion that reasonable people ought to show respect for one another in debate by offering the kinds of arguments and reasons that another person, from the standpoint of a different comprehensive doctrine, might find reasonable. Other liberal theorists have used "public reason" to denote what Rawls thinks is better called "secular reason" or reasons that do not require belief in God or adherence to any particular religious faith. Rawls wants to make clear, and says so in more than one place, that he is departing from that understanding of public reason. Rather, given the fact of reasonable pluralism and with a view to fundamental matters of basic justice and constitutional essentials Rawls's theory of public reason requires public officials

(and also citizens, who are to reason about constitutional fundamentals as though they were public officials) to avoid arguments sustained only by appealing to a comprehensive doctrine, whether religious or secular. (Dyer and Stuart 2013, 148–149)

10. On King's ethics, see E. Smith 1981.

11. King appears to have posed the same question as Arendt: Socrates or Heidegger? His answer seems to have been both. For Arendt's response, see Canovan 1990.

12. Heidegger found an unsettling ambiguity in Plato's rhetoric that, in its identification, may have enabled this form of politicization in Heidegger's thought. On his estimation of ambiguity in Plato's rhetoric, see Brogan 1997.

13. Relatedly, on Gnosis in the work of Jonas's friend and former Heidegger student Hannah Arendt, see Zawisza, 387.

14. On Tillich's philosophy of history, see Montgomery 1968.

15. Despite being well documented, the Heidegger-Arendt relationship, both as romance and as philosophical exchange, remains enigmatic. Among the countless attempts to decide the nature of either or both entanglements, see Villa 2007, Barash 2002, and Overenget 1995; on politics and remembrance; Bernauer 2013 on Arendt's "hallucinatinated" Heidegger; Jones 1998, on the two philosophers' "hidden dialogue"; Biskowski 1995 for Arendt's critique of Heidegger; Hinchman and Hiunchman 1984 for the philosopher's influence on Arendt's humanism; on their romantic intimacy, see Caladorne 2016 and Maier-Katkin and Maier-Katkin 2007.

16. Arendt's dissertation on Saint Augustine, directed by Jaspers, was in part a product of her association with Bultmann. On the dissertation's politics, see Breidenthal 1998. On Arendt, Jaspers, Heidegger, and politics, see Flakne 2002; and on Arendt and Christian theology more generally, see Davies 2014.

17. The German reads: "Paulus wird also gleichsam zur theologischen Metonymie der Kulturkrise, dies auch insofern, als in der Dialektik von Nomos und Pneuma die Gefahr jener gnostischen Interrelation aufbrechen konnte, die in Harnacks *Untersuchung über Marcion* von 1921 offenbar auch als Ausdruck der real gnostischen Gefahr der modernen Kultur und Kulturwissenschaft gedeutet werden möchte."

18. The enormous impact of Barth's thought includes the development of a Jewish Barthianism, described in Herskowitz 2017.

19. The German reads: "sieht Paulus nach Bultmann 'die Juden befangen,' da sie sich mittels der als Leistungen verstandenen 'Werke des Gesetzes' selbst sichern und vor Gott behaupten wollen und so ihr καύχημα suchen, statt der eigenen Geschopflichkeit und des Angewiesenseins auf die Gnade Gottes gewahr zu werden und Gott die Ehre zu geben."

20. The German reads: "Die zwei Faktoren, die wie keine anderen die maßgeblichen Impulse zur Dogmatisierung des Christentums gegeben haben, sind das . . . Scheitern der Eschatologie und eine konkurrierende Antwort auf die dadurch aufgeworfenen Probleme: die Gnosis."

21. Within eschatological Jewish thought in interwar and postwar Germany, particularly in the work of Franz Rosenzweig and Gershom Scholem, there is "a tension within the messianic idea of Judaism between this-worldly and otherworldly, temporal and eternal foci of redemption" (Kaplan 2004, 511). On Gnosis and Judaism, see also Broek 2014.

22. On Jonas and "classical Jewish sources," see Lawee 2015.

23. This view would be at odds with Hannah Arendt's, and the two acquaintances discussed their differences in correspondence and in print. Voegelin reviewed *The Origins of Totalitarianism* (1951) by request for *The Review of Politics*, and Arendt was invited to respond. The two exchanged letters in anticipation of the review. See Baehr and Wells 2012 and Feldman 2012. On Arendt and racism "in the theory canon," see Owens 2017. Arendt on race and Arendt on Little Rock do not form the same discussion. Of the numerous essays on Arendt and Little Rock, see Hinze 2009 for her specific treatment of King in the issue. On Voegelin's "race talk," see Henningsen 1992; and on Voegelin's racism, see Hund 2019. While Voegelin could be said to have an oppositional view to Arendt's embrace of politics, this would not prevent a reading of Voegelin's thought as strongly conservative. On the matter of Voegelin and "the practice of opposition," see Heilke 1994.

24. For a full account of Voegelin's historicism as understood by his American contemporaries, see Albright 1961.

25. Racially transfigured nature posits its own natural law. For Voegelin on natural law, see Schmidt Passos 2019.

26. On Voegelin and Gnosis, see Rossbach 2005.

27. Voegelin's theory was not without its detractors. Hans Kelsen, for instance, "categorically [rejected] Voegelin's diagnosis of modernity as being Gnostic; and, quite important, he traces back those Gnostic tendencies, not to secular ideologies, but to their own religious or philosophical sources" (Thomassen 2014, 439). For Kelsen, echoing Hans Blumenberg, because the term "secular religion" was oxymoronic, Gnosis was impossible as a political form in its sacral configuration (Thomassen 2014, 439). Indeed, Blumenberg sees modernity not as a process of increasing Gnostic belief but rather as Gnosticism's overcoming (Styfhals 2012, 193). Kelsen's and Blumenberg's critique applies to the idea of "political theology" championed by his opponent in constitutional theory, Carl Schmitt, whose notion of the Enemy fits in well with the concept of political religion (Gray 2014, 8n). Schmitt's eschatology, however, posits a different force at work structuring history. In the secularization of the sacred in the concept of the political, the eschaton is associated with cataclysm without eternal salvation. The purpose of the sovereign is to ward off the apocalyptic conclusion to history. In this sense, political theology's attempt "to preserve the political spirit of eschatological hope may also lead to the deformation of eschatology" (Ostovich 2007, 52). As Hugo Ball noticed in Schmitt's work in 1924,

> the concept of personality in Schmitt's oeuvre takes on a greater importance with each new work. I have already pointed out the degree to which the scientific problem and the personal problem are linked for this ideologist. Who seeks to give

longevity to his own person must be mindful of the identity of his expressions. The dignity and value of the person cannot be maintained otherwise. If this conviction coincides with a propensity for the absolute and the definitive, then one encounters the religious personality that aspires to an "eternal life," to immortality, to a sublime existence beyond death and chance. I called this attitude eschatological. (Ball 2013, 84)

Schmitt's eschatology is the perfection of the personality in an absolute human type, the eschatological, messianic figure without divine dispensation yet still capable of rendering sovereign justice.

28. I would strongly agree with Dyer and Stuart's assertion:

What is missing from the relevant literature regarding public reason and King's "Letter from Birmingham City Jail" is a close analysis of the examples of legal injustice King marshaled in support of his natural law argument. As we note, King's specific examples of unjust laws rely on a Thomistic framework that bedevils the attempt to reconcile his Letter with the constructivist underpinnings of Rawls's theory of public reason. If King's Letter is acceptable under the terms of public reason, then public reason simply cannot limit contemporary public discourse in the way Rawls has in mind. (Dyer and Stuart 2013, 148)

Chapter Five: Divine Nonviolence

1. On Arendt, race, and the Civil Rights Movement, see Allen 2004.

2. For a complete account of Arendt and Benjamin's long friendship and its afterlife, including key documents, see Schöttker and Wizisla 2006; Weissberg 2002.

3. Angela Y. Davis, in Germany at the time, recalls that Dutschke's shooting was "inspired" by King's murder. See Davis 1974, 143.

4. On Arendt's "critique of violence," see Finlay 2009; for "the political" and "the messianic" in Benjamin and Arendt, see Lindner 2011.

5. Schmitt's Catholicism does not prevent the charge of racism, as even the church's early history with Nazism shows. See Hastings 2018.

6. On Taubes and Schmitt, see Terpstra 2009.

7. On Schmitt's theology, see Gavin 2016.

8. See also Paipais 2016, 1603.

9. On the divisions of sovereignty, and political theology between immanence and transcendence, see Dickinson 2013. See also Dickinson 2016 for a good discussion of Benjamin and theology.

10. For more on Heidegger's Paul, particularly in relation to orthodoxy, see Klassen 2010.

11. See also Gorgone 2010 for Heidegger on Kairos and early Christianity.

12. For other views on reading Benjamin and Heidegger together, see Fenves 2016; Long 2001; Knoche 2000; Van Reijen 1998.

13. Sturm has written that the literary quality of the "Letter" distinguishes it as the ideogram of its era:

> King's Letter from a Birmingham Jail is significant in its testimony to the unremitting perseverance of racism in American. The import of the letter is to state the need for forcing the [structural] crisis of racism to the point of psychological and political explication. The strategy of King and his aides was to foster an open and eventful crisis with the expectation of moving toward a reconstruction institutional and cultural life of the city. But, on a profound level, the crisis was already inescapably present. It has been characteristic of the city since its founding, as it has been and remains an integral characteristic of American society since it begins. The letter, though addressed to a particular occasion, is the ideogram, revealing contradictory principles at the heart of the American social order. (Sturm 1984, 314)

14. As Enns and Myers note, the work is so strongly indebted to Pauline epistolary "that it is fruitful to read Ephesians as a sort of ancient 'Letter from Birmingham City Jail'" (Enns and Myers 2009,15). For "Ephesians challenges Christians, as King would later, to fully embrace both the gospel and their responsibilities in the historical moment. And both do so from behind bars of the system they are seeking to overturn" (Enns and Myers 2009, 17). "As peacemakers," Enns and Myers continue, "both King and Paul stressed repeatedly that members of the very group who had historically oppressed their people are welcome as full members in the movement. This was not easy for nationalists in their respective minority contexts to accept, and both men were accused of being 'traitors to their race'" (Enns and Myers 2009, 18).

15. For a detailed comparison of King's "Letter" and Paul's epistles, see Snow 1985.

16. Indeed, as Tiefenbrun argues, King's work is a literary masterpiece as well as an astonishing piece of rhetorical genius. See Tiefenbrun 1992, 255.

17. Police violence is an expression of power. "Although fully aware of how power and violence are frequently combined," Bernstein writes, "[Arendt] argues that they are conceptually distinct—even antithetical" (Bernstein 2011, 3).

18. As Anselm Haverkamp has pointed out, even the death penalty is for Benjamin preferable to police violence. Haverkamp explains:

> The death penalty draws its attraction from nothing less than this "dramatic" reinforcement of the "mystic" foundation It proves in its performance, but not—on the contrary—in its aims and as a means. . . . Violence in this sense is necessary for "justice," and the mournful mind of the critic (Benjamin) prefers it to the more pernicious, hideous enforcement of law through the police. There, the mere logic of conserving the law produces a less visible, but no less violent violence in whose mechanism even the undecidability of whether violence was "pure" or nothing but yet another instance of a means to an end is lost. (Haverkamp 1991, 1165)

19. Friedlander perfectly summarizes Benjamin's understanding of police violence:

> The police should be seen, similarly, to fill a gap between the general form that the law qua law takes and the specific circumstances in which it is to be enforced. It might seem as though the law applies itself to the particular circumstances, as though specific cases naturally "fall under" the already existing law, and thus that the violence the police musters is merely needed to enforce it. Yet the police is a hybrid force, like the imagination. It is both receptive (to law) and at the same time spontaneous (in producing ordinances). Its ordinances "mediate" between the universality of law and the particular circumstances that the law cannot determine out of its own ground. . . . Putting it this way makes clear that far from constituting a solution to the problem of application the police achieves the apparent determination by arrogating to itself force that is not its own. The police, so to speak, takes the law into its own hands. (Friedlander 2015, 161)

20. On the "Parrhesiastic enterprise of black philosophy," see Havis 2013.

21. As Witte writes: "Benjamin is cognizant of social phenomena that do indeed include a presaging of the effects of divine power. As an example, the fervent supporter of the youth movement cites education, which relies on communicative skills, rather than taking recourse to penalties and relegation to achieve its goals. Education is situated in the true sphere of communication, language, and is therefore inaccessible to violence" (Witte 2011, 10). The "true sphere of communication" is "inaccessible to violence." The language of the state is antithetical to that of education and thus conducive to violence. To remain free of violence, education must therefore avoid falling within the purview of the public sphere and the influence of the state.

22. Friedlander has also commented on the special place of education and student life in Benjamin's thought on divine violence: "It is only by holding to the identity of revelation of divine force with the highest actualization or articulation of meaning that one can begin to address Benjamin's initially extremely surprising claim that divine force is present in education understood in its highest sense (Friedlander 2015, 175–176n). See also Martel's definitive 2012 study on Benjamin, divine violence, and eschatology. On the distinction between divine and mythic violence in Benjamin, see Ross 2014.

23. For the relation between Schmitt's "messianism" and martyrdom, see Schmidt Passos 2018.

Conclusion: Eros as Nonviolence

1. Finding Heidegger's idiosyncratic lexical approach too constricting did not stop his students and other contemporaries from elaborating the basic structure of his thought in other ways. These usually highlighted the same milestones of philosophical history in the same way, seeing humanism as Platonism's historical expression (Grassi 1968, 509).

2. Nonviolent protest's refusal would not be "great" enough, because it does not reject consumer society in toto. On Marcuse's "great refusal," see Farr 2013.

3. Partisan violence and the New Left were not out of keeping with Marcuse's thought (Herf 1979, 24).

4. On King's thought and the tradition of "pedagogical personalism" at Morehouse, see Jensen 2017.

5. Woodson has noted the Heideggerian aspect of hooks's thought. See Woodson 2019. This is not surprising, given Woodson's work on Heidegger and interwar German theology.

6. This reading of "émigré" philosophers as "transmitters of American protest culture" is only from a very narrow perspective. On this, see Friedman 2014; Kettler and Lauer 2005; and Stephan 2000. See also Scott 2004.

7. On the Black Campus Movement and the institutionalization of Black studies, see Rogers 2012.

Bibliography

Aboutorabi, Rozita. 2015. "Heidegger, Education, Nation and Race." *Policy Futures in Education* 13 (4): 415–423.

Abron, JoNina M. 1986. "The Legacy of the Black Panther Party." *The Black Scholar* 17 (6): 33–37.

Adams, James Luther. 1965. *Paul Tillich's Philosophy of Culture, Science, and Religion*. New York: Harper & Row.

Adorno, Theodor. 2019. *Ontology and Dialectics*. Edited by Rolf Tiedemann. Translated by Nicholas Walker. Cambridge: Polity.

Aeschliman, M. D. 2005. "Enduring Documents and Public Doctrines: Martin Luther King's 'Letter from Birmingham Jail' After Forty Years." *Journal of Education* 186 (1): 29–46.

Agamben, Giorgio. 2011. *The Kingdom and the Glory: For a Theological Genealogy of Economy and Government*. Translated by Lorenzo Chiesa with Matteo Mandarini. Stanford, CA: Stanford University Press.

Agamben, Giorgio. 2009. "On the Limits of Violence." Edited by Lorenzo Fabbri. Translated by Elisabeth Fay. *Diacritics* 39 (4): 103–111.

Agamben, Giorgio. 1998. *Homo Sacer: Sovereign Power and Bare Life*. Stanford, CA: Stanford University Press.

Agamben, Giorgio, and Daniel Heller-Roazen. 1999. *Potentialities: Collected Essays In Philosophy*. Stanford, CA: Stanford University Press.

Albrecht, Johannes-Friedrich. 2019. "Das politische und die Kommunikation des Evangeliums." *Neue Zeitschrift für systematische Theologie und Religionsphilosophie* 61 (4): 533–548.

Albright, William Foxwell. 1961. "Eric Voegelin: Order and History." *Theological Studies* 22 (2): 270–279.

Allen, Anita L. 2013. "African-American Philosophers and the Critique of Law." *Black Scholar* 43 (4): 17–23.

Alsup, Royal. 2009. "Liberation Psychology." *Journal of Humanistic Psychology* 49 (4): 388.

Anderson, Joshua. 2012. "A Tension in the Political Thought of Huey P. Newton." *Journal of African American Studies* 16 (2): 249–267.

Ansbro, John J. 2004. *The Credos of Eight Black Leaders: Converting Obstacles Into Opportunities*. Lanham, MD: University Press of America.
Ansbro, John J. 1982. *Martin Luther King, Jr.: The Making of a Mind*. Maryknoll, NY: Orbis Books.
Ansell-Pearson, Keith. 1994. "Heidegger's Decline: Between Philosophy and Politics." *Political Studies* 42 (3): 505–518.
Appiah, K. Anthony. 1992. "African-American Philosophy?" *Philosophical Forum* 24 (1–3): 11–34.
Appiah, K. Anthony. 1985. "The Uncompleted Argument: Du Bois and the Illusion of Race." *Critical Inquiry* 12 (1): 21–37.
Arendt, Hannah. 1973. *Crises of the Republic*. Harmondsworth, UK: Penguin.
Arendt, Hannah. 1969. "Reflections on Violence." *Journal of International Affairs* 23 (1): 1–35.
Arendt, Hannah. *On Revolution*. 1977. Harmondsworth, UK: Penguin Books. (Originally published 1964.)
Arendt, Hannah. 1959. "Reflections on Little Rock." *Dissent* 6 (1): 45–56.
Arendt, Hannah. 1958. *The Human Condition*. 1958. Garden City, NY: Doubleday.
Arendt, Hannah. 1954. "Socrates." *The Promise of Politics*, 5–39. New York: Schocken Books.
Arendt, Hannah. 1951. *The Origins of Totalitarianism*. New York: Harcourt, Brace.
Arendt, Hannah. 1929. *Der Liebesbegriff bei Augustin: Versuch Einer Philosophischen Interpretation*. Berlin: J. Springer.
Arendt, Hannah, et al. 2002. "Hannah Arendt–Paul Tillich: Briefwechsel." *Zeitschrift für neuere Theologiegeschichte* 9 (1): 131–156.
Armitage, Duane. 2014. "Heidegger's Contributions to Philosophy: Pauline Meontology and Lutheran Irony." *Heythrop Journal* 55 (4): 576–583.
Armon, Adi. 2010. "Just before the 'Straussians': The Development of Leo Strauss's Political Thought from the Weimar Republic to America." *New German Critique* (111): 173–198.
Arndt, David. 2019. *Arendt on the Political*. Cambridge, UK: Cambridge University Press.
Austin, Curtis J. 2006. *Up Against the Wall: Violence In the Making and Unmaking of the Black Panther Party*. Fayetteville: University of Arkansas Press.
Austin, Tracy. 1979. "Huey on Trial in '79." *Umoja Sasa* 5 (7): 3.
Badiou, Alain, and Ray Brassier. 2003. *Saint Paul: the Foundation of Universalism*. Stanford, CA: Stanford University Press.
Bae, Aaron Byungjoo. 2017. "'The Struggle for Freedom, Justice, and Equality Transcends Racial and National Boundaries': Anti-Imperialism, Multiracial Alliances, and the Free Huey Movement in the San Francisco Bay Area." *Pacific Historical Review* 86 (4): 691–722.
Baehr, Peter, and Gordon C. Wells. 2012. "Debating Totalitarianism: An Exchange of Letters Between Hannah Arendt and Eric Voegelin." *History and Theory* 51 (3): 364–380.

Baldwin, Lewis V. 2010. *The Voice of Conscience: the Church in the Mind of Martin Luther King, Jr*. New York: Oxford University Press.

Baldwin, Lewis V. 1986. "Malcolm X and Martin Luther King, Jr.: What They Thought About Each Other." *Islamic Studies* 25 (4): 395–416.

Baldwin, Lewis V., Rufus Burrow, and Adam Fairclough. 2013. *The Domestication of Martin Luther King Jr.: Clarence B. Jones, Right-wing Conservatism, and the Manipulation of the King Legacy*. Edited by Lewis V. Baldwin and Rufus Burrow, Jr. Eugene, OR: Wipf and Stock Publishers.

Ball, Hugo. 2013. "Carl Schmitt's Political Theology." *October* (146): 65–92.

Barash, Jeffrey Andrew. 2002. "Martin Heidegger, Hannah Arendt and the Politics of Remembrance." *International Journal of Philosophical Studies* 10 (2): 171–182.

Barber, Benjamin R. 2006. "The Politics of Political Science: 'Value-Free' Theory and the Wolin-Strauss Dust-Up of 1963." *American Political Science Review* 100 (4): 539–545.

Baruzzi, Arno. 2001. "Kritik der Moderne nach Voegelin und Heidegger. Thesen und Fragen." *Zeitschrift für Politik* 48 (3): 257–267.

Bauer, Michelle. 2000. "An Essay Review: Implementing a Liberatory Feminist Pedagogy: Bell Hooks's Strategies for Transforming the Classroom." *Melus* 25 (3): 265–274.

Bell, Bernard W. 1993. "Malcolm, Martin, and the Black Jeremiadic Cry." *World & I* 8 (7): 452.

Benhabib, Seyla. 2010. *Politics in Dark Times: Encounters with Hannah Arendt*. New York: Cambridge University Press.

Benhabib, Seyla. 1996. *The Reluctant Modernism of Hannah Arendt*. Thousand Oaks, CA: Sage Publications.

Benjamin, Andrew E., and Peter Osborne. 1994. *Walter Benjamin's Philosophy: Destruction and Experience*. Warwick Studies in European Philosophy. London: Routledge.

Benjamin, Walter. 2018. "Ends and Means of Student Pedagogic Groups in German Universities (with Particular Attention to the 'Freiburg Direction')." *Boundary 2* 45 (3): 15–21.

Benjamin, Walter. 2011. *Early Writings, 1910–1917*. Edited by Howard Eiland. Cambridge, MA: Belknap Press of Harvard University Press.

Benjamin, Walter. 1986. *Reflections: Essays, Aphorisms, Autobiographical Writing*. Edited by Peter Demetz. New York: Schocken Books. (Originally published 1978.)

Benjamin, Walter. 1969. *Illuminations*. New York: Schocken Books. (Originally published 1968.)

Bennett, Lerone. 1956. "The King Plan for Freedom." *Ebony* 7: 65–69.

Benson, Thomas W. 1970. "Violence: Communication Breakdown? Focus on Recent Publications." *Today's Speech* 18 (1): 39–46.

Bernasconi, Robert. 2015. "'The Misinterpretation of Violence': Heidegger's Reading of Hegel and Schmitt on Gewalt." *Research in Phenomenology* 45 (2): 214–236.

Bernasconi, Robert. 2013a. "Heidegger, Nietzsche, National Socialism: The Place of Metaphysics in the Political Debate of the 1930s." In *The Bloomsbury Companion to*

Heidegger, edited by François Rafoul and Eric S. Nelson, 47–54. London: Bloomsbury Academic.

Bernasconi, Robert. 2013b. "Who Belongs? Heidegger's Philosophy of the Volk in 1933-4." In *Nature, History, State: 1933-1934*, edited by Gregory Fried and Richard Polt, 109–126. London: Bloomsbury.

Bernasconi, Robert. 2010. "Race and Earth in Heidegger's Thinking During the Late 1930s." *Southern Journal of Philosophy* 48 (1): 49–66.

Bernasconi, Robert. 2000. "Heidegger's Alleged Challenge to the Nazi Concepts of Race." In *Appropriating Heidegger*, edited by James E. Faulconer and Mark A. Wrathall, 49–67. Cambridge, UK: Cambridge University Press.

Bernauer, James William. 2013. "Hallucinating Heidegger: Reflections from Hannah Arendt's Thought." *Philosophy & Social Criticism* 39 (9): 877–883.

Bernauer, James William. 2007. "Bonhoeffer and Arendt at One Hundred." *Studies in Christian-Jewish Relations* 2 (1): 77–85.

Bernstein, Richard J. 2011. "Hannah Arendt's Reflections on Violence and Power." *Iris: European Journal of Philosophy & Public Debate* 3 (5): 3–30.

Berry, Edward. 2005. "Doing Time: King's 'Letter from Birmingham Jail.'" *Rhetoric and Public Affairs* 8 (1): 109–132.

Beshai, James A. 2017. "Martin Luther King Jr.—On Love and Justice." *The Humanistic Psychologist* 45 (4): 408–421.

Bevir, Mark. 2000. "Derrida and the Heidegger Controversy: Global Friendship Against Racism." *Critical Review of International Social and Political Philosophy* 3 (1): 121–138.

"Bibliography: Sources for Martin Luther King, Jr." 2005. *OAH Magazine of History* 19 (1): 11–12.

Birmingham, Peg. 2014. "Law's Violent Judgment: Does Agamben have a Political Aesthetics?" *CR: The New Centennial Review* 14 (2): 99–110.

Birmingham, Peg. 2010. "On Violence, Politics, and the Law." *Journal of Speculative Philosophy* 24 (1): 1–20.

Birt, Robert E., ed. 2012. "Introduction." *The Liberatory Thought of Martin Luther King Jr.: Critical Essays on the Philosopher King*. Lanham, MD: Lexington Books.

Biskowski, Lawrence J. 1995. "Politics Versus Aesthetics: Arendt's Critiques of Nietzsche and Heidegger." *Review of Politics* 57 (1): 59–89.

Blake, J. H. 2012. "The Caged Panther: The Prison Years of Huey P. Newton." *Journal of African American Studies* 16 (2): 236–248.

Blok, Vincent. 2011. "Establishing the Truth: Heidegger's Reflections on Gestalt." *Heidegger Studies* 27: 101–118.

Blok, Vincent. 2012. "Naming Being—Or the Philosophical Content of Heidegger's National Socialism." *Heidegger Studies* 28: 101–122.

Bloom, Jack M. 1987. *Class, Race, and the Civil Rights Movement*. Bloomington: Indiana University Press, 1987.

Bogues, Anthony. 2015. *Black Heretics, Black Prophets: Radical Political Intellectuals*. New York: Routledge.
Boxill, Bernard R. 2004. "Why We Should Not Think of Ourselves as Divided by Race." In *Racism in Mind*, edited by Michael R. Levine and Tamas Pataki, 209–224. Ithaca, NY: Cornell University Press.
Boxill, Bernard R. 2003. "A Lockean Argument for Black Reparations." *Journal of Ethics* 7 (1): 63–91.
Boxill, Bernard R. 1992. "Two Traditions in African American Political Philosophy." *Philosophical Forum* 24 (1–3): 119–135.
Boxill, Bernard R. 1984. *Blacks and Social Justice*. Totowa, NJ: Rowman & Allanheld.
Bradshaw, Leah. 2018. "Hannah Arendt: The German Years." *Political Science Reviewer* 42 (1): 89–118.
Breidenthal, Thomas E. 1998. "Jesus Is My Neighbor: Arendt, Augustine, and the Politics of Incarnation." *Modern Theology* 14 (4): 489–503.
Brenner, Michael. 1999. "Gnosis and History: Polemics of German-Jewish Identity from Graetz to Scholem." *New German Critique* (77): 45–60.
Britt, Brian. 2010. "The Schmittian Messiah in Agamben's *The Time That Remains*." *Critical Inquiry* 36 (2): 262–287.
Broek, Roelof van den. 2014. "Gnosis und Judentum: Alttestamentliche und jüdische Motive in der gnostischen Literatur und das Ursprungsproblem der Gnosis." *Vigiliae Christianae* 68 (2): 229–232.
Brogan, Walter. 1997. "Plato's Dialectical Soul: Heidegger on Plato's Ambiguous Relationship to Rhetoric." *Research in Phenomenology* 27: 3–15.
Brotz, Howard, and B. William Austin. 2017. *African-American Social and Political Thought, 1850-1920*. London: Routledge.
Buch, Robert. 2012. "Umbuchung: Säkularisierung als Schuld und als Hypothek bei Hans Blumenberg." *Zeitschrift für Religions- und Geistesgeschichte* 64 (4): 338–358.
Burrin, Philippe. 1997. "Political Religion." *History & Memory* 9 (1): 321–349.
Burrow, Rufus. 2014. *Martin Luther King, Jr., and the Theology of Resistance*. Jefferson, NC: McFarland & Company, Inc., Publishers.
Burrow, Rufus, Jr. 2006. *God and Human Dignity: The Personalism, Theology, and Ethics of Martin Luther King, Jr.* Notre Dame, IN: University of Notre Dame Press.
Burrow, Rufus, Jr. 2002. "Martin Luther King, Jr.'s Doctrine of Human Dignity." *Western Journal of Black Studies* 26 (4): 228–239.
Cahana, Jonathan. 2018. "A Gnostic Critic of Modernity: Hans Jonas from Existentialism to Science." *Journal of the American Academy of Religion* 86 (1): 158–180.
Caldarone, Rosaria. 2016. "'Eternity, from Afar into Intimacy': Time and History in the Letters of Martin Heidegger to Hannah Arendt." *Philosophy Today* 60 (4): 927–948.
Calloway, Carolyn R. 1977. "Group Cohesiveness in the Black Panther Party." *Journal of Black Studies* 8 (1): 55–74.

Campbell, Douglas A. 2013. "Paul's Apocalyptic Politics." *Pro Ecclesia* 22 (2): 129–152.
Canovan, Margaret. 1990. "Socrates or Heidegger? Hannah Arendt's Reflections on Philosophy and Politics." *Social Research* 57 (1): 135–165.
Carman, Taylor. 2003. *Heidegger's Analytic: Interpretation, Discourse, and Authenticity in Being and Time*. Cambridge: Cambridge University Press.
Carmichael, Stokely. 2007. "Free Huey." *Stokely Speaks: From Black Power to Pan-Africanism*, 111–130. Chicago: Lawrence Hill Books, 2007.
Carson, Clayborne. 2008. *The Martin Luther King, Jr. Encyclopedia*. Westport, CT: Greenwood Press.
Carson, Clayborne. 2005a. "Between Contending Forces: Martin Luther King, Jr., and the African American Freedom Struggle." *OAH Magazine of History* 19 (1): 17–21.
Carson, Clayborne. 2005b. "The Unfinished Dialogue of Martin Luther King, Jr. and Malcolm X." *OAH Magazine of History* 19 (1): 22–26.
Carson, Clayborne, Tenisha Armstrong, Susan Carson, Erin Cook, and Susan Englander. *The Martin Luther King, Jr., Encyclopedia*. Westport, CT: Greenwood, 2008.
Chakrabarty, Bidyut. 2014. *Confluence of Thought: Mahatma Gandhi and Martin Luther King, Jr*. New York: Oxford University Press.
Chappell, David L. 2021. "Martin Luther King, Jr.: Strategist of Force". *African American Political Thought: A Collected History*. Ed. Melvin L. Rogers, and Jack Turner. Chicago: The University of Chicago Press, 516–535.
Christiaens, Tim. 2021. "Agamben's Theories of the State of Exception: From Political to Economic Theology." *Cultural Critique* 110: 49–74.
Christophersen, Alf, and Claudia Schulze. 2002. "Chronologie eines Eklats: Hannah Arendt und Paul Tillich." *Zeitschrift für neuere Theologiegeschichte* 9 (1): 98–130.
Cimino, Antonio. 2016. "Agamben's Political Messianism in *The Time That Remains*." *International Journal of Philosophy and Theology* 77 (3): 102–118.
Clavey, Charles. 2016. "Arendt Among the Americans." *Chronicle of Higher Education* 62 (19): 9.
Cleaver, Eldridge. 1968. *Soul on Ice*. New York: McGraw-Hill.
Cleaver, Kathleen, and George N. Katsiaficas. 2001. *Liberation, Imagination, and the Black Panther Party: A New Look at the Panthers and Their Legacy*. New York: Routledge.
Cleghorn, Reese. 1963. "Martin Luther King, Jr., Apostle of Crisis." *Saturday Evening Post* 236 (23): 15–19.
Colaiaco, James A. 1988. *Martin Luther King, Jr.: Apostle of Militant Nonviolence*. Basingstoke, UK: Macmillan.
Colaiaco, James A. 1984. "The American Dream Unfulfilled: Martin Luther King, Jr. and the 'Letter from Birmingham Jai.'" *Phylon* 45 (1): 1–18.
Comay, Rebecca. 1992. "Framing Redemption: Aura, Origin, Technology in Benjamin and Heidegger." In *Ethics and Danger: Essays on Heidegger and Continental Thought*,

edited by Arleen B. Dallery and Charles E. Scott with P. Holley Roberts, 139–168. Albany: State University of New York Press.

Cone, James H. 1986. "The Theology of Martin Luther King, Jr." *Union Seminary Quarterly Review* 40 (4): 21–39.

Congdon, David W. 2014. "Kerygma and Community: A Response to R. W. L. Moberly's Revisiting of Bultmann." *Journal of Theological Interpretation* 8 (1): 1–21.

Conyers, James L. 2007. *Engines of the Black Power Movement: Essays on the Influence of Civil Rights Actions, Arts, and Islam*. Jefferson, NC: McFarland & Co.

Cooper, John C. 1969. "Paul Tillich's Philosophy of Science." *Southern Humanities Review* 3 (4): 365–374.

Corlett, J. A. 1995. "Political Integration, Political Separation, and the African-American Experience: Martin Luther King, Jr. and Malcolm X on Social Change." *Humboldt Journal of Social Relations* 21 (2): 191–207.

Courtright, John A. 1974. "Rhetoric of the Gun: An Analysis of the Rhetorical Modifications of the Black Panther Party." *Journal of Black Studies* 4 (3): 249–267.

Crawford, Vicki L., and Lewis V. Baldwin. 2019. *Reclaiming the Great World House: The Global Vision of Martin Luther King Jr*. Athens: University of Georgia Press.

Danz, Christian. 2018. "Prophetic Interruptions. Critical Theory, Emancipation, and Religion in Paul Tillich, Theodor Adorno, and Max Horkheimer (1929–1944)." *International Yearbook for Tillich Research* 13 (1): 302–306.

Davies, Alan. 2014. "Hannah Arendt and Christian Theology." *Touchstone* 32 (3): 30.

Davis, Angela. 1974. *An Autobiography*. New York: Random House.

Davis, Jack E. 2001. *The Civil Rights Movement*. 3 vols. Malden, MA: Blackwell Publishers.

De Wilde, Marc. 2011. "Meeting Opposites: The Political Theologies of Walter Benjamin and Carl Schmitt." *Philosophy & Rhetoric* 44 (4): 363–381.

Demos, Raphael. 1958. "Tillich's Philosophical Theology." *Philosophy and Phenomenological Research* 19 (1): 74–85.

Demske, James M. 1994. "Heidegger: A Political Life?" *America* 170: 16–30.

Denker, Alfred. 2013. "Martin Heidegger's Being and Time: A Carefully Planned Accident?" *The Cambridge Companion to Heidegger's* Being and Time. Edited by Mark A. Wrathall. Cambridge: Cambridge University Press, 54–82.

Derks, H. 1999. "Social Sciences in Germany, 1933–1945." *German History* 17 (2): 177–219.

Derrida, Jacques. 1989. *Of Spirit: Heidegger and the Question*. Chicago: University of Chicago Press.

Derrida, Jacques, Geoffrey Bennington, Thomas Dutoit, and Marguerite Derrida. 2016. *Heidegger: The Question of Being & History*. Chicago University of Chicago Press.

Derrida, Jacques, Hans-Georg Gadamer, Philippe Lacoue-Labarthe, and Mireille Calle-Gruber. 2016. *Heidegger, Philosophy, and Politics: The Heidelberg Conference*. New York: Fordham University Press.

Dickinson, Colby. 2013. "'The Divisions of Sovereignty': Political Theology Caught Between Immanence and Transcendence." *Political Theology* 14 (1): 88–99.

Dickinson, Colby. 2016. *Walter Benjamin and Theology*. Perspectives in Continental Philosophy. New York: Fordham University Press.

Dorrien, Gary. 2018. "Religious Socialism, Paul Tillich, and the Abyss of Estrangement." *Social Research: An International Quarterly* 85 (2): 425–452.

Downing, Frederick L. 1987. "Martin Luther King, Jr. as Public Theologian." *Theology Today* 44 (1): 15–31.

Dreisbach, Donald F. 1975. "Paul Tillich's Hermeneutic." *Journal of the American Academy of Religion* 43 (1): 84–94.

Driver, Tom F. 1965. "St. Paul and Tillich." *Union Seminary Quarterly Review* 21 (1): 30–32.

Dyer, Justin Buckley, and Kevin Stuart. 2013. "Rawlsian Public Reason and the Theological Framework of Martin Luther King's 'Letter from Birmingham City Jail.'" *Politics and Religion* 6 (1): 145–163.

Earle, Elizabeth R. 2017. "The Rhetoric of Kairos: Paul Tillich's Reinterpretation." *Journal of Communication & Religion* 40 (4): 1–13.

Eccel, Daiane. 2015. "Eric Voegelin e o gnosticismo: da estreita relação entre religião, política e os regimes totalitários." *Numen: Revista de Estudos e Pesquisa da Religião* 18 (2): 40–58.

Enns, Elaine, and Ched Myers. 2009. "'Ambassadors in Chains': Evangelizing the Powers: Ephesians 2–3 and M. L. King's Letter from Birmingham City Jail." *The Conrad Grebel Review* 27 (3): 4–27.

Erskine, Noel Leo. 1991. "King and the Black Church." *Journal of Religious Thought* 48 (2): 9–16.

Fairclough, Adam. 1986. "Martin Luther King, Jr. and the Quest for Nonviolent Social Change." *Phylon (1960-)* 47 (1): 1–15.

Fairclough, Adam. 1983. "Was Martin Luther King a Marxist?" *History Workshop* (15): 117–125.

Fanon, Frantz. 2004. *The Wretched of the Earth*. Translated by Richard Philcox. Commentary by Jean-Paul Sartre and Homi K. Bhabha. New York: Grove Press.

Farber, Marvin. 1958. "Heidegger on the Essence of Truth." *Philosophy and Phenomenological Research* 18: 523–532.

Farías, Víctor, Joseph Margolis, and Tom Rockmore. 1989. *Heidegger and Nazism*. Philadelphia: Temple University Press.

Farmer, Ashley D. 2019. *Remaking Black Power: How Black Women Transformed an Era*. Chapel Hill, NC: University of North Carolina Press.

Farr, Arnold L., et al. 2013. 2009. *Critical Theory and Democratic Vision: Herbert Marcuse and Recent Liberation Philosophies*. Lanham, MD: Lexington Books.

Faye, Emmanuel. 2009. *Heidegger: the Introduction of Nazism into Philosophy in Light of the Unpublished Seminars of 1933–1935*. New Haven, CT: Yale University Press.

Feenberg, Andrew. 2013. "Heidegger and Marcuse: On Reification and Concrete Phi-

losophy." In *The Bloomsbury Companion to Heidegger*, edited by François Rafoul and Eric S. Nelson, 171–176. London: Bloomsbury Academic.
Feenberg, Andrew. 2009. "The Liberation of Nature?" *Western Humanities Review* 63 (3): 85–96.
Feenberg, Andrew. 2005. *Heidegger and Marcuse: The Catastrophe and Redemption of History*. New York: Routledge.
Feenberg, Andrew. 2003. "Heidegger and Marcuse: Zerfall und Rettung der Aufklärung." In *Kritische Theorie der Technik und der Natur*, edited by Gernot Böhme and Alexandra Manzei, 39–53. Munich: Wilhelm Fink Verlag.
Feldman, Matthew. 2005. "Between Geist and Zeitgeist: Martin Heidegger as Ideologue of 'Metapolitical Fascism.'" *Totalitarian Movements & Political Religions* 6 (2): 175–198.
Feldman, Stephen M. 2012. "Democracy and Dissent: Strauss, Arendt, and Voegelin in America." *Denver University Law Review* 89 (3): 671–697.
Feller, Yaniv. 2013. "From Aher to Marcion: Martin Buber's Understanding of Gnosis." *Jewish Studies Quarterly* 20 (4): 374–397.
Fenves, Peter. 2016. "The Problem of Popularization in Benjamin, Schrödinger, and Heidegger Circa 1935." *The Germanic Review* 91 (2): 112–125.
Ferguson, Stephen C. 2015. *Philosophy of African American Studies: Nothing Left of Blackness*. African American Philosophy and the African Diaspora. New York: Palgrave Macmillan.
Finlay, Christopher J. 2009. "Hannah Arendt's Critique of Violence." *Thesis Eleven* 97 (1): 26–45.
Finzsch, Norbert. 1999. "'Picking Up the Gun': Die Black Panther Party zwischen gewaltsamer Revolution und sozialer Reform, 1966–1984." *Amerikastudien / American Studies* 44 (2): 223–254.
Fitts, Mako. 2011. "Theorizing Transformative Revolutionary Action: The Contribution of Bell Hooks to Emancipatory Knowledge Production." *CLR James Journal* 17 (1): 112–132.
Flakne, April N. 2002. "Beyond Banality and Fatality: Arendt, Heidegger and Jaspers on Political Speech." *New German Critique* (86): 3–18.
Fleming, Katie. 2012. "Heidegger, Jaeger, Plato: The Politics of Humanism." *International Journal of the Classical Tradition* 19 (2): 82–106.
Foner, Philip Sheldon. 2014. *The Black Panthers Speak*. Chicago: Haymarket Books. (Originally published 1970.)
Fosdick, Harry Emerson. 1947. *On Being Fit to Live With: Sermons on Post-War Christianity*. London: S.C.M. Press.
Frady, Marshall. 2006. *Martin Luther King, Jr.: A Life*. New York: Penguin Group.
Franklin, Robert Michael. 1990. "In Pursuit of a Just Society: Martin Luther King, Jr, and John Rawls." *Journal of Religious Ethics* 18 (2): 57–77.

Freer, Joanna. 2013. "Thomas Pynchon and the Black Panther Party: Revolutionary Suicide in *Gravity's Rainbow*." *Journal of American Studies* 47 (1): 171–188.

Friedlander, Eli. 2015. "Assuming Violence: A Commentary on Walter Benjamin's 'Critique of Violence.'" *Boundary 2: An International Journal of Literature and Culture* 42 (4): 159–185.

Friedman, Max Paul. 2014. "Émigrés as Transmitters of American Protest Culture." *Journal of Modern Jewish Studies* 13 (1): 87–98.

Fritsche, Johannes. 2018. "Heidegger on Machination, the Jewish Race, and the Holocaust." *Critical Horizons* 19 (4): 312–333.

Fritsche, Johannes. 2016. "National Socialism, Anti-Semitism, and Philosophy in Heidegger and Scheler: On Peter Trawny's *Heidegger & the Myth of a Jewish World-Conspiracy*." *Philosophy Today* 60 (2): 583–608.

Fuchs, Christian. 2015. "Anti-Semitism, Anti-Marxism, and Technophobia: The Fourth Volume of Martin Heidegger's *Black Notebooks* (1942–1948)." *TripleC (Cognition, Communication, Co-Operation): Open Access Journal for a Global Sustainable Information Society* 13 (1): 93–100.

Fulkerson, Richard P. 1979. "The Public Letter as a Rhetorical Form: Structure, Logic, and Style in King's 'Letter from Birmingham Jail.'" *Quarterly Journal of Speech* 65: 121–136.

Gaipa, Mark. 2007. "'A Creative Psalm of Brotherhood': The (De)Constructive Play in Martin Luther King's 'Letter from Birmingham Jail.'" *Quarterly Journal of Speech* 93 (3): 279–307.

Gaiter, Colette. 2020. "The Black Panther Newspaper and Revolutionary Aesthetics." In *Art, Global Maoism and the Chinese Cultural Revolution*, edited by Jacopo Galimberti, Noemi de Haro García, and Victoria H. F. Scott, 87–108. Manchester: Manchester University Press.

Gandhi, Mohandas Karamchand. 1993. *The Penguin Gandhi Reader*. Edited by Rudrangshu Mukherjee. New York: Penguin Books.

Garber, Paul R. 1975. "Black Theology: The Latter-Day Legacy of Martin Luther King, Jr." *Journal of the Interdenominational Theological Center* 2 (2): 100–113.

Garrow, David J. 2001. *The FBI and Martin Luther King, Jr.: from "Solo"" to Memphis*. New Haven, CT: Yale University Press.

Garrow, David J. 1986. "The Intellectual Development of Martin Luther King, Jr.: Influences and Commentaries." *Union Seminary Quarterly Review* 40 (4): 5–20.

Gates, Henry Louis, Jr. 1992. "African American Studies in the 21st Century." *Black Scholar* 22 (3): 3–9.

Gelven, Michael. 1973. "Eros and Projection: Plato and Heidegger." *Southwestern Journal of Philosophy* 4 (3): 125–136.

Gerolin, Alessandra. 2015. "The Influence of Alfred North Whitehead on Eric Voegelin." *Journal of the History of Ideas* 76 (4): 633–655.

Gilkey, Langdon. 1990. *Gilkey on Tillich*. New York: Crossroad.

Glazer, Nathan. 1975. "Hannah Arendt's America." *Commentary* 60: 61–67.

Godzieba, Anthony J. 1995. "Ontotheology to Excess: Imagining God without Being." *Theological Studies*. 56 (1): 3-20.
Gontier, Thierry. 2013. "From 'Political Theology' to 'Political Religion': Eric Voegelin and Carl Schmitt." *Review of Politics* 75 (1): 25–43.
Gonzalez, Francisco J. 2015. "'I Have to Live in Eros': Heidegger's 1932 Seminar on Plato's Phaedrus." *Epoché: A Journal for the History of Philosophy* 9 (2): 217--240.
Gordon, Lewis R. 2020. "Shifting the Geography of Reason in Black and Africana Studies." *Black Scholar* 50 (3): 42–47.
Gordon, Lewis R. 2019. "Decolonizing Philosophy." *Southern Journal of Philosophy* 57: 16–36.
Gordon, Lewis R. 2018. "Thoughts on Two Recent Decades of Studying Race and Racism." *Social Identities* 24 (1): 29–38.
Gordon, Lewis. 2017. "Thoughts on Afropessimism." *Contemporary Political Theory* 17 (1) (2017): 105–112.
Gordon, Lewis. 2014. Disciplinary Decadence and the Decolonisation of Knowledge. *Africa Development* 39 (1): 81-92.
Gordon, Lewis R. 2013a. "Africana Philosophy and Philosophy in Black." *Black Scholar* 43 (4): 46–51.
Gordon, Lewis R. 2013b. "Race, Theodicy, and the Normative Emancipatory Challenges of Blackness." *South Atlantic Quarterly* 112 (4): 725–736.
Gordon, Lewis R. 2012. "Black Existence in Philosophy of Culture." *Diogenes* 59 (3–4): 96–105.
Gordon, Peter Eli. 2007. "The Concept of the Apolitical: German Jewish Thought and Weimar Political Theology." *Social Research* 74 (3): 855–878.
Gorgone, Sandro. 2010. "Vom Kairós zum Ereignis: Martin Heideggers Auseinandersetzung mit dem Urchristentum." *Zeitschrift für Religions- und Geistesgeschichte* 62 (4): 367–383.
Graf, Friedrich Wilhelm. 2017. "Zur Publikationsgeschichte von Paul Tillichs *Systematic Theology*. Teil 2." *Journal for the History of Modern Theology / Zeitschrift für Neuere Theologiegeschichte* 24 (1): 51–121.
Grant, Carl A. 2012. "Cultivating Flourishing Lives: A Robust Social Justice Vision of Education." *American Educational Research Journal* 49 (5): 910–934.
Grassi, Ernesto. 1980. "Italian Humanism and Heidegger's Thesis of the End of Philosophy." *Philosophy & Rhetoric* 13 (2): 79–98.
Grassi, Ernesto. 1968. "G. B. Vico und das Problem des Beginns des modernen Denkens." *Zeitschrift für Philosophische Forschung* 22: 491–509.
Gray, Phillip W. 2014. "Vanguards, Sacralisation of Politics, and Totalitarianism: Category-Based Epistemology and Political Religion." *Politics, Religion and Ideology* 15 (4): 521–540.
Greenberg, Udi E. 2008. "Orthodox Violence: 'Critique of Violence' and Walter Benjamin's Jewish Political Theology." *History of European Ideas* 34 (3): 324–333.

Gregg, Richard B., and James Tully. 2018. *The Power of Nonviolence*. Cambridge, UK: Cambridge University Press.

Grunenberg, Antonia, and Adrian Daub. 2007. "Arendt, Heidegger, Jaspers: Thinking Through the Breach in Tradition." *Social Research* 74 (4): 1003–1028.

Habermas, Jürgen. 1989. "Work and Weltanschauung: The Heidegger Controversy from a German Perspective." Translated by John McCumber. *Critical Inquiry* 15 (2): 431–456.

Habermas, Jürgen. 1971. *Knowledge and Human Interests*. Boston: Beacon Press. (Originally published 1968.)

Hadad, Yemima. 2019. "Hasidic Myth-Activism: Martin Buber's Theopolitical Revision of Volkish Nationalism." *Religions* 10 (2): 96–129.

Hamilton, Amy. 1993. "Insurgent Black Intellectual Life: Bell Hooks and Cornel West Break Bread." *Off Our Backs* 23 (7): 1–3.

Hammann, Konrad. 2012. "Der Glaube als freie Tat des Gehorsams: Herkunft, Bedeutung und Problematik einer Denkfigur Rudolf Bultmanns." *Zeitschrift für Theologie und Kirche* 109 (2): 206–234.

Hammann, Konrad. 2005. "Rudolf Bultmanns Begegnung mit dem Judentum." *Zeitschrift für Theologie und Kirche* 102 (1): 35–72.

Hammer, Espen. 2020. "Adorno's Critique of Heidegger." *A Companion to Adorno*. Edited by Max Pensky, Peter Gordon, and Espen Hammer. New York: Wiley-Blackwell, 473-87.

Hanssen, Beatrice. 2005. "Benjamin or Heidegger: Aesthetics and Politics in an Age of Technology." In *Walter Benjamin and Art*, edited by Andrew Benjamin. 73-92. New York: Continuum.

Harris, Jessica C. 2001. "Revolutionary Black Nationalism: The Black Panther Party." *Journal of Negro History* 86 (3): 409–421.

Hastings, Derek. 2018. "Nation, Race, and Religious Identity in the Early Nazi Movement." *Religions* 9 (10): 1–14.

Haverkamp, Anselm. 1991. "How to Take it (and Do the Right Thing): Violence and the Mournful Mind in Benjamin's Critique of Violence." *Cardozo Law Review* 13 (4): 1159–1171.

Havis, Devonya N. 2013. "The Parrhesiastic Enterprise of Black Philosophy." *The Black Scholar* 43 (4): 52–58.

Headley, Clevis. 2001. "Race, African American Philosophy, and Africana Philosophy: A Critical Reading of Lewis Gordon's *Her Majesty's Other Children*." *Philosophia Africana* 4 (1): 43.

Hegel, Georg Wilhelm Friedrich. 2018. *The Phenomenology of Spirit*. Translated by M. J. Inwood. Oxford: Oxford University Press.

Hegel, Georg Wilhelm Friedrich. 2011. *Lectures on the Philosophy of World History*. Translated by Robert F. Brown and Peter Crafts Hodgson. Oxford: Oxford University Press.

Heidegger, Martin. 2016. *Ponderings: Black Notebooks*. Bloomington: Indiana University Press.

Heidegger, Martin. 2013. *The Essence of Truth: On Plato's Cave Allegory and* Theaetetus. Translated by Ted Sadler. New York: Bloomsbury.

Heidegger, Martin. 1998. *Pathmarks*. Translated by William McNeill. Cambridge, UK: Cambridge University Press.

Heidegger, Martin. 1996. *Being and Time*. Translated by Joan Stambaugh. Albany: State University of New York Press.

Heidegger, Martin. 1993. *Basic Writings*. Edited by David Farrell Krell. San Francisco: HarperSanFrancisco.

Heidegger, Martin. 1980. "A Heidegger Seminar on Hegel's *Differenzschrift*." Translated by William Lovitt. *Southwestern Journal of Philosophy* 11 (3): 9–45.

Heiden, Gerrit Jan van der. 2016. "Paul's Dialectic in Present-Day Philosophy." *Zeitschrift für dialektische Theologie* 32 (1): 39–55.

Heilke, Thomas W. 1994. "Science, Philosophy, and Resistance: On Eric Voegelin's Practice of Opposition." *Review of Politics* 56 (4): 727–752.

Henderson, Errol A. 1997. "The Lumpenproletariat as Vanguard? The Black Panther Party, Social Transformation, and Pearson's Analysis of Huey Newton." *Journal of Black Studies* 28 (2): 171–199.

Henningsen, Manfred. 1992. "Politics and Race Talk in Voegelin." *Review of Politics* 54 (4): 706–707.

Henry, Paget. 2006. "Afro-American Studies and the Rise of African-American Philosophy." In *A Companion to African-American Studies*, edited by Lewis R. Gordon and Jane Anna Gordon, 223–246. Oxford, UK: Blackwell Publishing.

Herf, Jeffrey. 1979. "The Critical Spirit of Herbert Marcuse." *New German Critique* 18: 24–27.

Herskowitz, Daniel. 2017. "An Impossible Possibility? Jewish Barthianism in Interwar Germany." *Modern Theology* 33 (3): 348–368.

Hérubel, Jean-Pierre V. M. 1991. "The Darker Side of Light: Heidegger and Nazism: A Bibliographic Essay." *Shofar* 10 (1): 85–105.

Hills, Darrius D., and Tommy J. Curry. 2015. "State Violence, Black Bodies, and Martin Luther King's Black Power: Cries of the Unheard." *Journal of Africana Religions* 3 (4): 453–469.

Hinchman, Lewis P., and Sandra K. Hinchman. 1984. "In Heidegger's Shadow: Hannah Arendt's Phenomenological Humanism." *Review of Politics* 46 (2): 183–211.

Hinton, Elizabeth. 2018. "On Violence and Nonviolence." In *Fifty Years since MLK*, edited by Brandon M. Terry. Cambridge, MA: MIT Press, 45–52.

Hinze, Christine Firer. 2009. "Reconsidering Little Rock: Hannah Arendt, Martin Luther King Jr., and Catholic Social Thought on Children and Families in the Struggle for Justice." *Journal of the Society of Christian Ethics* 29 (1): 25–50.

Holman, Christopher. 2012. "Marcuse's Affirmation: Nietzsche and the Logos of Gratification." *New German Critique*. 115: 67-112.
hooks, bell. 1994. *Outlaw Culture: Resisting Representations*. New York: Routledge.
hooks, bell. 1993. "A Revolution of Values: The Promise of Multi-Cultural Change." *Journal of the Midwest Modern Language Association* 26 (1): 4–11.
hooks, bell. 1990. "An Aesthetic of Blackness: Strange and Oppositional." In *Yearning: Race, Gender, & Cultural Politics*. Boston: South End Press.
hooks, bell. 1989. "Choosing the Margin as a Space of Radical Openness." *Framework: The Journal of Cinema and Media* 36: 15–23.
Horkheimer, Max, and Theodor W. Adorno. 2002. *The Dialectic of Enlightenment*. Edited by Gunzelin Schmid Noerr. Translated by Edmund Jephcott. Stanford, CA: Stanford University Press. (Originally published 1947.)
Horowitz, Irving Louis. 2012. *Hannah Arendt: Radical Conservative*. New Brunswick, NJ: Transaction Publishers.
Hotam, Yotam. 2007. "Gnosis and Modernity—a Postwar German Intellectual Debate on Secularisation, Religion and 'Overcoming' the Past." *Totalitarian Movements & Political Religions* 8 (3–4): 591–608.
Hrynkow, Christopher. 2015. "Confluence of Thought: Mahatma Gandhi and Martin Luther King Jr." *Political Studies Review* 13 (4): 594-594.
Hughey, Matthew W. 2007. "The Pedagogy of Huey P. Newton: Critical Reflections on Education in His Writings and Speeches." *Journal of Black Studies* 38 (2): 209–231.
Hughey, Matthew W. 2005. "The Sociology, Pedagogy, and Theology of Huey P. Newton: Toward a Radical Democratic Utopia." *Western Journal of Black Studies* 29 (3): 639–655.
Hund, Wulf D. 2019. "The Racism of Eric Voegelin." *Journal of World Philosophies* 4: 1–22.
Ingraffia, Brian D. 1999. "'Neither Jew Nor Greek': Judaism, Christianity, and Ontotheology." *Christianity and Literature*. 48 (4): 497-510.
Inwood, J. F. 2009. "Searching for the Promised Land: Examining Dr Martin Luther King's Concept of the Beloved Community.'" *Antipode* 41 (3): 487-508.
Irwin, Alexander C. 1990. "The Faces of Desire: Tillich on 'Essential Libido,' Concupiscence and the Transcendence of Estrangement." *Encounter* 51 (4): 339–358.
Jahanbegloo, Ramin. 2020. *Revolution of Values: The Origins of Martin Luther King Jr.'s Moral and Political Philosophy*. Lanham, MD: Lexington Books.
Janicaud, Dominique. 1969. "Marcuse hors de la mode." *Les Études philosophiques* (2): 159–171.
Janicaud, Dominique. 1989. "Heidegger's Politics: Determinable or Not?" Translated by Pierre Adler. *Social Research* 56 (4): 819–847.
Jaspers, Karl. 1947. *The Question of German Guilt*. New York: Fordham University Press.
Jensen, Kipton E. 2017. "Pedagogical Personalism at Morehouse College." *Studies in Philosophy and Education* 36: 147–165.

Johnson, Davi. 2007. "Martin Luther King Jr.'s 1963 Birmingham Campaign as Image Event." *Rhetoric and Public Affairs* 10 (1): 1-26.

Jones, Charles E. 1988. "The Political Repression of the Black Panther Party 1966-1971: The Case of the Oakland Bay Area." *Journal of Black Studies* 18 (4): 415-434.

Jones, Michael T. 1998. "Heidegger the Fox: Hannah Arendt's Hidden Dialogue." *New German Critique* 73: 164-192.

Jones, Richard A. 2004. *African-American Sociopolitical Philosophy: Imagining Black Communities*. Lewiston, NY: Edwin Mellen Press.

Joseph, Peniel E. 2020. *The Sword and the Shield: The Revolutionary Lives of Malcolm X and Martin Luther King Jr.* New York: Basic Books.

Joseph, Peniel E. 2009a. "The Black Power Movement, Democracy, and America in the King Years." *American Historical Review* 114 (4): 1001-1016.

Joseph, Peniel E. 2009b. "The Black Power Movement: A State of the Field." *The Journal of American History* 96 (3): 751-776.

Joseph, Peniel E. 2009c. "Rethinking the Black Power Era." *The Journal of Southern History*. 75 (3): 707-716.

Joseph, Peniel E. 2008. "Historians and the Black Power Movement." *OAH Magazine of History* 22 (3): 8-15.

Joseph, Peniel E. 2006. *The Black Power Movement: Rethinking the Civil Rights-Black Power Era*. New York: Routledge.

Joseph, Peniel E. 2001. "Black Liberation Without Apology: Reconceptualizing the Black Power Movement." *The Black Scholar* 31 (3): 2-19.

Kakkori, Leena, and Rauno Huttunen. 2012. "The Sartre-Heidegger Controversy on Humanism and the Concept of Man in Education." *Educational Philosophy & Theory* 44 (4): 351-365.

Kaplan, Gregory. 2004. "In the End Shall Christians Become Jews and Jews, Christians? On Franz Rosenzweig's Apocalyptic Eschatology." *Cross Currents* 53 (4): 511-529.

Kavka, Martin. 2020. "A Mystic Conception of History: Negative Political Theology in Jacob Taubes." *Modern Theology* 36 (1): 13-28.

Kazin, Michael. 2009. "Martin Luther King, Jr. and the Meanings of the 1960s." *American Historical Review* 114 (4): 980-989.

Keedus, Liisi. 2014. "Thinking Beyond Philosophy: Hannah Arendt and the Weimar Hermeneutic Connections." *TRAMES: A Journal of the Humanities & Social Sciences* 18 (4): 307-325.

Kegley, Charles W. 1960. "Paul Tillich on the Philosophy of Art." *Journal of Aesthetics and Art Criticism* 19 (2): 175-184.

Kelley, Shawn. 1997. "Aesthetic Fascism: Heidegger, Anti-Semitism, and the Quest for Christian Origins." *Semeia* 77: 195-225.

Kelly, Robert, and Erin Cook. 2005. "Martin Luther King, Jr., and Malcolm X: A Common Solution." *OAH Magazine of History* 19 (1): 37-40.

Kennedy, Randall. 1989. "Martin Luther King's Constitution: A Legal History of the Montgomery Bus Boycott." *Yale Law Journal* 98 (6): 999–1067.

Kettler, David, and Gerhard Lauer. 2005. *Exile, Science, and Bildung: The Contested Legacies of German Emigre Intellectuals.* New York: Palgrave Macmillan.

Kierkegaard, Søren. 2013. *Fear and Trembling: And the Sickness unto Death.* Translated by Walter Lowrie. Princeton, NJ: Princeton University Press.

Kierkegaard, Søren. 1987. *Either/or.* Edited by Howard V. Hong and Edna H. Hong. Princeton, NJ: Princeton University Press.

King, Martin Luther, Jr. 2013. *The Essential Martin Luther King, Jr.* Ed. Clayborne Carson. Boston: Beacon Press.

King, Martin Luther, Jr. 2011. *Why We Can't Wait.* Boston: Beacon Press.

King, Martin Luther, Jr. 2010a. *Where Do We Go from Here: Chaos or Community?* Boston: Beacon Press.

King, Martin Luther, Jr. 2010b. *Stride Toward Freedom.* Boston: Beacon Press.

King, Martin Luther, Jr. 2000. *A Knock at Midnight.* Edited by Clayborne Carson and Peter Holloran. New York: Warner Books.

King, Martin Luther, Jr. 1998. *The Autobiography of Martin Luther King, Jr.* Edited by Clayborne Carson. New York: IPM in Association with Warner Books.

King, Martin Luther, Jr. 1994a. *The Papers of Martin Luther King, Jr., Volume I: Called to Serve, January 1929–June 1951.* Edited by Clayborne Carson. Berkeley: University of California Press.

King, Martin Luther, Jr. 1994b. *The Papers of Martin Luther King, Jr., Volume II: Rediscovering Precious Values. July 1951–November 1955.* Edited by Clayborne Carson. Berkeley: University of California Press.

King, Martin Luther, Jr. 1994c. *The Papers of Martin Luther King, Jr., Volume III: Birth of a New Age, December 1955–December 1956.* Edited by Clayborne Carson. Berkeley: University of California Press.

King, Martin Luther, Jr. 1994d. *The Papers of Martin Luther King, Jr., Volume IV: Symbol of the Movement. January 1957–December 1958.* Edited by Clayborne Carson. Berkeley: University of California Press.

King, Martin Luther, Jr. 1994e. *The Papers of Martin Luther King, Jr., Volume V: Threshold of a New Decade, January 1959–December 1960.* Edited by Clayborne Carson. Berkeley: University of California Press.

King, Martin Luther, Jr. 1994f. *The Papers of Martin Luther King, Jr., Volume VI: Advocate of the Social Gospel, September 1948–March 1963.* Edited by Clayborne Carson. Berkeley: University of California Press.

King, Martin Luther, Jr. 1986. *A Testament of Hope: The Essential Writings and Speeches of Martin Luther King, Jr.* Edited by James M Washington. New York: Harper Collins.

King, Richard H. 2004. *Race, Culture, and the Intellectuals, 1940–1970.* Washington, DC: Woodrow Wilson Center Press.

Kirk, John A. 2005. *Martin Luther King, Jr. Profiles in Power.* Harlow, UK: Pearson/Longman.

Klassen, Justin D. 2010. "Heidegger's Paul and Radical Orthodoxy on the Structure of Christian Hope." In *Paul, Philosophy, and the Theopolitical Vision: Critical Engagements with Agamben, Badiou, Žižek and Others,* edited by Douglas Harink, 64–89. Eugene, OR: Cascade Books.

Kleffmann, Tom. 2009. "Philosophie und Theologie: Der Briefwechsel zwischen Bultmann und Heidegger 1925–1975." *Theologische Rundschau* 74 (3): 249–262.

Klein, Mia. 1981. "The Other Beauty of Martin Luther King, Jr.'s 'Letter from Birmingham Jail.'" *College Composition and Communication* 32 (1): 30–37.

Knoche, Stefan. 2000. *Benjamin—Heidegger: Über Gewalt: Die Politisierung der Kunst.* Wien: Turia + Kant.

Korycki, Kate. 2020. "*African American Philosophers and Philosophy: An Introduction to the History, Concepts, and Contemporary Issues*: By John H. McClendon III and Stephen C. Ferguson II." *Bloomsbury Ethnic & Racial Studies* 43 (13): 2480–2482.

Kovacs, George. 2003. "Being, Truth, and the Political in Heidegger (1933–1934)." *Heidegger Studies* 19: 31–48.

Kreiss, Daniel. 2008. "Appropriating the Master's Tools: Sun Ra, the Black Panthers, and Black Consciousness, 1952–1973." *Black Music Research Journal* 28 (1): 57–81.

Krell, David Farrell. 2015. *Ecstasy, Catastrophe: Heidegger from Being and Time to the Black Notebooks.* Albany: State University of New York Press.

Krishnamurthy, Meena. 2015. "(White) Tyranny and the Democratic Value of Distrust." *Monist.* 98 (4):391-406.

Kroeker, P. Travis. 2005. "Whither Messianic Ethics? Paul as Political Theorist." *Journal of the Society of Christian Ethics.* 25 (2): 37-58.

Lafont, Cristina. 2018. "Hermeneutics and the Linguistic Turn." In *The Habermas Handbook,* edited by Hauke Brunkhorst, Regina Kreide, and Cristina Lafont, 49–57. New York: Columbia University Press.

Laing, Bonnie Young. 2009. "The Universal Negro Improvement Association, Southern Christian Leadership Conference, and Black Panther Party: Lessons for Understanding African American Culture-Based Organizing." *Journal of Black Studies* 39 (4): 635–656.

Lamarche, Pierre. 2001. "Tradition, Crisis, and the Work of Art in Benjamin and Heidegger." *Philosophy Today* 45 (5): 37–45.

Lampert, Laurence. 1974. "On Heidegger and Historicism." *Philosophy and Phenomenological Research* 34 (4): 586–590.

Landmesser, Christof. 2013. "Rudolf Bultmann als Paulusinterpret." *Zeitschrift für Theologie und Kirche* 110 (1): 1–21.

Lanzetta, Beverly J. 2018. "The Heart of a World Citizen: Martin Luther King Jr. as Social Mystic." In *Revives My Soul Again: The Spirituality of Martin Luther King Jr.,* edited by Lewis V. Baldwin and Victor Anderson, 239–270. Minneapolis: Augsburg Fortress.

Lasater, Phillip Michael. 2019. "Not So Vain After All: Hannah Arendt's Reception of Ecclesiastes." *Journal of the Bible & Its Reception* 6 (2): 163–196.

Lawee, Eric. 2015. "Hans Jonas and Classical Jewish Sources: New Dimensions." *Journal of Jewish Thought & Philosophy* 23 (1): 75–125.

Lazerow, Jama, and Yohuru R. Williams. 2006. *In Search of the Black Panther Party: New Perspectives on a Revolutionary Movement*. Durham, NC: Duke University Press.

Lazier, Benjamin. 2008. "On the Origins of 'Political Theology': Judaism and Heresy Between the World Wars." *New German Critique* 105: 143–164.

Ledger-Lomas, Michael. 2014. "God's Own Story? German Theology and its Nineteenth-Century Readers." *Reviews in Religion & Theology* 21 (4): 444–453.

Leff, Michael, and Ebony A. Utley. 2004. "Instrumental and Constitutive Rhetoric in Martin Luther King Jr.'s 'Letter from Birmingham Jail.'" *Rhetoric and Public Affairs* 7 (1): 37–51.

Lewis, David Levering. 2013. *King: A Biography*. 3rd ed. Urbana: University of Illinois Press.

Lier, Tiago. 2018. "The Rhetoric of the Non-Lover in Plato's *Phaedrus*." *Phoenix* 72 (1): 62–85.

Lindner, Burkhardt. 2011. "Das Politische und das Messianische: Hannah Arendt und Walter Benjamin. Mit einem Rückblick auf den Streit Arendt-Adorno." In *Affinität wider Willen? Hannah Arendt, Theodor W. Adorno Und Die Frankfurter Schule*, edited by Liliane Weissberg, 209–230. Frankfurt: Campus Verlag.

Ling, Peter J. 2015. *Martin Luther King, Jr.* 2nd ed. London: Routledge.

Livingston, Alexander. 2020. "Power for the Powerless: Martin Luther King, Jr.'s Late Theory of Civil Disobedience." *The Journal of Politics* 82 (2020): 700 - 713.

Long, Christopher P. 2001. "Art's Fateful Hour: Benjamin, Heidegger, Art and Politics." *New German Critique* 83: 89–115.

Long, Fiachra. 2017. "Transhuman Education? Sloterdijk's Reading of Heidegger's 'Letter on Humanism.'" *Journal of Philosophy of Education* 51 (1): 177–192.

Loomer, Bernard. 1956. "Tillich's Theology of Correlation." *Journal of Religion* 36 (1): 150–156.

Loose, Donald. 2009. "Saint Paul of the Philosophers: An Introduction to Recent Interpretations." *Bijdragen* 70 (2): 135–151.

Lott, Tommy Lee. 2020. "African American Philosophers and Philosophy: An Introduction to the History, Concepts, and Contemporary Issues." *Choice: Current Reviews for Academic Libraries* 57 (8): 869–870.

Lott, Tommy Lee, and John P. Pittman. 2003. *A Companion to African-American Philosophy*. New York: Blackwell.

Love, Jeff, and Michael Meng. 2018. "Heidegger's Metapolitics." *Cultural Critique* 99: 97–122.

Löwith, Karl. 1995. *Martin Heidegger and European Nihilism*. Edited by Richard Wolin. New York: Columbia University Press.

Luft, David S. 1994. "Being and German History: Historiographical Notes on the Heidegger Controversy." *Central European History* 27 (4): 479-502.

Lynd, Staughton. 1969. "The New Left." *Annals of the American Academy of Political and Social Science* 382: 64-72.

Mack, Michael. 2000. "Law, Charity and Taboo or Kant's Reversal of St Paul's Spirit-Letter Opposition and its Theological Implications." *Modern Theology* 16 (4): 417-441.

Macquarrie, John. 1967. "Heidegger's Earlier and Later Work Compared." *Anglican Theological Review*. 49 (1): 3-16.

Macquarrie, John, and J. H. Randall. 1964. "Tillich's *Systematic Theology, Vol. 3*." *Union Seminary Quarterly Review* 19 (4): 345.

Maier, Hans, and Jodi Cockerill. 2000. "Eric Vogelin and German Political Science." *Review of Politics* 62 (4): 707-727.

Maier-Katkin, Daniel, and Birgit Maier-Katkin. 2007. "Love and Reconciliation: The Case of Hannah Arendt and Martin Heidegger." *Harvard Review* (32): 34-48.

Malpas, Jeff. 2012. "'The House of Being': Poetry, Language, Place." In *Paths in Heidegger's Later Thought*, edited by Günter Figal, Diego D'Angelo, Tobias Keiling, and Guang Yang, 15-44. Bloomington: Indiana University Press.

Marcuse, Herbert. 2014. "Afterword to Walter Benjamin's *Critique of Violence*." In *Marxism, Revolution, and Utopia, Collected Papers of Herbert Marcuse, Volume Six*, edited by Douglas Kellner and Clayton Pierce. London and New York: Routledge, 123-127.

Marcuse, Herbert. 2007. *The Essential Marcuse: Selected Writings of Philosopher and Social Critic Herbert Marcuse*. Edited by Andrew Feenberg and William Leiss. Boston: Beacon Press.

Marcuse, Herbert. 2005a. "The Problem of Violence and the Radical Opposition." In *Herbert Marcuse, The New Left and the 1960s, Volume Three, The Collected Papers of Herbert Marcuse*, edited by Douglas Kellner. New York and London: Routledge, 57-76.

Marcuse, Herbert. 2005b. "German Philosophy, 1871-1933." In *Heideggerian Marxism*, edited by Richard Wolin and John Abromeit. Lincoln: University of Nebraska Press, 151-164.

Marcuse, Herbert. 1955. *Eros and Civilization: A Philosophical Inquiry into Freud*. 1955. Boston: Beacon Press.

Martel, James R. 2012. *Divine Violence: Walter Benjamin and the Eschatology of Sovereignty*. Abingdon, UK: Routledge.

Martin, Wayne. 2013. "The Semantics of 'Dasein' and the Modality of *Being and Time*." In *The Cambridge companion to Heidegger's* Being and Time, edited by Mark A. Wrathall. Cambridge: Cambridge University Press, 100-128.

Marx, Karl. 1990. *Capital: A Critique of Political Economy*. London: Penguin Books in association with New Left Review.

Marx, Karl, and Friedrich Engels. 1985. *The Communist Manifesto*. Translated by A. J. P. Taylor. London: Penguin Books.

May, William Francis. 1971. "Marcuse: Apologist for Intolerance." *Christianity and Crisis* 31 (4): 47–50.

McClendon, John H., and Stephen C. Ferguson. 2019. *African American Philosophers and Philosophy: An Introduction to the History, Concepts, and Contemporary Issues*. London: Bloomsbury Academic.

McDonald, Henry. 2010. "Levinas, Heidegger, and Hitlerism's Ontological Racism." *European Legacy* 15 (7): 891–896.

McGary, Howard. 2009. "Liberalism and the Problem of Racism." *Southern Journal of Philosophy* 47: 1–15.

McKinney, Jason Thomas. 2011. "Secret Agreements and Slight Adjustments: On Giorgio Agamben's Messianic Citations." *Journal of Religion* 91 (4): 496–518.

McManus, Denis. 2013. "Heidegger, Wittgenstein and St Paul on the Last Judgement: On the Roots and Significance of 'The Theoretical Attitude.'" *British Journal for the History of Philosophy* 21 (1): 143.

McNulty, Tracy. 2015. "Modernist Political Theologies: Carl Schmitt's Political Theology (1922) and Walter Benjamin's 'Critique of Violence' (1921)." In *1922: Literature, Culture, Politics*, edited by Jean-Michel Rabaté, 248–260. New York: Cambridge University Press.

McNulty, Tracy. 2007. "The Commandment Against the Law: Writing and Divine Justice in Walter Benjamin's 'Critique of Violence.'" *Diacritics* 37 (2): 34–60.

Mehring, Reinhard. 1996. "Karl Löwith, Carl Schmitt, Jacob Taubes und das 'Ende Der Geschichte.'" *Zeitschrift für Religions- Und Geistesgeschichte* 48 (3): 231–248.

Mendes-Flohr, Paul. 2019. "Gnostic Anxieties: Jewish Intellectuals and Weimar Neo-Marcionism." *Modern Theology* 35 (1): 71–80.

Mikelson, Thomas J. 1990. "Cosmic Companionship: The Place of God in the Moral Reasoning of Martin Luther King, Jr." *Journal of Religious Ethics* 18 (2): 1–14.

Miller, Donna R., and Monica Turci. 2006. "Construing the 'Social Gospel' of Martin Luther King Jr.: A Corpus-Assisted Study of *Free*." *Linguistics and Human Sciences* 2 (3): 399–429.

Miller, Keith D. 1998. *Voice of Deliverance: The Language of Martin Luther King, Jr., and Its Sources*. Athens: The University of Georgia Press.

Mills, Charles W. 2000. "Race and the Social Contract Tradition." *Social Identities* 6 (4): 441–462.

Mitchell, Andrew J., and Peter Trawny. 2017. *Heidegger's Black Notebooks: Responses to Anti-Semitism*. New York: Columbia University Press.

Monahan, Michael J. 2011. "Emancipatory Affect: Bell Hooks on Love and Liberation." *CLR James Journal* 17 (1): 102–111.

Montgomery, John Warwick. 1968. "Tillich's Philosophy of History: The Bearing of His Historical Understanding on His Theological Commitment." *Lutheran Scholar* 25 (1): 8.

Morales, Bernat Torres, and Josep Monserrat Molas. 2017. "The Significance of Plato's Philebus in the Philosophy of Eric Voegelin." *Political Science Reviewer* 41 (1): 33–51.

Morgan, Jo-Ann. 2018. *The Black Arts Movement and the Black Panther Party in American Visual Culture*. New York: Routledge, Taylor & Francis Group.

Morgan, Benjamin. 2007. "Undoing Legal Violence: Walter Benjamin's and Giorgio Agamben's Aesthetics of Pure Means." *Journal of Law and Society* 34 (1): 46–64.

Moses, Greg. 1998. *Revolution of Conscience: Martin Luther King, Jr. and the Philosophy of Nonviolence*. New York: Guilford.

Moten, Fred. 2008. "The Case of Blackness." *Criticism: A Quarterly for Literature and the Arts* 50 (2): 177–218.

Moten, Fred. 2007. "Preface for a Solo by Miles Davis." *Women & Performance* 17 (2): 217–246.

Mott, Wesley T. 1975. "The Rhetoric of Martin Luther King, Jr.: 'Letter from Birmingham Jail.'" *Phylon: The Clark Atlanta University Review of Race and Culture* 36 (4): 411–421.

Mueller, David L. 1966. "Paul Tillich's Philosophy of Culture, Science, and Religion." *Review & Expositor* 63 (4): 499–513.

Müller, Tim B. 2002. "Bearing Witness to the Liquidation of Western Dasein: Herbert Marcuse and the Holocaust, 1941–1948." *New German Critique* 85: 133–164.

Murphy, John W. 1984. "Paul Tillich and Western Marxism." *American Journal of Theology & Philosophy* 5 (1): 13–24.

Naishtat, Francisco. 2019. "Benjamin's Profane Uses of Theology: The Invisible Organon." *Religions* 10 (2): 1–18.

Nash, Jennifer C. 2011. "Practicing Love: Black Feminism, Love-Politics, and Post-Intersectionality." *Meridians* 11 (2): 1–24.

Naveh, Eyal. 1992. "Dialectical Redemption: Reinhold Niebuhr, Martin Luther King, Jr., and the Kingdom of God in America." *Journal of Religious Thought* 48 (2): 57–76.

Neddens, Christian. 2012. "'Politische Religion': Zur Herkunft eines Interpretationsmodells totalitärer Ideologien." *Zeitschrift für Theologie und Kirche* 109 (3): 307–336.

Negri, Antonio. 2010. "The Eclipse of Eschatology: Conversing with Taube's Messianism and the Common Body." *Political Theology* 11 (1): 35–41.

Nesbitt, Nick. 2013. "Revolutionary Inhumanism: Fanon's 'De la violence.'" *International Journal of Francophone Studies* 15 (3–4): 395–413.

Nesbitt, Rita. 1972. "Conflict and the Black Panther Party: A Social Psychological Interpretation." *Sociological Focus* 5 (4): 105–119.

Neugebauer, Fritz. 1959. "Die hermeneutischen Voraussetzungen Rudolf Bultmanns in ihrem Verhältnis zur paulinischen Theologie." *Kerygma und Dogma* 5 (4): 289–305.

Newton, Huey P. 1995. *Revolutionary Suicide*. New York: Writers and Readers Publishing.

Nietzsche, Friedrich Wilhelm. 1989. *On the Genealogy of Morals*. Translated by Walter Kaufmann. New York: Vintage Books.

Nietzsche, Friedrich Wilhelm. 1967. *The Will to Power*. Translated by Walter Kaufmann and R. J. Hollingdale. New York: Random House.

Noschka, Michael. 2014. "Extended Cognition, Heidegger, and Pauline Post/Humanism." *Literature and Theology* 28 (3): 334–347.

Nussbaum, Martha C. 2018. "From Anger to Love: Self-Purification and Political Resistance." In *To Shape a New World: Essays on the Political Philosophy of Martin Luther King, Jr.*, edited by Tommie Shelby and Brandon M. Terry. Cambridge, MA: The Belknap Press of Harvard University Press.

Nussbaum, Martha C. 2004. "On Hearing Women's Voices: A Reply to Susan Okin." *Philosophy & Public Affairs* 32 (2): 193–205.

Nussbaum, Martha C. 1997. *Cultivating Humanity: A Classical Defense of Reform in Liberal Education*. Cambridge, MA: Harvard University Press.

O'Mahoney, Paul. 2011. "Opposing Political Philosophy and Literature: Strauss's Critique of Heidegger and the Fate of the 'Quarrel Between Philosophy and Poetry.'" *Theoria* 126: 73–96.

O'Meara, Thomas, F. 1968. "Tillich and Heidegger: A Structural Relationship." *Harvard Theological Review* 61 (2): 249–261.

Ongiri, Amy Abugo. 2020. "Seize the Time! Military Aesthetics, Symbolic Revolution and the Black Panther Party." In *Making War on Bodies*, edited by Catherine Baker, 242–268. Edinburgh: Edinburgh University Press.

Osborn, Michael. 2004. "Rhetorical Distance in 'Letter from a Birmingham Jail.'" *Rhetoric and Public Affairs* 7 (1): 23–36.

Ostovich, Steven. 2007. "Carl Schmitt, Political Theology, and Eschatology." *KronoScope: Journal for the Study of Time* 7 (1): 49–66.

Ott, Hugo. 1993. *Martin Heidegger: A Political Life*. London: HarperCollinsPublishers.

Outlaw, Lucius. 1987. "African-American Philosophy: Social and Political Case Studies." *Social Science Information* 26 (1): 75–97.

Outlaw, Lucius, and Michael D. Roth. 1997. "Is There a Distinctive African-American Philosophy?" *Academic Questions* 10 (2): 29–46.

Overenget, Einar. 1995. "Heidegger and Arendt." *Philosophy Today* 39 (4): 430–444.

Owens, Patricia. 2017. "Racism in the Theory Canon: Hannah Arendt and 'the One Great Crime in Which America Was Never Involved.'" *Millennium* 45 (3): 403–424.

Paipais, Vassilios. 2016. "Overcoming 'Gnosticism'? Realism as Political Theology." *Cambridge Review of International Affairs* 29 (4): 1603–1623.

Pangle, Thomas L. 2004. "Leo Strauss's Perspective on Modern Politics." *Perspectives on Political Science* 33 (4): 197-203.

Parr, Patrick. 2018. *The Seminarian: Martin Luther King, Jr. Comes of Age*. Chicago: Lawrence Hill Books.

Patton, John H. 2004. "A Transforming Response: Martin Luther King Jr.'s ' 'Letter from Birmingham Jail.'" *Rhetoric and Public Affairs* 7 (1): 53–66.
Pégny, Gaëtan. 2018. "Beyond the Human: Heidegger's Self-Interpretation of Being and Time in the *Black Notebooks*." *Critical Horizons* 19 (4): 292–311.
Peterson, Thomas E. 2005. "Notes on Heidegger's Authoritarian Pedagogy." *Educational Philosophy & Theory* 37 (4): 599–623.
Polt, Richard F. H. 1999. *Heidegger: An Introduction*. Ithaca, NY: Cornell University Press.
Popkes, Enno Edzard. 2006. "'Phänomenologie frühchristlichen Lebens': Exegetische Anmerkungen zu Heideggers Auslegung paulinischer Briefe." *Kerygma und Dogma* 52 (3): 263–282.
Porter, Clifford F. 2002. "Eric Voegelin on Nazi Political Extremism." *Journal of the History of Ideas* 63 (1): 151–171.
Rabinbach, Anson. 1994. "Heidegger's 'Letter on Humanism' as Text and Event." *New German Critique* 62: 3–38.
Rae, Gavin. 2010. "Re-Thinking the Human: Heidegger, Fundamental Ontology, and Humanism." *Human Studies: A Journal for Philosophy and the Social Sciences* 33 (1): 22–39.
Rae, Gavin. 2016. "The Theology of Carl Schmitt's Political Theology." *Political Theology* 17 (6): 555–572.
Raeder, Linda C. 2007. "Voegelin on Gnosticism, Modernity, and the Balance of Consciousness." *Political Science Reviewer* 36: 344–370.
Rathburn, John. 1968. "Martin Luther King: The Theology of Social Action." *American Quarterly* 20 (1): 38–53.
Rauschenbusch, Walter. 1907. *Christianity and the Social Crisis*. New York: Macmillan.
Rawls, John. 2007. *Lectures on the History of Political Philosophy*. Edited by Samuel Richard Freeman. Cambridge, MA: Belknap Press of Harvard University Press.
Richardson, William J. 2012. *Heidegger*. Routledge Philosophers. Abington, UK: Routledge.
Richardson, William J. 1963. "Heidegger and Plato." *Heythrop Journal* 4 (3): 273–279.
Röbel, Marc. 2017. "Die Frage nach der Frage: Paul Tillichs Korrelationsmethode und ihre existentialontologische Fundierung." *International Yearbook for Tillich Research* 12 (1): 9–17.
Roberts, Adam. 1968. "Martin Luther King and Non-Violent Resistance." *The World Today* 24 (6): 226–236.
Robinson, Dean E. 2001. *Black Nationalism in American Politics and Thought*. Cambridge, UK: Cambridge University Press.
Robinson, Scott, Lee Trepanier, and David N. Whitney, eds. 2019. *Eric Voegelin Today: Voegelin's Political Thought in the 21st Century*. Lanham, MD: Lexington Books.
Rockmore, Tom. 2016. "A Progress Report on the Ongoing Heidegger Reception." *Studies in East European Thought* 68 (2): 229–239.

Rockmore, Tom. 1992. *On Heidegger's Nazism and Philosophy*. Berkeley: University of California Press.

Rogers, Ibram H. 2012. "The Black Campus Movement and the Institutionalization of Black Studies, 1965–1970." *Journal of African American Studies* 16 (1): 21–40.

Rogers, Melvin L., and Jack Turner. 2021. *African American Political Thought: A Collected History*. Chicago: The University of Chicago Press.

Rojas, Fabio. 2006. "Social Movement Tactics, Organizational Change and the Spread of African-American Studies." *Social Forces* 84 (4): 2147–2166.

Rojcewicz, Richard. 1997. "Platonic Love: Dasein's Urge Toward Being." *Research in Phenomenology* 27: 103–120.

Roman, Meredith. 2016. "The Black Panther Party and the Struggle for Human Rights." *Spectrum: A Journal on Black Men* 5 (1): 7–32.

Rose, Justin. 2019. *The Drum Major Instinct: Martin Luther King Jr.'s Theory of Political Service*. Athens: University of Georgia Press.

Ross, Alison. 2014. "The Distinction Between Mythic and Divine Violence: Walter Benjamin's 'Critique of Violence' from the Perspective of Goethe's *Elective Affinities*." *New German Critique* 121: 93–120.

Rossbach, Stefan. 2005. "'Gnosis' in Eric Voegelin's Philosophy." *Political Science Reviewer* 34: 77–121.

Rubenstein, Mary-Jane. 2008. *Strange Wonder: The Closure of Metaphysics and the Opening of Awe*. New York: Columbia University Press.

Rubini, Rocco. 2011. "Humanism Is an Existentialism: Renaissance and Vichian Legacies in Italian Philosophy Between Hegel and Heidegger." *Annali d'Italianistica* 29: 431–458.

Sabl, Andrew. 1999. "The Paradox of Equality and the Trials of Martin Luther King, Jr." *Society* 3: 32–42.

Scaer, David P. 1975. "Gnosis in the Church Today." *Springfielder* 38 (4): 334–344.

Scharff, Robert. 2007. "Andrew Feenberg, Heidegger and Marcuse: The Catastrophe and Redemption of History." *Continental Philosophy Review* 40 (1): 91–97.

Schatzki, Theodore R. 1989. "Early Heidegger on Being, the Clearing, and Realism." *Revue internationale de philosophie* 43 (168): 80–102.

Scheuerman, William E. 2015. "Recent Theories of Civil Disobedience: An Anti-Legal Turn?" *Journal of Political Philosophy* 23 (4): 427–449.

Schmidt, Christoph. 1998. "Der häretische Imperativ: Gershom Scholems Kabbala als politische Theologie?" *Zeitschrift für Religions- und Geistesgeschichte* 50 (1): 61–83.

Schmidt Passos, Eduardo. 2019. "Eric Voegelin and the Natural Law Tradition." *Perspectives on Political Science* 48 (3): 210–217.

Schmidt Passos, Eduardo. 2018. "The Blood of the Martyrs: Erik Peterson's Theology of Martyrdom and Carl Schmitt's Political Theology of Sovereignty." *Review of Politics* 80 (3): 487–510.

Schmutz, Jacob. 2009. "Eric Voegelin (1901–1985)." *Cités* 37: 157–165.

Schöttker, Detlev, and Erdmut Wizisla. 2006. *Arendt und Benjamin: Texte, Briefe, Dokumente*. Frankfurt am Main: Suhrkamp.

Schrijvers, Joeri. 2006. "On Doing Theology 'After' Ontotheology: Notes on a French Debate." *New Blackfriars* 87 (1009): 302–314.

Schüssler, Werner. 1995. "Metaphysik und Theologie: Zu Paul Tillichs 'Umwendung' der Metaphysik in der 'Dogmatik' von 1925." *Zeitschrift für katholische Theologie* 117 (2): 192–202.

Scott, Joanna Vecchiarelli. 2004. "Alien Nation: Hannah Arendt, the German Émigrés and America." *European Journal of Political Theory* 3 (2): 167–176.

Seale, Bobby. 1972. "The Black Scholar Interviews: Bobby Seale." *The Black Scholar* 4 (1): 7–16.

Seale, Bobby. 1970. *Seize the Time: The Story of the Black Panther Party and Huey P. Newton*. New York: Random House.

Shakur, Assata. 2001. *Assata: An Autobiography*. Chicago: Lawrence Hill Books.

Sharpe, Matthew. 2018a. "On Reading Heidegger—After the 'Heidegger Case'?" *Critical Horizons* 19 (4): 334–360.

Sharpe, Matthew. 2018b. "Rhetorical Action in *Rektoratsrede*: Calling Heidegger's Gefolgschaft." *Philosophy and Rhetoric* 51 (2): 176–201.

Sheehan, Thomas. 2015. "Emmanuel Faye: The Introduction of Fraud into Philosophy?" *Philosophy Today* 59 (3): 367–400.

Sheehan, Thomas. 1992. "The Heidegger Controversy: A Critical Reader." *Ethics* 103 (1): 178–181.

Shelby, Tommie. 2010. "Reflections on Boxill's 'Blacks and Social Justice.'" *Journal of Social Philosophy* 41 (3): 343-353.

Shelby, Tommie, and Brandon M. Terry, eds. 2018. *To Shape a New World: Essays on the Political Philosophy of Martin Luther King, Jr.* Cambridge, MA: The Belknap Press of Harvard University Press.

Simmons, Gwendolyn Zoharah. 2008. "Martin Luther King Jr. Revisited: A Black Power Feminist Pays Homage to the King." *Journal of Feminist Studies in Religion* 24 (2): 189–213.

Simpson, G. M. 2008. "'Changing the Face of the Enemy': Martin Luther King, Jr., and the Beloved Community." *Word & World* 28 (1): 57–65.

Smith, David Norman. 1992. "Introduction to Herbert Marcuse, 'On the Critique of Sociology.'" *Mid-American Review of Sociology* 16 (2): 1–13.

Smith, Ervin. 1981. *The Ethics of Martin Luther King, Jr.* 2 vols. New York: E. Mellen Press.

Smith, Gregory Bruce. 1997. "Leo Strauss and the Straussians: An Anti-Democratic Cult?" *PS: Political Science and Politics* 30 (2): 180–189.

Smith, Kenneth L., and Ira G. Zepp. 1974. *Search for the Beloved Community: The Thinking of Martin Luther King, Jr.* Valley Forge, PA: Judson Press.

Smith, Steven B. 1995. "Heidegger and Political Philosophy: The Theory of His Practice." *Nomos* 37: 440–463.

Smith, Steven B. 1997. "Destruktion or Recovery? Leo Strauss's Critique of Heidegger." *Review of Metaphysics* 51: 345–377.
Snow, Malinda. 1985. "Martin Luther King's 'Letter from Birmingham Jail' as Pauline Epistle." *Quarterly Journal of Speech* 71 (3): 318–334.
Soffer, Gail. 1996. "Heidegger, Humanism, and the Destruction of History." *Review of Metaphysics* 49: 547–576.
Sokolsky-Tifft, Samuel. 2020. "Heidegger and Marcuse: A History of Disenchantment." *Journal of European Studies* 50 (2): 162–177.
Sowers, Brian P. 2017. "The Socratic Black Panther: Reading Huey P. Newton Reading Plato." *Journal of African American Studies* 21 (1): 26–41.
Spencer, Robyn C. *The Revolution Has Come: Black Power, Gender, and the Black Panther Party in Oakland*. Durham, NC: Duke University Press, 2016.
Stanley, Timothy. 2007. "Heidegger on Luther on Paul." *Dialog* 46 (1): 41–45.
Steinkraus, Warren E. 1973. "Martin Luther King's Personalism and Non-Violence." *Journal of the History of Ideas* 34 (1): 97–111.
Stephan, Alexander. 2000. *"Communazis": FBI Surveillance of German Emigré Writers*. New Haven, CT: Yale University Press.
Strauss, Leo, Eric Voegelin, Peter Emberley, and Barry Cooper. 2004. *Faith and Political Philosophy: The Correspondence between Leo Strauss and Eric Voegelin, 1934-1964*. Columbia: University of Missouri Press.
Strenski, Ivan. 1982. "Heidegger Is No Hero." *The Christian Century* 99 (18): 153–165.
Sturm, Douglas. 1990. "Martin Luther King, Jr., as Democratic Socialist." *Journal of Religious Ethics* 18 (2): 79–105.
Sturm, Douglas. 1984. "Crisis in the American Republic: The Legal and Political Significance of Martin Luther King's Letter from a Birmingham Jail." *Journal of Law and Religion* 2 (2): 309–324.
Sturm, Erdmann. 2016. "Paul Tillich: Contemporary German Philosophy." *International Yearbook for Tillich Research* 11 (1): 181–216.
Sturm, Erdmann. 1994. "'Holy Love Claims Life and Limb': Paul Tillich's War on Theology." *Zeitschrift für neuere Theologiegeschichte* 1 (1): 275–304.
Styfhals, Willem. 2015. "Evil in History: Karl Löwith and Jacob Taubes on Modern Eschatology." *Journal of the History of Ideas* 76 (2): 191–213.
Styfhals, Willem. 2012. "Gnosis, Modernity and Divine Incarnation: The Voegelin-Blumenberg Debate." *Bijdragen* 73 (2): 190–211.
Sundquist, Eric J. 2009. *King's Dream*. New Haven, CT: Yale University Press.
Svenungsson, Jayne. 2017. "Law and Liberation: Critical Notes on Agamben's Political Messianism." *European Judaism* 50 (1): 68–77.
Taminiaux, Jacques. 1989. "Heidegger and the Earth." *Diacritics* 19 (3): 76–81.
Terpstra, Marin. 2009. "'God's Love for His Enemies': Jacob Taubes' Conversation with Carl Schmitt on Paul." *Bijdragen* 70 (2): 185–206.
Terry, Brandon M. 2018a. "Requiem for a Dream: The Problem-Space of Black Power."

In *To Shape a New World: Essays on the Political Philosophy of Martin Luther King, Jr.*, edited by Tommie Shelby and Brandon M. Terry. Cambridge, MA: The Belknap Press of Harvard University Press, 290–323.

Terry, Brandon M. 2018b. "A Revolution in Values." In *Fifty Years since MLK*, edited by Brandon M. Terry. Cambridge, MA: MIT Press, 53–58.

"The Theses of Martin Luther King, Jr." 1991. Editorial. *First Things*, February 1991.

Thiem, Annika. 2013. "Theological-Political Ruins: Walter Benjamin, Sovereignty, and the Politics of Skeletal Eschatology." *Law & Critique* 24 (3): 295–315.

Thomas, J. H. 1953. "Tillich on Philosophy and Theology." *Union Seminary Quarterly Review* 8 (3): 10–16.

Thomas, Owen C. 1996. "Tillich and the Perennial Philosophy." *Harvard Theological Review* 89 (1): 85–98.

Thomassen, Bjørn. 2014. "Debating Modernity as Secular Religion: Hans Kelsen's Future Exchange with Eric Voegelin." *History & Theory* 53 (3): 435–450.

Thompson, Mark Christian. 2022. *Phenomenal Blackness: Black Power, Philosophy, and Theory*. Chicago: University of Chicago Press.

Thompson, Mark Christian. 2007. *Black Fascisms: African American Literature and Culture Between the Wars*. Charlottesville: University of Virginia Press.

Thomson, Iain. 2000. "From the Question Concerning Technology to the Quest for a Democratic Technology: Heidegger, Marcuse, Feenberg." *Inquiry* 43 (2): 203–216.

Tiebout, Harry M. 1959. "Tillich, Existentialism, and Psychoanalysis." *Journal of Philosophy* 56 (14): 605–612.

Tiefenbrun, Susan. 1992. "Semiotics and Martin Luther King's 'Letter from Birmingham Jail.'" *Cardozo Studies in Law and Literature* 4 (2): 255–287.

Tillich, Paul. 2000. *The Courage to Be*. New Haven, CT: Yale University Press.

Tillich, Paul. 1995. *Morality and Beyond*. Louisville, KY: Westminster John Knox Press.

Tillich, Paul. 1951. *Systematic Theology: Volume One*. Chicago: University of Chicago Press.

Tillich, Paul, et al. 2007. "Streit über John F. Kennedy: Ein kurzer Briefwechsel zwischen Paul Tillich und Herbert Marcuse." *Zeitschrift für neuere Theologiegeschichte* 14 (2): 312–325.

Tillich, Paul, Max Horkheimer, and Erdmann Sturm. 1994. "Paul Tillich und Max Horkheimer im Dialog: Drei bisher unveröffentlichte Texte (1942/45)." *Zeitschrift für Neuere Theologiegeschichte* 1 (2): 275–304.

Trawny, Peter. 2017. "Anti-Semitism and History: On the Role of 'World Judaism' in Heidegger's History of Being." *Tópicos: Revista de Filosofía* 53: 437–453.

Trawny, Peter. 2018. *Heidegger: A Critical Introduction*. Cambridge, UK: Polity Press.

Trawny, Peter, and Andrew J. Mitchell. 2015. *Heidegger and the Myth of a Jewish World Conspiracy*. Chicago: University of Chicago Press.

Trepanier, Lee. 2018. "Eric Voegelin's Contribution to Political Science." *Perspectives on Political Science* 47 (3): 177–181.

Trepanier, Lee, and Steven F. McGuire. 2011. *Eric Voegelin and the Continental Tradition: Explorations in Modern Political Thought*. Columbia: University of Missouri Press.

Ture, Kwame, and Charles V. Hamilton. 1992. *Black Power: The Politics of Liberation in America*. New York: Vintage Books.

Tyner, James A. 2006. "'Defend the Ghetto': Space and the Urban Politics of the Black Panther Party." *Annals of the Association of American Geographers* 96 (1): 105–118.

Valls, Andrew. 2010. "A Liberal Defense of Black Nationalism." *American Political Science Review* 104 (3): 467–481.

Van Deburg, William L. 1992. *New Day in Babylon: The Black Power Movement and American Culture, 1965–1975*. Chicago: University of Chicago Press.

Van Hook, Jay M. 1977. "Tillich on the Relation Between Philosophy and Theology." *Journal of the American Academy of Religion* 45 (1): 73.

Van Reijen, Willem. 1998. *Der Schwarzwald und Paris: Heidegger und Benjamin*. Munich: W. Fink.

Vandiver, Josh. 2016. "Plato in Folsom Prison; Eldridge Cleaver, Black Power, Queer Classicism." *Political Theory* 44 (6): 764–796.

Varshizky, Amit. 2012. "Alfred Rosenberg: The Nazi Weltanschauung as Modern Gnosis." *Politics, Religion & Ideology* 13 (3): 311–331.

Varshizky, Amit. 2019. "The Metaphysics of Race: Revisiting Nazism and Religion." *Central European History* 52 (2): 252–288.

Vatter, Miguel E. 2019. "'Only a God Can Resist a God': Political Theology Between Polytheism and Gnosticism." *Political Theology* 20 (6): 472–497.

Vaughan, William. 1995. "The Phenomenology of Time in Pauline Epistles." *Encounter* 56 (2): 147–173.

Vedder, Ben. 2009. "Heidegger's Explication of Religious Phenomena in the Letters of Saint Paul." *Bijdragen* 70 (2): 152–167.

Velkey, Richard L. 2011. *Heidegger, Strauss, and the Premises of Philosophy on Original Forgetting*. Chicago; London: University of Chicago Press.

Velkey, Richard L. 2008. "On the Roots of Rationalism: Strauss's *Natural Right and History* as Response to Heidegger." *Review of Politics* 70 (2): 245–259.

Villa, Dana. 2007. "Arendt, Heidegger, and the Tradition." *Social Research* 74 (4): 983–1002.

Voegelin, Eric. 2000. *The Collected Works of Eric Voegelin*. Edited by Ellis Sandoz and Paul Caringella. Baton Rouge: Louisiana State University Press.

Voegelin, Eric. 1998. *The History of the Race Idea: From Ray to Carus*. Baton Rouge: Louisiana State University Press.

Voegelin, Eric. 1997. *Race and State*. Edited by Klaus Vondung. Baton Rouge: Louisiana State University Press.

Voegelin, Eric. 1987. *The New Science of Politics: An Introduction*. Chicago: University of Chicago Press. (Originally published 1952.)

Voegelin, Eric. 1940. "The Growth of the Race Idea." *Review of Politics* 2: 283–317.

Voegelin, Eric, William Petropulos, and Gilbert Weiss. 2004. "Man in Political Institutions: Excerpts from the Discussion." *The Drama of Humanity and Other Miscellaneous Papers, 1939-1985*. Columbia: University of Missouri Press, 150-173.
Voegelin, Eric, and Ellis Sandoz. 2011. *Autobiographical Reflections*. Columbia: University of Missouri Press.
Waddell, Robby. 2012. "Letters from Jail: The Apostle Paul and the Rev. Dr. Martin Luther King, Jr.: An Open Letter to the Church of the Brethren." *Brethren Life and Thought* 57 (1): 43-53.
Waite, Geoff. 2008. "Heidegger, Schmitt, Strauss: The Hidden Monologue, or Conserving Esotericism to Justify the High Hand of Violence." *Cultural Critique* 69: 113-144.
Walton, Hanes. 1971. *The Political Philosophy of Martin Luther King, Jr*. Westport, CN: Greenwood Pub. Corp.
Ward, James F. 1987. "Political Philosophy and History: The Links Between Strauss and Heidegger." *Polity* 20 (2): 273-295.
Warnek, Peter. 1997. "Reading Plato Before Platonism (After Heidegger)." *Research in Phenomenology* 27: 61-89.
Watson, Martha Solomon. 2004. "The Issue Is Justice: Martin Luther King Jr.'s Response to the Birmingham Clergy." *Rhetoric and Public Affairs* 7 (1): 1-22.
Webb, Eugene. 2005. "Voegelin's 'Gnosticism' Reconsidered." *Political Science Reviewer* 34: 48-76.
Weissberg, Liliane. 2002. "On Friendship in Dark Times: Hannah Arendt Reads Walter Benjamin." In *Literary Paternity, Literary Friendship: Essays in Honor of Stanley Corngold*, edited by Gerhard Richter, 278-293. Chapel Hill: University of North Carolina Press.
West, Cornel. 1977. "Philosophy and the Afro-American Experience." *Philosophical Forum* 9 (2): 117-148.
Westbrook, Robert. 2013. "MLK's Manifesto: 'Letter from Birmingham Jail' at 50." *Christian Century* 130 (8): 22-27.
Willhelm, Sidney M. 1979. "Martin Luther King, Jr. and the Black Experience in America." *Journal of Black Studies* 10 (1): 3-19.
Williams, Dana M. 2015. "Black Panther Radical Factionalization and the Development of Black Anarchism." *Journal of Black Studies* 46 (7): 678-703.
Williams, Preston N. 1990. "An Analysis of the Conception of Love and Its Influence on Justice in the Thought of Martin Luther King, Jr." *Journal of Religious Ethics* 18 (2): 15-31.
Williams, Yohuru. 2008. "'Some Abstract Thing Called Freedom': Civil Rights, Black Power, and the Legacy of the Black Panther Party." *OAH Magazine of History* 22 (3): 16-21.
Williams, Yohuru R. 2001. "No Haven: From Civil Rights to Black Power in New Haven, Connecticut." *The Black Scholar* 31 (3-4): 54-66.
Williams, Yohuru R. 1998. "In the Name of the Law: The 1967 Shooting of Huey New-

ton and Law Enforcement's Permissive Environment." *Negro History Bulletin* 61 (2): 6–18.

Williams, Yohuru R. 1997. "American Exported Black Nationalism: The Student Nonviolent Coordinating Committee, the Black Panther Party, and the Worldwide Freedom Struggle, 1967–1972." *Negro History Bulletin* 60 (3): 13–20.

Williamson, Clark M. 1972. "Tillich's 'Two Types of Philosophy of Religion': A Reconsideration." *Journal of Religion* 52 (3): 205–222.

Williamson, Joy Ann. 2005. "Community Control with a Black Nationalist Twist: The Black Panther Party's Educational Programs." *Counterpoints* 237: 137–157.

Wills, Richard W. 2011. *Martin Luther King, Jr. and the Image of God*. New York: Oxford University Press.

Wilson, Robert McLachlan. 1974. "Jewish Gnosis and Gnostic Origins: A Survey." *Hebrew Union College Annual* 45: 177–189.

Witte, Bernd. 2011. "Politics, Economics, and Religion in the Global Age: Walter Benjamin's Critique of Violence and Capitalism as Religion." *Symposium: A Quarterly Journal in Modern Literatures* 65 (1): 5–15.

Woessner, Martin. 2011. "Reconsidering the Slaughter Bench of History: Genocide, Theodicy, and the Philosophy of History." *Journal of Genocide Research* 13 (1): 85–105.

Wolfe, J. E. 2019. "The Eschatological Turn in German Philosophy." *Modern Theology* 35 (1): 55–70.

Wolin, Richard. 2015. *Heidegger's Children: Hannah Arendt, Karl Löwith, Hans Jonas, and Herbert Marcuse*. Princeton, NJ: Princeton University Press.

Wolin, Richard. 1995. "Hannah and the Magician." *New Republic* 213 (15): 27–37.

Wolin, Richard, ed. 1993. *The Heidegger Controversy: A Critical Reader*. Cambridge, MA: MIT Press.

Wolin, Richard. 1991. "Introduction to Herbert Marcuse and Martin Heidegger: An Exchange of Letters." *New German Critique* (53): 19–27.

Woodson, Hue. 2019. "Between Activism, Religiosity, and the Public Sphere: The Intellectual Insurgency of Bell Hooks." *Journal of African American Studies* 23 (3): 187–202.

Woodson, Hue. 2018. *Heideggerian Theologies: The Pathmarks of John Macquarrie, Rudolf Bultmann, Paul Tillich, and Karl Rahner*. Eugene, OR: Wipf and Stock.

Worthington, Bruce. 2013. "Martin Luther King, Jr. as Identificatory Conglomerate." *Black Theology* 11 (2): 219–239.

Wrathall, Mark A. 2005. *How to Read Heidegger*. How to Read. London: Granta Books.

Wrathall, Mark A. and Max Murphey. 2013. "An Overview of Being and Time." In *The Cambridge Companion to Heidegger's* Being and Time, edited by Mark A. Wrathall. Cambridge: Cambridge University Press, 1–53.

Yancy, George. 2015. "Through the Crucible of Pain and Suffering: African-American Philosophy as a Gift and the Countering of the Western Philosophical Metanarrative." *Educational Philosophy & Theory* 47 (11): 1143–1159.

Yancy, George. 2012a. *Look, a White!: Philosophical Essays on Whiteness*. Philadelphia, PA: Temple University Press.

Yancy, George. 2012b. *Reframing the Practice of Philosophy: Bodies of Color, Bodies of Knowledge*. Albany: State University of New York Press.

Yancy, George. 2011. "African-American Philosophy: Through the Lens of Socio-Existential Struggle." *Philosophy & Social Criticism* 37 (5): 551–574.

Yancy, George. 2004. *What White Looks Like: African-American Philosophers on the Whiteness Question*. New York: Routledge.

Young, Julian. 1997. *Heidegger, Philosophy, Nazism*. Cambridge, UK: Cambridge University Press.

Zack, Naomi. 1999. "Philosophy and Racial Paradigms." *The Journal of Value Inquiry* 33 (3): 299-317.

Zawisza, Raphael. 2018. "Thank God We Are Creatures: Hannah Arendt's Cryptotheology." *Religions* 9 (11).

Zepp, Ira G. 1989. *The Social Vision of Martin Luther King, Jr*. Brooklyn, NY: Carlson.

Index

Abernathy, Ralph, 7
Abron, JoNina M., 74
absolutism, practical, 42
activism: African American/Black, 14, 74–76; and agape, 90; collective, 17; social, 48–49, 52, 70, 90, 123, 152n15; spiritual, 145–46. *See also* inaction; social responsibility
Adorno, Theodor, 137–38, 140, 153n1
"Advice for Living" (King), 66
African American philosophy: academic, 150n24; and activism, 14; basic critical assumptions/truths, 12; and Blackness, 15; and ethnophilosophy, 15; existentialist, 17; and history, 10, 14, 17, 74; King and, 9–19, 24; and meontology, 14; and metaphysics, 12–13; and nonviolence, 10–19; and ontology, 9–19, 24, 94; and onto-theological truth., 94; and racial ontology, 14; and racism, 30, 94; roles of, 17; and socio-existential context, 15; and sociological critique, 150n24; sociopolitical, 150n24; and white Euro-American/Western philosophical tradition, 13, 18; as world-historical, 94. *See also* Africana philosophy; Afro-American philosophy; Black philosophy
African American studies, 143–44, 146–47. *See also* Africana studies; Afro-American studies; Black studies
African American theory, 17–18

African Americans: in beloved community, 134–35; exploitation and gradual elimination of in U.S., 79; and law, 18; and racial clustering, 75; racially normative principles for, 79–80; and redemption of white Americans, 91–92; state of exception, as constant/norm for, 135–36
Africana philosophy, 14–19. *See also* African American philosophy; Afro-American philosophy; Black philosophy; ethnophilosophy
Africana studies, 16. *See also* African American studies; Afro-American studies; Black studies
Afro-American philosophy, 12–13. *See also* African American philosophy; Africana philosophy; Black philosophy
Afro-American studies, 150n23. *See also* African American studies; Africana studies; Black studies
Agamben, Giorgio, 22, 117, 119, 124, 133–34
agape: and activism, 90; as anti-essentialism, 26; as Being Itself, 90; as Being-in-love, 26, 88, 90–91; and beloved community, 25, 123; as brotherly love, 66; Christianized, 87–89; of cosmic importance, 91; and creativity, 86; and eros, 25, 56, 61, 82–91, 137, 151n29; as essential libido, 25, 151n29; and existentialism, 56;

agape (*continued*)
and forgiveness, 83; and freedom, 61; God's love as, 61, 83; goodwill, 82–83, 86–88; and interrelatedness, 91; and justice, 61, 88; and libido, 25, 151n29; and love, 61, 66, 82–89, 91; and metaphysics, 90; and nonviolence, 25, 83, 90; and objectivity, 85, 89; and philia, 61, 82–84, 87, 91; and philosophy, 89–90, 92; and Platonism, 25, 88–89; and power, 84–85, 151n29; primitive Christian, 89; and purity of its divine source, 83; and racial essentialism, 25; and redemption/salvation, 83, 86, 91; and separatism, 26; as spontaneous, 82, 89; and subjectivism, 89; and theology, 88–90; unconditional love, 61
Agape and Eros (Nygren), 86–89
Allen, Anita, 17–19, 160n1
Anger and Forgiveness: Resentment, Generosity, Justice (Nussbaum), 39–40
"Annabel Lee" (Poe), 86
anthropocentrism, 17, 30
anthropology, 16–17, 41, 136
antichrist, *katechon as*, 115–16
anti-essentialism, 4, 9, 25–26, 63, 76, 92. *See also* essentialism
anti-historicism, 103, 106, 119. *See also* historicism
anti-humanism, 17, 22, 25–30, 104; King and, 3, 27–30, 45–46, 149n5. *See also* humanism
anti-racism, 3, 25–26, 32–33, 35, 76, 134. *See also* racism
anti-Semitism, 23, 31, 35, 96, 104, 106, 141, 151n4. *See also* Judaism
apotheosis, 108, 111
Appiah, Kwame Anthony, 14–15, 18
Arcades Project, The (Benjamin), 120
Arendt, Hannah, 158n11; and Agamben, 124; and Benjamin, 113–14, 160n2, 160n4; and Bultmann, 102, 158n16; and Christian theology, 158n16; and Civil Rights Movement, 160n1; and critique of violence, 113–14, 160n4; and eschatology, 102; Gnosis, 158n13; and Heidegger, 23, 95, 102, 158n13, 158n15; and humanism, 102, 158n15; and Jaspers, 158n16; and Jonas, 158n13; on Little Rock, 159n23; and Marcuse, 23, 113–14; and messianic, 160n4; on past and future in the now, 153n5; and politics, 158n16, 159n23, 160n4; on power and violence, 161n17; on race/racism, 159n23, 160n1; on Saint Augustine, 158n16; and Tillich, 153n1; and violence, 114, 161n17; and Voegelin, 159n23
Aristotle, 37, 49, 60
assimilation, and separatism, 13, 150n18
atheism, 38, 51, 152n16
Augustine, Saint, 3, 55–58, 62, 89, 110, 118, 135, 158n16
Austin, B. William, 7
Austin, Curtis J., 7
Austin, Tracy, 78
authoritarianism, 137–39, 149n3. *See also* totalitarianism
Autobiographical Reflections (Voegelin), 95, 108–9

Badiou, Alain, 157n6
Baldwin, Lewis V., 71, 134
Ball, Hugo, 159–60n27
Bandung, Indonesia, Black Power in, 5–6
Barth, Karl: and anti-historicism, 103, 106, 119; on Christian revelation, 103; and crisis philosophy, 104; and crisis theology, 28; and existentialism, 29; and German academic debates, 24; on God's radical Otherness, 104; hermeneutic approach, 103; and Jewish Barthianism, 158n18; and Marcion, 104; and method in theology, 103; and ontology, 52; and philosophy, 29, 57; and

political theology, 116; on Saint Paul, 103; and theology, 33, 57, 103; and Tillich, 52; on Wholly Other, 58

Baur, Ferdinand Christian, 100–101

Being and Time (Heidegger), 28, 33–37, 107, 138–41

Being Itself: agape as, 90; and anti-essentialism, 92; and finitude, 45; and Gnosticism, 137; God as, 45–47, 51–52, 65, 92–93, 96; and God's love, 59, 92–93; and history, 36, 137; and love, 51, 66, 90–91, 93; and nonbeing/Nonbeing, 91; and nonviolence, 52; as political, 146; and redemption of self, 68; and self, 51, 66, 68; Tillich and, vii, 11–12, 49–52, 63, 66, 70, 90, 92

being/Being: African American/Black, 18, 80, 94; and anti-humanism, 27–30; being-for-itself and being-for-us, 53–54, 56; and being-in-love, 143; and being-in-the-world, 57; and being-there, 58; and beloved community, 21–22, 66–67; and Black power/Power, 3; and Blackness, 2–3, 94; and communion between self and other, 21; contingent, 58; and creativity, 58–59; and critical belief (doxa), 53; and death, 105; and dignity, 40; divine, 24, 62; and divine love, 24; as divine omnipotence, 57; and eschatology, 3; and existentialism, 21–22, 26, 29, 33–34, 46, 52–57, 65, 96, 104, 137; and finitude, 29, 52, 55, 57; and freedom, 48, 55, 58–60, 66; German academic debates on, 24; and Gnosticism, 3; and God, 46–47, 56–58, 60, 62, 96, 118; history of, 32, 35, 50, 67, 141; house of, 19–20, 22, 58; human, 56; human *vs.* animal, 33; and metaphysics, 12, 46; and nihilism, 52; and Nonbeing, struggle between, 29, 52, 56, 69; and nonviolence, 25, 27–44, 61–69, 151–53n; and objectivity, 84; oneness of, 110–11; and ontology, 96; as Other, 20; and philosophy, 57, 120; as political force, 64; and positive law, 111; as power, 46–47, 94; as preference rather than substance, 96; and race, 2–3, 96; racial, 2–3; and racial essentialism, 64; and racism, 31–37; and social action, 48; term, usage, 30; theology of, 118; and time, 48, 155n15; unconditional, 58; underminded, 40. *See also* Dasein; nonbeing/Nonbeing; ontotheology

Being-in-love, 9, 21, 24, 26, 88, 90, 100, 143, 145–46

being-in-the-world, 19, 41, 48, 55–59, 91, 140, 145

beloved community: African Americans in, 134–35; and agape, 25, 123; and being/Being, 21–22, 65–66; and Being-in-love, 26; and Black power/Power, 4; as brotherly society, 67; and City of God, 99; and color-blind society, 40; and creativity or divine spontaneity, 66, 86; and divine goodness, 66; and divine love, 91; and divine nonviolence, 26; as earthly kingdom, 67; and epistemology, 145; and equality, 4; and eschatology, 91, 99, 115; and essentialism, 40; and existentialism, 21, 26, 66; and fellowship, 63; and freedom, 63, 66, 69, 146; and God's love, 22, 65, 69; and love, 66, 94, 134, 146; and messianism, 134–35; and neighborly love, 66; and nonviolence, 21–22, 65–66, 125; ontological expression of, 145; and oppressed communities, 92; of others, 21, 145; and promised land attained, 22; and purification, 97; and racial segregation, 134; and reconciliation, 67; and redemption, 134–35; and salvation, 22, 115; and self-care, 21, 145–46; and sovereignty, 125;

200 Index

beloved community (*continued*)
teleological development toward, 26; and unconditional love, 94; and universalism, 97; and World House, 21–22, 65–66, 69
Benjamin, Walter: and Arendt, 113–14, 160n2, 160n4; and Christian theology, 117; and death penalty, 161n18; and debates in Germany, 22; on divine force, 162n22; and divine power, 162n21; on divine violence, 26, 125, 132–33, 136, 162n22; and eschatology, 117, 162n22; on Gnosticism, 100; and Heidegger, 119–21, 134, 161n12; and historically grounded philosophical ideology critique, 121; and historicity, 119–20; on *Jetztzeit*, 117–18, 135; King and, 24, 26; on law, 136; on localized use of force, 100; and meontology, 117–18, 133–34; on messianism, 113, 117–19, 133, 160n4; on moral action, 129; on nonviolence, 22, 113; on ontotheology, 120; and police violence, 22, 26, 124, 126–36, 162n19; and politics, 133, 160n4; and race, 111–12; and racial politics, 113; and revolutionary liberation, 134; on Saint Paul, 116, 119–22; on soma over pneuma, 118; and sovereignty, 100; and state violence, 136; and Taubes, 118; and theology, 160n9; on violence, 113, 119, 124, 129, 132; and world politics of nihilism, 116
Bennett, Lerone, 150n13
Bentham, Jeremy, 37
Bernasconi, Robert, 31–32
Berry, Edward, 154n8
Birmingham, Alabama, 97–100, 122–26, 153n5, 154n8, 157n7
Birmingham, Peg, 120
Black Bourgeoisie (Frazier), 81
Black Campus Movement, 147, 163n7
Black Fascisms (Thompson), 149n3

Black Freedom Movement, and Black Power, 5
Black Lives Matter, 8
Black nationalism, 5–6, 74–76, 80–81
Black Notebooks (Heidegger), 35, 152n9
Black Panther Party (BPP): and African American culture-based organizing, 76; beliefs, 6–7; and Black cultural production, 150n13; and Black nationalism, 74–76; and Black power/Power, 72–82, 156n10; and Black radicalism, 150n13; and Black revolutionaries, 73, 75; and civil rights, 73; as community-control movement, 76; and ethnic pluralism, 6; on ghettoes, defensive theorization of, 150n14; history of, 73; and human rights, 73; imagery, 149n8; and metaphysics of race and power, 79; as militant, 72–73, 149n8; newspaper, 149n8; and Platonism, 78–80; and racial essentialism, 25; and racial types, 76, 82; and racially normative principles, 79–80; as radical, 73, 75, 150n13; as revolutionary, 6, 73–74, 149n8, 156n10; rhetoric of, 156n10; and rhetoric of the gun, 155n7; schism in, 155n7; studies, 74; and transformation, 6; and underground, 6; and violence, 156n10
Black Panther Party for Self-Defense. *See* Black Panther Party (BPP)
Black philosophy, 16, 162n20. *See also* African American philosophy; Africana philosophy; Afro-American philosophy
Black power, 3–9; basic truths, 12; as Being-in-love, 24; and Black freedom, 5; and Black nationalism, 5; and Black personhood, 8; and Black radicalism, 3, 5–6; and Black separatism, 4; and BPP, 72–82; as civil disobedience, 147; and forgiveness, 4; imagery, 8; and integration, 4; as justice, 147; King and, 1–10, 12, 25,

72–73, 147; as love beyond the law, 147; meaning of as contested, 75; and nonviolence, 1–10, 70–94, 155–56n; and ontology, 1–10; and philosophy, 3, 5–6, 9, 12, 149n3; and Platonism, 79, 90–94; as self-love, 147; studies, 74–75, 147, 150n10, 155n5; and Third World, 149n7

Black Power Movement, 2–6; and African American liberation, 75; in Bandung, Indonesia, 5; and Black Campus Movement, 147; and Black culture, 143; and Black Freedom Movement, 5; and Black nationalism, 5; and Black radicalism, 3, 5–6, 149n3; and Black separatism, 149n3; and BPP, 25, 72–82; and Civil Rights Movement, 5–6, 72–75; and class, 4; as community advocacy, 4; comprehensive cartography of, 8; and eroticism, 144; formulation of, 1; and geopolitics, 8; imagery, 4; as law, 156n10; as militant, 74, 156n10; and Platonism, 79; popular, negative misconception of, 5; powerful forces combining to form complex, multifaceted concept of, 150n9; and race, 4; and racial essentialism, 149n3; and racial particularity, 144; as self-defense, 4; slogan, 2, 4, 72; as social and economic control, 79; and violence, 72, 156n10

Black Power: Politics of Liberation in America (Ture and Hamilton), 149n1, 149n7

Black radicalism, 3, 5–7, 72, 75, 143, 149n3, 150n13. *See also* radicalism

Black separatism, 2, 4, 26, 149n3. *See also* separatism

Black studies, 16–17, 146–47, 163n7. *See also* African American studies; Africana studies; Afro-American studies

Blackness: and being/Being, 19, 30, 94; and Black power/Power, 4; and existentialist humanism, 17; and ontology, 3; and philosophical anthropology, 16; as superior, 80; term, usage, 94; as truth, 93; and whiteness, 15, 94. *See also* whiteness

Blake, J. H., 78
Blok, Vincent, 152n12
Blumenberg, Hans, 107, 116, 159n27
Bogues, Anthony, 5
Boston University, 9, 40, 42–43, 71, 134
Boxill, Bernard R., 13–14, 24, 150n18
BPP. *See* Black Panther Party (BPP)
Brecht, Bertolt, 120
Brenner, Michael, 105–6
Broek, Roelof van den, 100, 159n21
Brotz, Howard, 7
Buber, Martin, 111, 114
Buch, Robert, 104
Buddha, 62
Bultmann, Rudolf: and Arendt, 102, 158n16; on being/Being, 118; and Continental theology, 22, 28; and crisis theology, 28; and eschatology, 102; and existentialism, 27–29, 104; and German academic debates, 24, 33; on Gnosticism, 105–7; and Heidegger, 28, 103, 105, 118–19, 121; and hermeneutic approach, 103; and Jonas, 105–6; on *kerygma,* 104; and philosophy, 27; on Saint Paul, 104, 107, 118–19, 121; and theology, 27, 33, 105, 107
Buttrick, George, 47

Cahana, Jonathan, 101, 107
Calloway, Carolyn R., 76
Capital (Marx), 38
capitalism, 5, 8, 38, 40, 133
Carmichael, Stokely, 1–2, 4, 25, 156n10
Carson, Clayborne, 27, 71, 83, 156n11
caste, 17, 93
Catholicism, 160n5
Chappell, David L., 7
Christian philosophy, 30, 37–39, 53, 84, 88

Christian theology, 28, 90, 96–97, 100, 117, 158n16

Christianity: and agape, 87–89; and antisemitism, 96; and carnality, 88; and civil disobedience, 11, 112; critique of, 38; dogma of, 104, 118; and eros, 84, 88; and eschatology, 104, 112, 116–17; and eschaton, 108; and ethics, 112; and existentialism, 27, 33, 45–46, 104; and Gnosticism, 100–109; Hellenization of, 106; history of, 112, 116–17; and humanism, 102; and inequality, 37; Judaic roots, 97; and justice, 69, 98, 123; and Kairos, 160n11; and law, 112, 123; and love, 84, 87–90; and morality, 112, 126; and natural law, 11; and nonviolence, 11, 39, 97; and pneuma, 117–18; and political religion, 96; and rebirth, 33; and religiosity, 118; and Saint Paul, 118; and salvation, 104; and sectarian movements, 109; and segregation, 100, 112; and social activism, 123; and social mission, 37–38; and socialism, 97; socially conscious, 69; spiritual religion of, 96; and theocentricism, 30; and universalism, 69; and violence, 11

Christianity and the Social Crisis (Rauschenbusch), 37

church: black, 134–35; black Baptist, 71; history of, 112; and Nazism, 160n5; and state, 115. *See also* religion

citizenship, 10–11, 146

City of God, 99, 126

civil disobedience: armed, 141–42; and beloved community, 99; Black power/Power as, 147; and Christian morality, 112; and divine law, 112; domesticated portrayals of, 10; as eschatological, 99; and Gnosticism, 26, 100, 136; and humanist tradition, 136; and justice, 40, 100, 110, 115; and law, 11, 98, 100, 112, 115; and messianism, 113; and metaphysics, 136; and morality, 112; nonviolent, 7–8, 11, 47, 112–13, 115, 125, 135; and peace, 112; philosophy of law in practices of, 112; and police violence, 136; and political theology, 26; and racist police violence, 136; and racist state power, 7–8; and self-love, 147; and sovereignty, 113, 125; strict rules of, 40; when permissible, 13

civil rights: and anti-essentialism, 9, 25; and Black demands for reform, 71; and Black power/Power, 5–6, 143; and freedom, 150n13; laws/legislation, 80–81; moral appeals for, 155n19; and nonviolence, 11, 71, 80, 114, 126; organizations and marches, 1, 70, 81; and racial essentialism, 36; and racial ontology, 9; revolution, 154n8; rhetoric of, 154n7–8. *See also* human rights

Civil Rights Movement: and Arendt, 160n1; and Black politics, 75; and Black power/Power, 5–6, 72–75; and Black radicalism, 6, 75; class and race in, 149n6; historiography/history of, 70–71, 155n6; and local interventions by little known groups, 155n6; and nonviolent protests, 142; and practice of freedom, 144; and race, 149n6, 160n1; rhetoric of, 154n7–8; and violence against workers, 156n10

class/classism, 4, 6–7, 17, 74, 111, 113, 149n6, 157n6

classical thought, 95–100

Cleaver, Eldridge, 155n7

Cleaver, Kathleen, 6

Cold War: geopolitics, 8; liberalism, 72

colonialism, 5, 16–17; anti-, 156n15; neo-, 74. *See also* imperialism

Comay, Rebecca, 120–21

communism, 38, 48, 107. *See also* fascism; Marxism

Communist Manifesto, The (Marx), 38

community, beloved. *See* beloved community
Cone, James H., 134
Conference on Christian Faith and Human Relations (Nashville, 1957), 85
Congdon, David W., 104
Congress of Racial Equity (CORE), 1
Contemporary Continental Theology (Horton), 28, 89
Continental theology, 22, 28, 89, 156n2
CORE. *See* Congress of Racial Equity (CORE)
Courage to Be, The (Tillich), 48, 50–51
creativity, 50–51, 54, 58–60, 63–69, 86, 104. *See also* Dasein
critical belief (doxa), and being, 53
critical theory, 26, 41, 75–76, 136, 138, 142
"Critique of Violence" (Benjamin), 22, 26, 112–25, 129, 132–33, 160n4
Crozer Theological Seminary, 9, 27, 72
culture: African-American, 17, 76; Black, 143–44, 150n13; and crises, 22; and cultural critique, 103–4; and Gnosticism, 105; and ontology, 22; Western, 105
Curry, Tommy J., 8

damnation, 22, 66–67. *See also* salvation
Dasein: and Being Itself, 45, 59, 65; and being/Being, 21, 46, 65, 90–91, 105, 118, 139; and being-there/being-in-the-world, 19, 58; and beloved community, 22, 146; and creativity, 59; and diversity, 36; and existentialism, 14, 20–22, 37, 45, 59, 65, 139; and finitude, 20, 58–59, 105; and fundamental ontology, 140; and God's love, 20–22, 59; and historicality, 12–13; and house of being, 20; and ontology, 21; and self-care, 20, 146; as socially responsible, 63; term, usage, 19. *See also* being/Being; creativity

Davis, Angela Y., 160n3
Davis, George Washington, 27–28
Davis, Jack E., 155n6
death penalty, 99, 161n18
Debs, Eugene, 72
democracy, 11, 72, 90, 147
Demos, Raphael, 155n15
Denkformen (thought), King and, 45–61
Derrida, Jacques, 31, 151n3
desegregation, 61, 76, 91. *See also* segregation
Dewey, John, 13, 95
DeWolf, L. Harold, 42, 134
Dexter Avenue Baptist Church (Montgomery, Alabama), 87
divine law, 68, 99, 104, 110–12, 121–24
divine love, 24, 39, 44, 61, 63–66, 86, 91–92. *See also* God's love
divine nonviolence, 22, 24–26, 110–36, 160–62n. *See also* divine violence
divine spontaneity. *See* creativity
divine violence, 22, 26, 64, 68, 114, 119, 125, 132–36, 162n22. *See also* divine nonviolence
divinity, 39, 48–49, 52, 85, 96, 105, 136
Douglass, Frederick, 3
doxa (critical belief), and being, 53
Dreisbach, Donald F., 154n14
Driver, Tom F., 101
Du Bois, W. E. B., 3, 7, 80
dualism, 42, 52, 100, 105–7, 117, 126
Dutschke, Rudi, shooting of, 114, 160n3
Dworkin, Ronald, 13
Dyer, Justin Buckley, 157–58n9, 160n28

Ebenezer Baptist Church, 85
Ebony magazine, 150n13
education, 146–47, 162n21–22
eidos (essence), 137
Emancipation Day Rally (NAACP, 1957), 87–88
Engels, Friedrich, 38
Enns, Elaine, 161n14
epistemology, 11, 17, 20, 42–43, 78–79, 111, 114, 125, 129, 144–45

equality: human, 4, 93, 134; racial, 2, 10–11. *See also* inequality
eros: as aesthetic love, 82, 85–89, 156n11; and agape, 25, 56, 61, 82–91, 137, 151n29; and Being-in-love, 143; and Black love, 26; and carnal/sexual love, 83, 86, 88, 143, 156n11; as civilization, 84, 141; as divine-human power, 151n29; as essential libido, 25, 151n29; and existentialism, 56; and Gnosis, 101; King and, 25, 82–89, 137, 143, 151n29; and logos, 90; and love, 25, 87; and love of power, 61; and metaphysics, 88; and nonviolence, 82–89, 137–47, 162–63n; as phenomenological ground of all knowledge, 145; and philia, 61, 82–84, 87, 91; Platonic, 25, 82, 85–89, 92, 101, 143, 156n13; as political and pedagogical, 145; and power, 84–85; and revolutionary love, 25–26; and self-care, 145; and subjectivity, 85, 89; as veiled social Being, 142–43
Eros and Civilization (Marcuse), 141
eschatology: and Being-in-love, 100; and beloved community, 91, 99, 115; Christian, 104, 112, 116–17; and class conflict, 111; and debates in Germany, 22; and divine nonviolence/violence, 125–26, 162n22; epistemological-critical contradictions in, 111; and Gnosticism, 3, 25–26, 101–4, 108; and God's creativity, 60; and history, 59; intersubjective, 64; and Judaism, 159n21; and *katechon*, 115; and messianism, 110, 117, 159n21, 160n27; Pauline, 134; and political power, 115; and political theology, 26, 115–16, 116–17, 159–60n27; and racial Gnosticism, 108
eschaton, 108, 115, 159n27
essentialism, 9, 17–18, 21, 24, 33, 40, 92, 143, 155n3. *See also* anti-essentialism; existentialism; racial essentialism
eternal life, 67, 160n27
eternity, 60, 85, 154n8
ethics, 8–11, 37, 63, 107, 112, 145–46, 158n10
ethnophilosophy, 14–15, 18–19. *See also* Africana philosophy
evil, 52, 59, 92–93
exception, state of. *See* state of exception
existentialism: and African American philosophy, 15, 17–18; and being/Being, 21–22, 26, 29, 33–34, 46, 52–57, 65, 96, 104, 137; and Being-in-love, 21; and beloved community, 21, 26, 134; Christian, 28, 33, 45–46, 104; and Dasein, 14, 20–22, 37, 45, 59, 65, 139; and essentialism, 17, 151n29; and freedom, 56, 59; and Gnosticism, 100; and God, 57; and humanism, 17, 27–28, 36; and idealism, 40–41; and libido, 151n29; and love, 21–22; and Marxism, 140; and nonbeing/Nonbeing, 52; and personalism, 41, 135; and philosophy, 12, 25, 46, 51, 105; psychological, 45; and race, 21; and racial segregation, 111, 134; and self-love, 51; and subjectivity, 45; and theology, 40; Tillich and, 40–41, 45–46, 51, 59. *See also* essentialism; Existenzphilosophie
Existentialism and Theology (Davis), 27–28
Existenzphilosophie, 21, 24, 41, 45, 51, 56–57, 92, 137–38, 145–46. *See also* existentialism; German idealism
exploitation, 4, 38, 40, 79, 145

"Facing the Challenge of a New Age" (King), 86–87
Fairclough, Adam, 70, 72
faith, 30, 38–39, 42, 48, 52, 68, 96, 134
Fanon, Frantz, 3, 149n5
Farmer, James, 7

Farr, Arnold L., 141, 162n2
fascism, 32, 38, 140. *See also* communism; Marxism
Feenberg, Andrew, 140
Feldman, Matthew, 32, 101–3
Feller, Yaniv, 106–7
fellowship, 62–63
Ferguson, Stephen, 10
finitude, 20–21, 29, 45, 50, 52, 55–60, 63, 105
First Things magazine, 134
Fosdick, Harry Emerson, 83, 87, 156n11
Fourcade, Dominique, 124
Fränkel, Hilda, 153n1
Frankfurt School, 138
Franklin, Robert Michael, 135
Frazier, E. Franklin, 81
freedom: and agape, 61; and being/Being, 48, 55, 58–60, 66; and being-in-the-world, 48, 59; and beloved community, 63, 66, 69, 146; Black, 5–6, 70; and civil rights, 144; and creativity, 48, 51; critical, 144–46; denied/deprived by communism, 48; and destiny, 45, 55, 60–61; existential, 66; and fellowship, 62–63; and finitude, 59; and God's love, 50, 60, 64; and goodness, 62–63; and human unity, 69; and intelligence, 63; and justice, 69; and love, 51, 69, 144, 146; and nonbeing/Nonbeing, 59; and nonviolence, 40; and peace, 65, 69; practice of, 40, 144–46; and redemption, 68; and revolutionary action, 146; and salvation, 58, 60; teaching as practice of, 145; term, usage, 151n28; and truth, 151n5; and universalism, 144
Freud, Sigmund, 138–40
Friedlander, Eli, 162n19, 162n22
Fritsche, Johannes, 31, 34–35
Fulkerson, Richard P., 152n13
fundamental ontology: and African American experience/philosophy, 12–14; anti-humanist, 26; anti-racist, 25–26; and eschatology, 25–26; and Gnosticism, 25–26; and history, 36, 141; and philosophy, 24–25, 33–35, 63; and race/racism, 13, 23–24; reimagined, 134; Tillich and, 26, 63

Gaipa, Mark, 157n8
Gandhi, Mahatma (Mohandas Karamchand), 38–40, 47, 66, 70, 153n17
Gates, Henry Louis, Jr., 16–17
Genealogy of Morals, The (Nietzsche), 38
geopolitics, 8
German Hellenism. *See* Hellenism
German idealism, 24, 41, 43, 45, 57. *See also Existenzphilosophie*
German philosophy, 9, 12, 22, 24–26, 37, 51, 62, 104, 139–40
"German Philosophy, 1871–1933" (Marcuse), 139–40
German Romanticism, 88
German theology, 22, 24, 26, 37, 103–4, 163n5
ghettoes, 7–8, 78, 150n14
Gnosticism: basic tenets, 107; and being/Being, 137, 143; in Christianity, 101–2, 106; and church/state, 115; and civil disobedience, 26, 100, 136; and classical thought, 95–100; and debates in Germany, 22; and demythologizing of theology, 106–7; and divine nonviolence, 26; and dualism, 42, 104–5, 112, 117; and eros, 101; and eschatology, 3, 25–26, 101–4, 108; German academic debates on, 24; and Hellenism, 106; and history, 107–8; and humanism, 136; and immanentization, 109; Jewish/and Judaism, 106, 159n21; and justice, 100; and metaphysics, 93, 108, 136; modernity as, 108, 159n27; and nonviolence, 26, 95–109, 125, 156–60n; and ontotheology, 102; philosophical, 107; and Platonism, 93, 105–6; and police violence, 26, 124, 136; political, 108, 116, 159n27; and political theology, 100; as political

Gnosticism (*continued*)
  theology, 26, 100, 112, 115; and primal man (*Urmensch*), 107; racial, 100–109; revolutionary, 101; and salvation, 116; and sovereignty, 26, 100; and state of exception, 136; as theory of revelation, 101; in Western culture, 105
God: alienation from, 28, 61; as Being Itself, 45–47, 51–52, 65, 92–93, 96; as being/Being, 46–47, 56–58, 60, 62, 96, 118; City of, 99, 126; and freedom, 60; human beings/individuals as aspects of, 64; and humanity, existential relation between, 45; and humanity, unbreakable bond between, 59; laws of, 99, 110–14, 121, 132; as logos, 52, 57, 64; as love, 61; and omnipotence, 56–58; and omnitemporality, 60; personal, 11, 42, 51–52; power of, 46–47, 49; sovereignty of, 136; transcendent power of, 135
God's love: acceptance of, 60, 62; African Americans redeemed by, 92; as agape, 61, 83; alienation from, 22, 137; and Being, 137; and Being Itself, affirmation of, 59; and beloved community, 22, 65, 69; divine law of, 99; as faith, 60; and fellowship, 62–63; and finitude, 60; and freedom, 50, 60, 64; power of, 69; as spontaneous, 86; as unconditional, 20, 94; and violence, rejection of, 39. *See also* divine love
goodwill/good will, 2, 82–83, 86–88, 90
Gordon, Lewis, 15–19
Gordon, Peter Eli, 157n5
Grassi, Ernesto, 36, 162n1
Greek philosophy, 62, 78, 84–88, 102, 105
Greenberg, Udi E., 119
Gregg, Richard, 43, 153n18

Habermas, Jürgen, 33, 138–40
Hamilton, Amy, 146
Hamilton, Charles V., 149n1, 149n7

Hamlet (Shakespeare), 29
Hanssen, Beatrice, 120–21
Harnack, Adolf von, 103–4
Harris, Jessica C., 74
Haverkamp, Anselm, 161n18
Hegel, Georg Wilhelm Friedrich, 43, 45, 49–53, 57–64, 67, 80, 107
hegemony, anti-racist, 76
Heidegger, Martin: and Adorno, 137, 140; and Agamben, 124; and anti-historicist hermeneutic of negative transcendence, 103; and anti-humanism, 22; and anti-racism, 25, 33; and anti-Semitism, 23, 35, 151n4; and Arendt, 23, 95, 102, 158n13, 158n15; and authoritarian pedagogy, 138; authoritarian pedagogy of, 138; on being/Being, 12, 34, 36, 45, 50, 65–66, 90–92, 96, 103, 105–6, 120, 137, 140, 146, 151n1; and Benjamin, 119–21, 134, 161n12; on Blackness, 94, 151n2; and Bultmann, 28, 103, 105, 118–19, 121; on the clearing, 155n18; controversy, 35, 151n3, 152n10; and Dasein, 59; on earth, 150n26; on eros, 156n13; and essentialism, 21, 24; and existentialism, 12, 21, 25, 34, 45–46, 53, 57, 92, 137, 139–41, 145–46; on freedom, 151n5; and fundamental ontology, 12, 19, 24–25, 30–31, 33–37, 45–46, 63, 92, 134, 138–41, 154n13; and German academic debates, 24; and German philosophy, 12, 24, 45; and German theology, 163n5; and Gnosticism, 101; and Grassi, 36; and Hellenism, 36–37, 105–6; hermeneutic approach, 103; on historicality, 12–13; and historicism/historicity, 120, 141; on history, 32; and Hitlerism/Nazism, 30, 33–36, 139, 152n8; and Hölderlin, 32–33, 103; on humanism, 30, 37, 96, 162n1; and Jonas, 101, 105–6; on Kairos and early Christianity, 160n11; King and,

24–26, 44; and language, 150n25, 155n18, 162n1; and Marcuse, 23, 138–41; and messianism, 119–20; and metaphysics, 12, 14, 34, 46, 90, 92–93, 120; and National Socialism, 34, 95, 103, 138–40, 151n3; and nihilism, 152n7; and ontology, 12–14, 19, 24–25, 30, 35, 37, 52, 91, 118, 140; on ontotheology, 102; on Parousia, 118; and philosophy, 12–14, 19, 22–25, 30, 33, 35–37, 46, 56, 106, 120–21, 138–41; on philosophy of being, 120; and Plato/Platonism, 36–37, 90, 92–93, 101, 105–6, 137–38, 143, 152n12, 156–57n3, 156n13, 158n12, 162n1; and politics, 158n12; and politics of heroism, 139–40; and racism, 22–25, 30–37, 96, 113, 139–40, 152n8; on Saint Paul, 118–19, 120, 160n10; on science, 33; and Taubes, 118; and theology, 36, 105–6, 163n5; and theology of being, 28, 118; on thrownness, 141; and Tillich, 25–26, 44–46, 52, 56–57, 118, 154n13; and Voegelin, 95, 156n3
"Heidegger and Theology" (Jonas), 106
Hellenism, 36–37, 106
hermeneutics, 4, 79, 103–4
Hills, Darrius D., 8
Hinton, Elizabeth, 11
historical materialism, 25, 94
historicality, 12–13, 118
historicism, 32, 36, 101, 106–9, 119–20, 159n24. *See also* anti-historicism
historicity: and being/Being, 141; and being/Nonbeing, 118; and dialectical image, 120; and finitude, 50; and hiddenness, 118; of human being, 62; human diversity's, 36; and nihilism of finitude, 50; and positive law as police violence., 122; reflective structure of, 119; and soteriology, 118; of spirit, 103
history: African American, 73–74, 134; and African American philosophy, 10; of African American political thought, 13; agency in, 116–17; of anthropocentric humanism, 30; apocalyptic forces of, 115; beginning of, 69; of being/Being, 32, 35, 50, 67, 141; and beloved community, 26; of Black power/Power, 74; of Black studies, 146; of Christianity, 112, 116–17; of church, 112; of Civil Rights Movement, 70–71, 155n6; creative moments in, 48; of dehumanization, 13; end of, 59, 67, 69, 91, 108–9, 124–25, 156n14; and eschatology, 59; and Gnosticism, 107–8; of human diversity, 36; idealist philosophy of, 67; as logos, 54; of Man, 149n7; of metaphysics, 61, 102, 118; order of, 59; philosophical, 17, 162n1; of philosophical violence, 113; and philosophy, 5, 14, 24, 32, 74, 102, 107; of philosophy, 32, 137, 152n16; philosophy of, 67, 138, 141, 158n14; of racism, 13; radical redemption of, 113; of radicalism, interracial, 75; of religious ideas, 116; of segregation, 137; soteriological, 91; of theology, 24; of Western philosophies, 17; of World House, 69
Hitler, Adolf, 34–35, 152n8. *See also* National Socialism; Nazism
Hobbes, Thomas, 37
Hölderlin, Friedrich, 32–33, 103
"Homecoming/To the Relatives" (Hölderlin), 32–33
homophobia, 17
hooks, bell, 26, 144–46, 163n5
hope: and Black church's faith in Jesus Christ, 134; and love, 39–40; and pessimism, 8
Horkheimer, Max, 137, 153n1
Horton, Walter Marshall, 28–30, 89
human nature: and philosophical anthropology, 16, 41; transfiguration of through human action in history, 108

human rights, 48, 73. *See also* civil rights
humanism: and anthropocentrism, 30; and anthropology, 136; and anthropomorphic thought, 29; and being/Being, 96; and being-unto-death, 29; Christian, 102; and civil disobedience, 136; and epistemology, 42–43; and existentialism, 17, 27–28, 36; German academic debates on, 24, 36–37; Gnostic, 136; and idealism, 29; and messianism, 135; and metaphysics, 33, 136; modern, 30, 96; and National Socialism/Nazism, 37, 96; and *paideia*, 36; and personalism, 42; and Platonism, 37, 162n1; and racial ontology, 136; and racism, 96; and segregated state, 112; Socratic, 32, 103; and sovereignty, 136; and universalism, 37, 100. *See also* anti-humanism

idealism, German, 24, 41, 43, 45, 57. *See also Existenzphilosophie*
identity: African-American, 17; and culture, 8; of freedom and destiny in God, 60; and law, 157n6; moral and progressive, 157n7; and personality, 159–60n27. *See also* racial identity
immanence, 101, 117, 160n9
immanentization, and Gnosticism, 108–9
imperialism, 5, 10–11, 74. *See also* colonialism
inaction, 64, 66–67, 132. *See also* activism
individualism, 6
inequality, 9–11, 37–38, 42, 76, 93, 142. *See also* equality
injustice, 9–10, 52, 61, 67–69, 71, 97–98, 114, 122–26, 156n10, 160n28. *See also* justice
integration, 8, 11, 24, 51, 75, 146. *See also* segregation
intercommunalism, 73–76
irrationalism, 11, 43, 63–64, 143

Janicaud, Dominique, 31, 138
Jaspers, Karl, 12, 34, 158n16
Jefferson, Thomas, 122–23
jeremiadic cry, 155n2
Jeremiah, 29–30
Jetztzeit, 117–18, 135
Johnson, Davi, 157n7
Jonas, Hans, 24, 95, 101, 105–8, 158n13, 159n22
Jones, Charles E., 150n12
Jones, E. S., 47
Jones, Michael T., 158n15
Jones, Richard A., 150n24
Joseph, Peniel E., 5–6, 74–75, 150n10, 151n27, 156n10
Judaism, 31, 104–6, 120–21, 140, 157n5, 158n18, 159n21–22. *See also* anti-Semitism
just law, 110–11, 115. *See also* unjust law
just war theory, 10–11
justice: and agape, 61, 88; Black power as, 8, 147; Christian, 69, 98, 123; and civil disobedience, 40, 100, 110, 115; in classical thought, 95; divine, 64, 126; and divine love, 63; as divine nonviolence, 25–26; and eschatology, 126; and Gnosticism, 100, 107–8; and God's love, 69; and law, 124, 128–29; and love, 66, 68, 93, 156n1, 156n12; and nonviolence, 25–26, 93; and peace, 94–95, 98; and public reason, 158n9; and purification, 97; revolutionary, 40; as sacred temporality, 126; secular, 98; sovereign, 159n27; universal, 100, 124, 157n6; and violence, 107–8, 124. *See also* injustice; social justice
"Justice Without Violence" (King), 65–66

Kairos (creative moments/rhetorical timing), 47–48, 118–19, 123–24, 153n4–5, 154n7, 160n11
Kant, Immanuel, 50, 96, 102, 121

katechon, as antichrist, 115–16
Katsiaficas, George N., 6
Kazin, Michael, 72
Keedus, Liisi, 103
Kelsen, Hans, 116, 159n27
Kennedy, John F., assassination of, 112
Kennedy, Randall, 70
Kennedy, Robert, killing of, 114
kerygma, 104
Kierkegaard, Søren, 12, 28–29
King, Coretta Scott, 47–48
King, Martin Luther, Jr.: and African American philosophy, 9–19, 24; and anti-essentialism, 25; and anti-humanism, 25, 27–30, 45, 149n5; as apostle of crisis, 135, 154n8; as apostle of nonviolence, 152n16; assassination/murder of, 114, 160n3; attitudes, 37–44; on being/Being, 45, 61–69; and Black power, 1–10, 12, 25, 72–73, 147; and Black separatism, 26; and civil rights, 25; as civil rights activist/champion, 9, 153n2; and classical thought, 95–100; as combination of opposing qualities, 71; as conciliatory element in diverse social movement, 70–71; and correlations, 48, 52, 70–76, 99; on courage to be, 48, 50–51; critical methodology of, 53; critics of, 7–8; and *Denkformen* (thought), 45–61; "Dream" speech, 8, 134, 150n15, 153n5; on eros/love, 25, 82–89, 137, 143, 151n29; and eschatological messianism, 110; ethics of, 158n10; and existentialism, 25, 41, 104; and fundamental ontology, 24–25; and German academic philosophical debates, 24–25, 33; and Gnosticism, 25–26; on humanism, 30; and idealism, 41, 67; as identificatory conglomerate, 155n3; intervention in ontology from philosophically imminent perspective, 151n27; legacy, 10; and militant nonviolence, 150n17; militant opponents of, 7; moral reasoning of, 154n11; Nobel Lecture (1964), 64–66; and nonviolence, 4, 7–8, 11–12, 22, 25–26, 39, 43, 67, 71, 82–83, 90, 92–93, 99, 111, 113–14, 125, 135, 142–43, 152n16, 155n4; and ontology, 4, 9–11, 19–25, 39, 41, 84, 92, 94, 151n27; and pedagogical personalism, 163n4; as philosopher who took action, 40; and philosophical anthropology, 41; and philosophy, 9, 18, 22–25, 36–39, 41, 43, 47, 53, 57, 67, 69, 84, 89–90, 93, 123, 134, 143, 146, 151n27, 152n16, 153n2; and philosophy of social action and revolutionary political change, 123; and plagiarism, 153n2; and Platonism, 90–94; political philosophy of, 23–24, 149n4; and political theology, 25–26, 100, 110–15; on race, and legal theory, 111–12; as radical, 10–11; as religious thinker, 41; rhetoric of, 44, 49, 70–76, 110, 150n16, 152n13, 153n5, 154n7, 154n10, 155n3, 155n19, 157n6–8, 161n16; as social activist, 70; and state of exception, 134–36; as theologian, 70, 153n2; and theology, 22, 24, 36–38, 40–41, 43, 47–48, 53, 57, 89, 134, 153n2; and theology of social action, 152n15; and universalism, 155n19, 157n6; unpublished works of, 10
"King Plan for Freedom, The" (Bennett), 150n13
Klee, Paul, 120
Kreiss, Daniel, 150n13
Kroeker, P. Travis, 117, 133–34

Lacoue-Labarthes, Philippe, 31
Lafont, Cristina, 33
Laing, Bonnie Young, 76
Lamarche, Pierre, 121

law: and African Americans, 18; and Black power/Power, 156n10; Christian, 112, 123; and civil disobedience, 11, 98, 100, 112, 115; collective, and violence, 119; critique of, 17; eternal, 110–11; federal, 110, 124; God of, 103; God's, 99, 110–14, 121, 132; just, 110–11, 115; and justice, 124, 128–29; and police violence, 136; and political theology, 123; secular, 104, 119; and sovereignty, 113; state, 110, 131; universality of, 162n19; unjust, 110–11, 132, 160n28; and violence, 119, 126–27, 130. *See* divine law; lawlessness; natural law; positive law

lawlessness, 7, 97–98, 115, 136

Lazerow, Jama, 7, 150n11

Lectures of the Philosophy of History (Hegel), 43

Leff, Michael, 155n3

"Letter from a Birmingham Jail" (King), 25–26, 49, 95, 97–98, 110, 114–15, 123, 136, 150n16, 153n5, 154n7–8, 160n28, 161n13–16

"Letter on Humanism" (Heidegger), 17, 19–20, 30–36, 102

Lewis, David Levering, 152n16

liberalism, 34, 72, 106, 157n9

Lincoln, Abraham, 122

Little Rock, Arendt on, 159n23

Livingston, Alexander, 10

Locke, John, 13, 37

logos, 52, 54, 57–58, 63–64, 90, 142–43

Loomer, Bernard, 154n9

Loose, Donald, 119

love: aesthetic, 82, 85–89, 156n11; African Americans redeemed by, 92; and agape, 61, 66, 82–89, 91; and Being Itself, 51, 66, 90–91, 93; and being-in-the-world, 91; and beloved community, 66, 94, 134, 146; Black, 26; Black power as, 147; brotherly, 66–67; carnal/sexual, 24, 83, 86, 88, 156n11; Christian, 84, 88–90; and creativity, 51, 66; and divine goodness, 66; divine law of, 68; and divine nonviolence, 122–26; and eros, 25, 87; erotic, 83, 85–86, 137, 143, 145; eternal, 58, 87–88; ethics of, 146; and extremism, 122–26; faith in, 38–39; and freedom, 51, 69, 144, 146; Greek forms of, 84–85; and hope, 39–40; and justice, 66, 68, 93, 156n1, 156n12; neighborly, 21, 66; and nonviolence, 67, 122–26; and nonviolent resistance, 82; as ontological concept., vii; as ontotheological concept, 24; Platonic, 88–89; political ontology of, 146; political-pedagogical, 145; politics of, 146; power of, and redemption, 133; power of, and social reform, 38; power of, infinite, 51–52; redeeming/redemptive, 66, 83, 86, 133–34; and religion, 64; revolutionary, 25–26; romantic, 82, 85–88; selfless, 145; unconditional, 20, 52, 61, 94; universal, 90, 92; and universalism, 144. *See also* divine love; God's love; self-love

Love, Jeff, 32

Löwith, Karl, 95, 152n7

Luther, Martin, 89, 114, 118, 122

Macquarrie, John, 28, 101, 154n9

Mahatma Gandhi, Horns and Halo (Jones), 47

Malcolm X, 23, 25, 71, 73, 77, 112, 143, 150n18, 156n10

Marburg theology, 27–28, 102, 107

"March Against Fear" (1966), 1

Marcion of Sinope, 103–4, 158n17

Marcuse, Herbert, 162–63n2–3; and Arendt, 23, 113–14; and Benjamin, 113–14; and Black power/Power, 3; and critical theory, 26, 138; de-Nazification activities, 140–41; and existential Marxism, 140–41; and fundamental ontology, 138, 140–41; and ideology critique, 142–43; on

nonviolence/violence, 114, 141–43, 162n2, 163n3; and Nussbaum, 26; and political foundation of philosophy, 140; and psychoanalytic critical theory, 138; and Tillich, 153n1
Maritain, Jacques, 29–30, 45
Martel, James R., 162n22
Martin Heidegger and European Nihilism (Löwith), 152n7
martyrs/martyrdom, 99–100, 153n2, 162n23
Marx, Karl, 3, 7, 38, 133, 139, 141
Marxism, 33, 38, 120, 138–41, 154n6; anti-, 96. *See also* communism; fascism
Massey, Walter, 144
materialism, 6, 25, 38, 80, 94, 117, 121, 145
McClendon, John, 10
McGary, Howard, 15
McKissick, Floyd, 1
McNulty, Tracy, 121–22
Meng, Michael, 32
meontology, 14, 105, 117–18, 133–34. *See also* ontology
Meredith, James, shooting of, 1–2
Meredith's Mississippi Freedom March (1966), 1–2
messianism, 101, 110, 113, 116–19, 133–35, 159n21, 160n4, 160n27, 162n23
metaphysics: and anti-humanism, 3; and anti-racism, 3; and eros, 88; and Gnosticism, 107–8; and historicism, 36; history of, 102, 118; and humanism, 34; interregnum, 101; and liberalism, 34; and nonviolence, 155n4; and personalism, 134; and philosophy, 13, 42, 46, 92; and Platonism, 90, 92–93, 152n12; and police violence, 128; and political theology, 101; and race, 3, 108; of race and power, and BPP, 79; and religion, 102; and theology, 41, 93, 102, 153n3; and universalism, 31;

Western, 9, 12–13, 34, 46, 61, 84, 90, 93–94
militarism, 10, 40, 149n8, 150n17
Mill, John Stuart, 37
Miller, Donna R., 151n28
Miller, Keith D., 155n16
Mills, Charles, 15–16, 19
Mississippi Freedom March (1966), 1–2
modernity, 5, 29, 31, 96, 159n27
Monahan, Michael J., 146
monism, 42, 61–64; eude-, 86
monotheism, and dualism, 106
Montgomery, John Warwick, 158n14
Montgomery bus boycott (1955–1956), 11, 43, 90, 155n4
"Montgomery Story" (King), 90
morality, 15, 17, 38, 51, 66–67, 110–12, 126, 128–29, 157n7
Morality and Beyond (Tillich), 151n29
Morehouse College, 9, 144, 163n4
Morgan, Benjamin, 133
Morgan, Jo-Ann, 6, 149n8
mortality, 50–51, 160n27
Moten, Fred, 151n2
"My Trip to the Land of Gandhi" (King), 66–67
Myers, Ched, 161n14
mysticism, 57, 106, 152n16

NAACP. *See* National Association for the Advancement of Colored People (NAACP)
National Association for the Advancement of Colored People (NAACP), 73, 80–81, 87–88, 90
National Socialism, 32, 34–35, 95–97, 101, 103, 138–40, 151n3. *See also* Hitler, Adolf; Nazism
nationalism, 10–11, 37. *See also* Black nationalism
natural law, 11, 99, 110–11, 114–15, 125, 159n25, 160n28
Nazism, 30–37, 96–97, 107–8, 138–41, 160n5. *See also* Hitler, Adolf; National Socialism

Negri, Antonio, 118
Negroes, 80
New Left, 72, 142, 163n3
New Science of Politics, The (Voegelin), 108–9
Newton, Huey P.: and/on eros, 82; black nationalist philosophy of, 80; and BPP, 6, 75–76, 155n7; and intercommunalism, 73–74; and Platonic ontology of race and power, 80; on race and social conflict, 93; on racial essentialism, 94; and racial identification, cultural value for, 80; on racial ontology, 94; and racial Platonism, 25, 37, 75–76, 80–82, 93–94, 109; and racial types, 76, 80, 82; and republic (Platonic), 76–82; as revolutionary, 143; on revolutionary suicide, 76–77, 156n8; street philosophy of, 77–78
Nietzsche, Friedrich Wilhelm, 12, 36–38, 50, 152n16
nihilism, 40, 50, 64, 101, 107, 116
nonbeing/Nonbeing: and being, struggle between, 29, 52, 56, 69; and death, 22, 51; manifest antagonism of, 69; and nonviolence, 45–69, 153–55n; philosophy of, 117; power of, 91; and violence, 22. *See also* being/Being
nonviolence: as absolute commitment to way of love, 67; as act of spirit, 67; and anti-racist fundamental ontology, 25; as basic truth of human being, 25; and being/Being, 25, 27–44, 61–69, 151–53n; Black power and, 1–10, 70–94, 155–56n; and Christianized philosophy, 39; as cosmic ontology, 93; critique of, 132; and eros, 82–89, 137–47, 162–63n; and fundamental ontology, 25–26; and historical materialism, 25; as human dignity reflected in practice of freedom and right to self-invention, 40; and insurgency, 39; militant, 10, 150n17; and nonbeing/Nonbeing, 45–69, 153–55n; and ontology, 1–26, 39, 149–51n; ontotheological, 25–26; philosophy of, 11, 39, 43–44, 83, 92, 113; and political theology, 25–26; and racial forgiveness, 143; radical, 22; and social realism, 25; social theory of, 67; supernatural power of, 70. *See also* divine nonviolence; violence
"Nonviolence and Racial Justice" (King), 87–88
nonviolent protests, 65–66, 97–99, 111, 125–26, 142, 162n2
Nussbaum, Martha C., 26, 39–40, 83–84, 143–47
Nygren, Anders, 86–89

objectivity, 46, 52, 54–55, 77, 84–85, 89, 144, 157n6. *See also* subjectivity
On Being Fit to Live With (Fosdick), 87
One-Dimensional Man (Marcuse), 112
ontology: African American/Black, 9–19, 24, 94; anti-racist, 25; and Black power, 1–10; cosmic, 93; dialectical, 52–53; divine nonviolece as, 24; hierarchical, 105; King and, 19–23, 25; and nonviolence, 1–26, 39, 149–51n; and philosophy, 9, 34; political, 22, 146; social, 25, 141; and sociology, 140. *See also* fundamental ontology; meontology; racial ontology
ontotheology, 9, 24–26, 94, 102, 120. *See also* being/Being
oppression, 3–4, 8–9, 17, 58, 66, 73–74, 78–79, 81–82, 91–92, 141–42, 145, 161n14
Origin of German Tragic Drama (Benjamin), 116
Origins of Totalitarianism, The (Arendt), 159n23
orthodoxy, 160n10; neo-, 30
Osborn, Michael, 154n7
Outlaw, Lucius, 15, 18, 24

pacifism, 39, 125
paganism, and nihilism, 101
pan-Africanism, and Black nationalism, 74
Pangle, Thomas L., 156–57n3
pantheism, 64, 117
Pappas, Theodore, 153n2
Parables of Jesus, The (Buttrick), 47
Parmenides, 55
Parousia (Second Coming), in Saint Paul, 118–19
Parrhesia, 130–31, 157n6, 162n20
passion: and creativity, for rational thought, 54; and sympathy, 85
pathos, 154n7
Patton, John H., 154n7
Paul, Saint: agape Christianized by, 88; apocalyptic messianism of, 117; Barth on, 103; Benjamin, 118, 121; Bultmann on, 104, 118–19, 121; conversion narrative of, 62; and creative integration, 62; epistle to Romans, 103; epistles, 121, 161n15; and eschatology, 59, 134; and finitude, 59; and hermetical methodology, 103; and historicism, 120; on law, 104, 157n6; and messianism, 117, 119, 135; and Parousia/Second Coming, 118, 157n6; and pneuma/soma, 118; and police violence, 123; political ontology of, 22; and revolutionary liberation, 134; and theological-cultural crisis of interregnum, 103; and theology of being, 118; and universalism, 157n6
Pauline contradictions, and divine nonviolence, 115–22
peace: and civil disobedience, 112; and classical thought, 98; and freedom, 65, 69; and justice, 94–95, 98; and messianism, 113; politics of, 119; racial, 74; and security, 118
perfectionism, 30
personalism, 40–43, 51, 134–35, 163n4
pessimism, and hope, 8

Phaedrus (Plato), 86–90, 156n13
Phenomenal Blackness (Thompson), 149n3
phenomenology, 17, 43, 145
Phenomenology of Spirit (Hegel), 43
philia, and agape/eros, 61, 82–84, 87, 91
philosophical anthropology, 16–17, 41
Philosophical Library, 27
philosophy: academic, 23; and/of science, 33–34, 153n1; anti-Cartesian, 12, 14; anti-Platonic, 12; crisis, 17, 154n8; émigré, 95, 105, 163n6; ethno-, 14–15, 18–19; European, 3, 35; and fundamental ontology, 24–25, 33–35, 63; and history, 5, 14, 24, 32, 74, 102, 107; of history, 67, 138, 141, 158n14; history of, 32, 137, 152n16; materialist, 25; meta-, 12–14, 25; moral, 38, 51, 128–29; of nonviolence, 11, 39, 43–44, 83, 92, 113; and ontology, 9, 34; Platonic, 78, 82, 87, 137; political, 10, 23–24, 73, 76–77, 95–96, 149n4; of race, 8, 14, 24; and science, 33–34, 153n1; social, 43, 146; and sociological sources, 37; sociopolitical, 14, 150n24; theological, 50, 105; and theology, 23–26, 42, 46, 49, 53, 85–86, 89, 105, 153n2; and violence, 113; Western, 12–14, 17–18, 77. *See also* African American philosophy; Christian philosophy; German philosophy; Greek philosophy
Philosophy of Right (Hegel), 43
Pierson v. Ray (1967), 128
"Pilgrimage to Nonviolence"(King), 12, 35–36, 40–44, 49, 52, 92, 105
Plato: cave allegory, 37, 77–80, 93, 109; on Creator-God, 58; dialogues, 85, 87; on divinity, 85; Doctrine of Truth, 36–37, 101–2, 137–38, 143; and existentialism, 92; Greek language used in philosophy of, 82; on museum of moving image, 60; rhetoric of, 158n12

Platonism: anti-, 12; and authoritarianism, 138; and Black power/Power, 79, 90–94; and Black separatism, 26; and divine omnipotence, 56–57; and essentialism, 92; and Gnosticism, 93, 105–6; and humanism, 37, 162n1; and metaphysics, 90, 92–93, 152n12; neo-, 58, 89, 109; and nonbeing/Nonbeing, 55; and nonviolence, 90–94; and ontology of race and power, 79–80; and oppression, 81–82; and philosophy, 78, 82, 87, 137; racial, 25, 37, 75–76, 80–82, 93–94, 109; and racial types, 76, 80, 82; and separatism, 26; and theology, 92–93

"Plato's Doctrine of Truth" (Heidegger), 36–37, 101–2, 137–38, 143

pluralism, 6, 62–63, 158n9

pneuma, 103–4, 117–19

Poe, Edgar Allan, 86

police violence, 162n19; anti-Black, 26; critique of, 22, 133; and divine nonviolence, 22; and divine violence, 22, 133; and Gnosticism, 26, 124, 136; as ignominious force, 126–27; as illegitimate power, 22, 26; and injustice, 124; and lawlessness, 97–98, 136; as law-making/law-preserving violence, 26, 125–28, 130–32; legal character of, 113; and messianism, 133; as political, 135–36; and political theology, 22, 26, 124; as power, 161n17; power of, 127; racist, 22–23, 136; and sovereignty, 22, 26, 124, 128; and state of exception, 22, 124, 127, 132–33; as ungodly and unnatural, 99

political philosophy, 10, 23–24, 73, 76–77, 95–96, 149n4

political religion, 95–97, 101, 108, 159n27. *See also* political theology

Political Religions (Voegelin), 95–96

political science, 156n2. *See also* social sciences

political theology: and Christian justice/law, 123; and civil disobedience, 26; and debates in Germany, 22; democratic, 26; and divine nonviolence, 110–15; and eschatology, 26, 116–17, 159–60n27; and Gnosticism, 26, 100, 112, 115; interregnum, 101, 107; and law, 123; and metaphysics, 101; moral deficiency of, 112; and nonviolence, 25–26, 110–15; and ontotheology, 25; and police violence, 22, 26, 124; and secularization, 116; and sovereignty, 160n9; and violence, critique of, 124. *See also* political religion; theopolitics

politics: and apolitical in German Jewish thought between wars, 157n5; Black, 2, 73, 75; and Christian eschatology, 116–17; and emotions, 145; and fundamental ontology, 37; geo-, 8; Gnostic theological framework, 115; of heroism, 139–40; and history, 116–17; and humanism, 37; and ideology, 15; of love, 146; and nature, 56; of nihilism, 116; of peace, 119; racial, 113; and remembrance, 158n15; and revolutionary ideal, 144–45; of self-determination, 8; socio-, 19, 123, 130, 132, 150n24; theo-, 8, 99, 116–17. *See also* political philosophy; political religion; political theology

poor/poverty, 4, 8, 10–11

positive law, 99, 110–12, 122, 125–26

postindustrial capitalism, and social justice, 8

poverty/poor, 4, 8, 10–11

power: Black racial essence as, 93–94; divine, 162n21; of nonviolence, 43, 70; of state, 130–31; and violence, 161n17; of will, 50, 136–37. *See also* Black power

"Practice of Freedom, The" (hooks), 144–46

Prayer Pilgrimage for Freedom, 85

primal man *(Urmensch)*, and Gnosticism, 107

"Protestant Hegelianism" (King), 57
Protestantism, 57, 89, 135
protest(s), 11, 142, 163n6. *See also* nonviolent protests; violent protests
public reason, 99–100, 157–58n9, 160n28

Question of German Guilt, The (Jaspers), 34–35

race: and anti-Semitism, 23; and Civil Rights Movement, 149n6, 160n1; and class, 4, 149n6; as construct, 3; and eros, 92; ethics of, 8; and fundamental ontology, 24; ideology, 36–37, 79; and injustice, 9; and messianism, 135; and metaphysics, 3; philosophy of, 8, 14, 24; and power, 79–80
racial difference(s), 13, 63, 75, 94, 111
racial essentialism, 9, 16, 18, 25, 36, 64, 76, 81–82, 94, 109, 149n3
racial identity, 8, 80, 141–42
racial integration. *See* integration
racial ontology, 2–3, 8–9, 14, 19, 23, 76, 92, 94, 136
racial oppression. *See* oppression
racial segregation. *See* segregation
racial/racist realism, 22, 96, 113, 139–40
racism: and being/Being, 31–37; destruction/end of, 91, 94; and exploitation, 79; and fundamental ontology, 13, 23–24; history of, 13; institutional, 10; interpersonal, 10; Nazi, 140; ontological, 152n8; and philosophy, 23, 25; in philosophy, 23; and prejudice, 99; and racial ontology, 23; and rhetoric, 157n7; as science of sin, 134; scientific, 31–32; and sin, 134; spiritual, 31; theories of, 8; undermine human being, 40; understanding, 3; white, 11, 15. *See also* anti-racism
radicalism, 5–6, 39, 75, 149n2. *See also* Black radicalism; revolution

Rae, Gavin, 34, 37
Raeder, Linda C., 108
RAM. *See* Revolutionary Action Movement (RAM)
rational deduction, 57
rational thought, 54
Rauschenbusch, Walter, 37, 152n14
Rawls, John, 13, 23, 147, 157–58n9, 160n28
realism/reality: objective, 77; racial/racist, 22, 96, 113, 139–40
reason: public, 99–100, 157–58n9, 160n28; secular, 157–58n9
redemption: and agape, 83, 86, 91; and freedom, 58; and Gnosticism, 106–7; and goodwill, 82–83, 87; and infinite being, 56; and love, 66, 83, 86, 133–34; otherworldly, 159n21; and salvation, 58, 67, 91; and violence, 119; white, 91–92. *See also* salvation
relativism: anti-, 4; moral, 38; spiritual, and divinity, 48–49, 52
religion: and Black Baptist church, 71; political, 95–97, 101, 108, 159n27; secular, 159n27; spiritual, 96; true, 39, 64. *See also* church; theology; specific religion(s)
Renaissance, 89, 109
reparations, 10–11, 13, 146
Republic (Plato), 25, 76–82
Review of Politics, The, 159n23
revolution: and anti-humanism, 149n5; and beloved community, 146; and BPP, 6, 74–75, 149n8, 156n10; and Christianity, 112; and education, 146; and freedom, 146; and Gnosis, 101, 108; and inhumanism, 149n5; and justice, 3, 40; and liberation, 134; and love, 25–26, 39; and nationalism, 74–75; and nonviolence, 112; and political change, 123; and politics, 144–45; and social action, 123; and state of exception, 133; and violence, 39, 124, 143, 156n10; worldly, 119. *See also* radicalism

Revolutionary Action Movement (RAM), 6
revolutionary suicide, 76–77, 156n8
Revolutionary Suicide (Newton), 76–77, 156n8
rhetoric: of civil rights, 154n7–8; democratic, 155n19; of the gun, 155n7; of King, 44, 49, 70–76, 110, 150n16, 152n13, 153n5, 154n7–8, 154n10, 155n3, 155n19, 157n6–8, 161n16; Plato and, 158n12; political, 156n10; power of, 154n10; and racism, 157n7; and spirituality, 44; and supernatural power of nonviolence, 70; universalist, 155n19, 157n6. *See also* Kairos (creative moments/rhetorical timing)
Richardson, William, 19, 152n12
Riverside Church (New York), 135
Roberts, Adam, 155n4
Robinson, Dean E., 6, 73
Rockmore, Tom, 35–36, 151n3, 152n10
Rogers, Ibram H., 163n7
Romanticism, German, 88
Romeo and Juliet (Shakespeare), 86
Rose, Justin, 10
Rosenberg, Alfred, 36, 108
Rosenzweig, Franz, 118, 159n21
Roth, Michael D., 15
Rousseau, Jean-Jacques, 37
Rubenstein, Mary-Jane, 102
Rustin, Bayard, 7

Sabl, Andrew, 155n19
Saint Augustine. *See* Augustine, Saint
Saint Paul. *See* Paul, Saint
Saint Paul: The Foundation of Universalism (Badiou), 157n6
salvation: and agape, 91; and beloved community, 22, 115; and Christian eschaton, 108; and damnation, 22; eternal grace in, 103; and freedom, 58, 60; otherworldly, 120; as reconciliation, 52; and redemption, 58, 67, 91; of soul, 119; spiritual, 119. *See also* damnation; redemption
Sartre, Jean-Paul, 12, 17, 27, 29, 33–34, 51
Saturday Evening Post, 135
satyagraha (soul force), 38, 70
Schatzki, Theodore R, 155n18
Scheuerman, William E., 11
Schmidt, Christoph, 103–4
Schmidt Passos, Eduardo, 159n25, 162n23
Schmitt, Carl, 24, 115–16, 118–19, 131, 133, 159–60n27, 160n5–7, 162n23
Scholem, Gershom, 106–7, 120, 159n21
Schrijvers, Joeri, 102
science: and fundamental ontology, 33–34; and humanism, 30; and methodology, 16; and philosophy, 33–34, 153n1; of sin, and racism, 134; technology, 29, 65; theology as, 33, 102
Science, Politics, and Gnosticism (Voegelin), 108–9
SCLC. *See* Southern Christian Leadership Conference (SCLC)
Seale, Bobby, 6, 76–77, 79–82
Second Coming (Parousia), in Saint Paul, 118
segregation: critique of, 20; history of, 137; and integration, 24; as morally wrong, 111; racial, 20, 24, 134; sin of, 66, 111–12, 134; and slavery, 114; and social dislocation, 66; undermine human being, 40. *See also* desegregation; integration
Seize the Time (Seale), 80–81
self, and other, 20–21, 114, 145
self-affirmation, 50–52
self-care, 20–21, 145–46. *See also* self-love
self-deception, 152n16
self-determination, 8, 40
self-estrangement, and damnation, 66

self-love, 50–51, 67, 146–47. *See also* self-care
self-mystification, 152n16
separatism, 4, 13, 26, 71, 109, 143, 150n18. *See also* Black separatism
sexism, 6, 17, 40
Shakespeare, William, 28–29, 86–87
Shakur, Assata, 73
Sharpe, Matthew, 32, 37
Sheehan, Thomas, 35, 152n10
Shelby, Tommie, 10–11, 13, 149n2
sin/sinfulness: and alienation from God, 137; and damnation, 66; and death, 121; and dictators, 115; and nonbeing/Nonbeing, 67; as ontotheological concept, 24; and segregation, 66, 111–12, 137
Sixteenth Street Baptist Church, 68
slavery, 17, 114
Smith, Adam, 133
Smith, David Norman, 141
Smith, Ervin, 158n10
Smith, Steven B., 36
SNCC. *See* Student Nonviolent Coordinating Committee (SNCC)
social action/activism. *See under* activism
social conflict, 93, 130–31
social criticism/critique, 5, 75, 92
social gospel, 25, 37, 54, 152n14
social justice, 8, 10–11, 38, 63
social realism/reality, 25, 64
social reform, 38, 135
social responsibility, 8, 62–63, 67. *See also* activism
social sciences, 152n11. *See also* political science
social theory, 8, 37, 67
socialism, 71–72, 97, 154n6. *See also* National Socialism
sociology, 37, 140, 150n24
sociopolitics. *See under* politics
Socrates, 32, 78, 90–91, 98–100, 103, 118, 158n11

solidarity, 13, 17, 141–42
Sophist (Plato), 90, 156n13
soteriology, and history, 91, 118, 126
soul force (satyagraha), 38, 70
Southern Christian Leadership Conference (SCLC), 1, 73
sovereignty: and beloved community, 125; and civil disobedience, 113, 125; divine, 114; divisions of, 160n9; end of, 26; German academic debates on, 24; God's, 136; messianic, 113, 117, 119; and nonviolence, 113, 136; and police violence, 22, 26, 124, 128; state, 26, 99, 113; theological-political, 116–17; and violence, 26
Spencer, Robyn C., 6
Spengler, Oswald, 105
Spinoza, Baruch, 64
spiritual relativism, and divinity, 48–49, 52
spiritualism, 44, 49, 51, 90, 105
Stanley, Timothy, 118
state of exception, 22, 115–19, 128, 132–36
state violence, 26, 99, 125–27, 136
Steinkraus, Warren E., 152n16
Stoicism, 40
Strauss, Leo, 95, 156–57n3
Strenski, Ivan, 34–35
Stride Toward Freedom (King), 11, 47, 82
Stuart, Kevin, 157–58n9, 160n28
Student Nonviolent Coordinating Committee (SNCC), 1, 72
Sturm, Douglas, 72, 161n13
Sturm, Erdmann, 45
Styfhals, Willem, 116, 159n27
subjectivity, 9, 56, 89, 105, 114, 138. *See also* objectivity
subordination, 17
suffering, 52, 93–94, 135
Supreme Court. *See* United States Supreme Court
Symposium (Plato), 88

systematic theology, 25, 35, 47–49, 53, 71, 89
Systematic Theology (Tillich), vii, 47–49, 84

Taubes, Jacob, 22, 116–19, 160n6
Taylor, Charles, 9
technocracy, 32
Terpstra, Marin, 115–16, 160n6
Terry, Brandon M., 8–11
theodicy, 59, 107
theology: biblical, 102; commitment to, 45; Continental, 22, 28, 89, 156n2; of correlation, 154n9; cosmo-, 102; crisis, 28, 103; demythologizing of, 107; history of, 24; idealist-existential, 40; Marburg, 27–28, 102, 107; and metaphysics, 41, 93, 102, 153n3; method in, 103; philosophical, 11–12, 36, 47, 51; and philosophy, 23–26, 42, 46, 49, 53, 85–86, 89, 105, 153n2; as science, 33, 102; social, 64. *See also* Christian theology; German theology; ontotheology; political theology; religion; systematic theology
theology of being. *See* ontotheology
theopolitics, 8, 99. *See also* political theology
Third World, 74, 149n7
Thomas, J. H., 46
Thomas, Owen C., 45
Thomas Aquinas, Saint, 60, 89, 110–11, 160n28
Thomassen, Bjørn, 159n27
Thompson, Mark Christian, 149n3
Thoreau, Henry David, 13
Tillich, Paul: as activist, 41; and Adorno, 153n1; on agape/eros, 151n29; and anti-humanism, 46; and Arendt, 153n1; and Barth, 52; on Being Itself, 11–12, 51–52, 63, 66, 70, 90, 92; on Being-in-love, 26; and correlation, 52–53, 154n9; on courage to be, 48, 50–51; critical methodology of, 53;

dialectical method, 52–53, 57, 59; on divine omnipotence, 56–57; and eschatology, 59–60; on essential libido, 151n29; and existentialism, 41, 45–46, 50–52; on finitude, 56, 58; on freedom, 48, 55–56, 58, 62, 64; and fundamental ontology, 26, 154n13; and German academic debates, 24, 33; on Gnosticism in Platonic eros, 101; on God, 49–50, 56–64, 101; on God's infinity, 155n15; as great philosopher and theologian of our age, 50; and Heidegger, 25–26, 44–46, 52, 56–57, 118, 154n13; and Horkheimer, 153n1; idealist-existential theology of, 40–41; King and, 24–26, 153n17; King's doctoral work on, 25, 44–45, 53, 61–62, 96; on love, 61; and Marcuse, 153n1; and Marxism, 154n6; and metaphysics, 153n3; on National Socialism, 96; and Nazism, 96–97; and ontology, 46–47, 52–53; philosophical sources, 50, 153n1; philosophical theology of, 11–12, 47; and philosophy, 11–12, 41, 46, 53, 58, 62–63, 153n1; and philosophy of history, 158n14; and philosophy of science, 153n1; on political religion, 96–97; and psychology, 153n1; and religious socialism, 154n6; and religious symbols, 57, 154n14; on systematic theology, vii, 25, 47–48, 84; and theological *Existenzphilosophie*, 24, 45, 51; and theology, 11–12, 33, 40–41, 46, 49–50, 53, 61–63, 92, 101, 153n1, 153n3, 154n9, 154n14, 155n15; and theology of being, 118; and theology of correlation, 154n9; and Voegelin, 97; and Wieman, 11
time: and eternity, 154n8; and space, 21, 28–29. *See also under* being/Being
totalitarianism, 5, 35, 38, 107. *See also* authoritarianism
transcendence, 90, 94, 103, 106, 109, 136, 160n9

Trawny, Peter, 19–20, 33–34, 151n4
truth: commitment to, 98; and freedom, 151n5; metaphysical, 3; ontological, 21, 42–43; ontotheological, 94; pursuit of, 144
Turci, Monica, 151n28
Ture, Kwame, 149n1, 149n7

United States Supreme Court, 98, 110–11, 123–24
universalism: and Christianity, 69; and civil rights, 144, 155n19; democratic, 155n19; and freedom, 144; and Gnosticism, 100; and humanism, 100; and love, 21–22, 144; and metaphysics, 31; Pauline, 97, 157n6; and race, 37; racial, 15; theological, 69
unjust law, 110–11, 132, 160n28. *See also* just law
Urmensch. *See* primal man *(Urmensch)*
Utley, Ebony A., 155n3

Valls, Andrew, 75
Van Deburg, William L., 155n5
Varshizky, Amit, 96–97, 108
Vedder, Ben, 118
violence: as act of spirit, 67; breakdown in communication as, 155n1; coercive, 133; evil, 93; German academic debates on, 24; history of, 113; as lawmaking or law-preserving, 125, 128, 132–33; and legacy, 72–73; mythic, 162n22; as ontology, 93; partisan, 163n3; philosophical, 113; political, 8–9, 114, 124; pure, 130–31; and self-defense, 7, 40, 73, 82, 143, 156n10; and sovereignty, 26; statutory as legal intent, 130; tactical, 7; unlawful use of, 132, 142. *See also* divine violence; nonviolence; police violence; state violence
violent protests, 66, 142. *See also* nonviolent protests

Voegelin, Eric: and Arendt, 159n23; and classical thought, 95; as conservative, 159n23; and Continental tradition, 156n2; and German academic debates, 24; on Gnosticism, 107–9, 116, 159n26–27; and Heidegger, 95; and historicism, 159n24; on National Socialism, 95–96; on natural law, 159n25; on Nazism, 108; on peace and justice in classical thought, 95; on Plato, 108–9, 156–57n3; and political philosophy, 95–96; and political religion, 96–97, 108; and political science, 156n2; and political theology, 116; and politics, 159n23; and practice of opposition, 159n23; on race/racism, 159n23; and Strauss, 156–57n3; and Tillich, 97
voting rights, 10–11
Voting Rights Act (1965), 1

Waite, Geoff, 32–33
Watson, Martha Solomon, 153n5
"We Shall Overcome," 1–2
Wells, Ida B., 3
West, Cornel, 12–14, 24, 146
"What Is Man?" (King), 30, 154n12
Where Do We Go from Here: Chaos or Community? (King), 1, 10, 29
white racism, 11, 15
white supremacy, 3–4, 146
Whitehead, Alfred North, 11, 51, 95
whiteness, 15–16, 80, 94. *See also* Blackness
Wieman, Henry Nelson, 11, 51, 53, 62–63
Wilkins, Roy, 7
will to power, 137
Will to Power, The (Nietzsche), 38
Williams, Yohuru R., 7, 72–74, 79
Williamson, Clark M., 46
Williamson, Joy Ann, 76
Witte, Bernd, 162n21
Wittgenstein, Ludwig, 13
Wofford, Harris, 84

Wolfe, J. E., 101–2, 117
Wolin, Richard, 140–41
Woodson, Hue, 163n5
World House, 21, 64–66, 69, 144, 146
"World House" (King), Nobel Lecture (1964), 64–66
World War I, 106
World War II, 101, 113

world-historical, 31, 69, 94, 111, 125
worthiness, 89, 91

Yancy, George, 15, 18–19, 24
Youth Leadership Conference (April 1960), 155n17, 157n17

Zack, Naomi, 14

The authorized representative in the EU for product safety and compliance is:
Mare Nostrum Group
B.V Doelen 72
4831 GR Breda
The Netherlands

www.ingramcontent.com/pod-product-compliance
Lightning Source LLC
Chambersburg PA
CBHW022014220426
43663CB00007B/1074